THE WAY OF
SOUL LIGHTENING

Also by Aminah Raheem, Ph.D.

Soul Return: Integrating Body, Psyche & Spirit
Soul Lightning: Awakening Soul Consciousness

THE WAY OF
SOUL LIGHTENING

INTEGRATING BODY, MIND, AND SOUL
THROUGH ENERGY

Aminah Raheem, Ph.D.

Foreword by Arnold Mindell, Ph.D.

Soul Lightening International

www.SoulLightening.com.

ISBN: 1492203653
ISBN-13: 9781492203650
Published by Soul Lightening International, Borrego Springs, California 92004.

DEDICATION

This book is dedicated to all those amazing students I have shared learning with since 1965, here in the U.S., in Switzerland and England. They include my own remarkable children: Viviana, Philip, Rosalind and William Henry, who taught me, and are still teaching me, how to love, give generously and pay attention. We have feasted on such illuminating moments. I am most grateful for the insights, creativity, laughter, tears and reflections we have generated.

CONTENTS

APPRECIATIONS

It is impossible to thank all the wonderful people who have encouraged and supported me in the production of this book, principally because that would cover much of my lifetime as a teacher, in the U.S., England, and Switzerland. I'm thinking of all the fabulous hours we have spent together, following our processes, laughing, crying, hugging, always supporting, and loving each other. But beginning in this present time, I thank all the students who have partnered with me in the development of Soul Lightening work, and this book. Thank you, Cathy Miller, our Soul Lightening President, for your encouraging words, your love, and dedicated efforts for our work, and also for the illustrations here in the book. Thank you, Jim Mutch, for your integrity in shepherding Soul Lightening from its beginning, always faithful and true. Literally, I couldn't have completed this book without the positive encouragement of all of you. Thanks particularly to those students who sent heartfelt reports of their own processes.

I'm especially grateful for my incomparable editor, Hal Zina Bennett, who coached me through the rapids of finishing the book, and getting it to the publisher. Arny and Amy Mindell took time out from their incredibly busy schedule to read a summary of the book and write a foreword for it. Thanks so much, dear old friends for your love through all these years. I also thank Jan Alegretti for excellent copy editing. Special appreciation goes to Barbara Matson for the inspired painting on the cover. I'm grateful for April Bogdon and the very accommodating folks at CreateSpace for moving this book through publication and delivery.

My husband, Fritz Smith, has been a constant grounded partner and supporter in this production. There's no way to thank him enough; I just love him everyday. I thank all my extraordinary children: Viviana, Philip, Rosalind, and William Henry. God bless you for hanging in there with me, and supporting me, while I missed many special hours with you. I thank my granddaughter Lauren for her perceptive reading and feedback of part of the manuscript. And I especially thank my process partner, Laura Ramsay, who has flown by my side, participating in every venture, since I met her over thirty years ago. And a profound thank you to you, Laura, and to my entire, extraordinarily generous family for the 80th birthday present. I am deeply touched. I will never forget.

I feel so blessed by the large numbers of students, colleagues, and family who have loved me well. My gratitude to all of you, those mentioned by name and all the rest. Thanks for sharing part of this life with me.

FOREWORD

Aminah Raheem's *Way of Soul Lightening* is just that. Her well written and easy to read book describes how her work enables the deepest self, the Soul, to emerge fully into consciousness. She integrates not only process oriented psychology but the best of humanistic, transpersonal and integral ideas into her work.

Over the past four decades we have seen many discoveries in the worlds of physics, psychology, and healing. These have had a powerful impact on our approaches to personal growth, resulting in a much greater awareness of the role of consciousness in body wellness and quality of life.

The Way of Soul Lightening embraces ancient healing approaches to the challenges of the human condition. In the 1960s, throughout the U.S., physicians began exploring acupuncture, acupressure, and other ancient healing traditions from the east. The mind-body connection became part of an international dialogue and many people began looking for ways to bring together and treat all aspects of our being—the psychological, spiritual, mental and physical. Today millions of people are involved, either as practitioners or clients, in new, more wholistic approaches to healing and change.

Over the past 30 years Aminah has been at the forefront of these world-changing approaches. From a background in traditional psychology she expanded her work to include body and soul, by enfolding two very different methods into a wholistic approach. When I first met Aminah in 1982, she was working with the whole person through the body with the gentle but profound ancient practice of acupressure. She told me then that Process Work was the perfect method to work with the emotional and mental issues that arose from people during bodywork. Therefore, I invited her to create and teach *Process Acupressure*, her unique combination of acupressure and Process Work, which she would present at the first Process Work Intensive in Zurich, Switzerland, in 1986. She arrived with a foundation teaching of Process Acupressure. That work has evolved now into the whole curriculum of Soul Lightening, which she describes in detail in this book.

Aminah's work provides an excellent picture of how one gifted teacher and healer has brought together systems of healing from ancient traditions with many of the best methods of modern psychological and spiritual practices.

~Arnold Mindell, Ph.D., originator of *Process Oriented Psychology*

INTRODUCTION

Often when someone comes to ask my advice,
I hear him giving himself the answer to his
question and that is the way it ought to be.

~Martin Buber

A world-changing phenomenon is happening at this time in our history. It isn't covered in the Western media, hardly even noticed in mainstream publications, and is certainly not noted in our schools. But it is very real. It is an awakening of the soul.

In many people's minds the word "soul" has become a bit tarnished at best. Although the word and the experience are very real to me and many of my students, here's what I mean by it: essence, the core of our being, Divine spark, or inner knowing. I am not using the word in a conventional religious context but rather as it was used in psychology, originally by William James and Carl Jung. So I ask you to substitute whatever word best works for you, to denote that deepest, most sacred part of yourself.

We are in a new era of human evolution. As Jurriaan Kamp, founder and publisher of *The Intelligent Optimist*, said in 2013, "Humanity stands at the threshold of a new era: the era of consciousness. After conquering the external world, human beings will discover their inner selves."

Many things are changing rapidly and will continue to do so. Our belief systems, theories and trainings will need to be updated regularly. Gifted teachers have popped up to show the way to inner truth and a "new earth," as Eckhart Tolle described it. They pass on to us valuable methods for true self-inquiry.

The Indian avatar Sai Baba said, "You have been asleep for a thousand years. Now you must wake up." After thousands of years of soul sleep, thousands and perhaps millions of people, alone and in diverse groups, are discovering who they actually are and what their planetary purposes are in this life. They are freeing themselves from dysfunctional belief systems of the past and are envisioning the possibility of a "new Earth," as Eckhart Tolle put it in his book by that title: *A New Earth. Awakening to Your Life Purpose*[1]. And together we are discovering the wisdom of the Divine light within ourselves as the most reliable guide to righteous living.

The current awakening is not just a phenomenon of the intelligentsia; it is global and it is nothing short of revolutionary. I have observed it in individuals and groups during my thirty years of healing, therapeutic practice and widespread teaching in the U.S., Switzerland and England. As I taught psychology and bodywork, I was simultaneously researching full human development and soul realization. As I watched this individual soul awakening I saw happening in my own work and elsewhere, I became convinced that we are at the threshold of a global shift in spiritual consciousness, one that could revolutionize the way we organize life on our precious planet.

This book is about the specific work of Soul Lightening Acupressure to facilitate a spiritual awakening that can be realized through individual soul actualization. As the Dalai Lama has said, "Even though it seems very difficult, world peace can only come about through individual transformation."

---

1 Tolle, Eckhart. 2008. *A New Earth: Awakening to Your Life's Purpose*. New York, Penguin Books

The Evolution of Soul Lightening Acupressure

After years of investigating the *parts* of a person—body, mind, emotions and soul—I developed a model for *whole person* development, described in my first book, *Soul Return.* Simultaneously I worked with clients and students to apply the model in real life. As we worked, I began to observe a remarkable *light-en-ing* process in these students—a speedy progression that penetrated through the traumas and dramas of personal history to expose soul wisdom within them. I observed that once people realized the possibility of returning to their own soul wisdom, and followed that unfolding process faithfully, they came into a flowering of health, wholeness and personal vision that was life altering, and life fulfilling.

I witnessed how people could find soul strength and guidance long before all their "issues" were resolved and without long-term therapy. Long ago, as a graduate student in psychology, I had a strong intuition about the inadequacy of psychotherapy alone, as it was practiced then, to liberate mind, body and soul from past wounding. I was beginning to empirically observe the fallacy of what I had been taught, namely that human development was dictated by a five- to six-year period of fundamental conditioning in childhood that Freud said would shape our personalities for life. I was beginning to see that while the programming of those first years was extremely important, it was still a very small part of a more vast intelligence that contains centuries of ancestral patterns, a multitude of past lives and an eternal soul blueprint.

I was seeing clients and students move toward greater health and integration, faster and more expansively than I could have imagined. They had either found, or were working swiftly toward, their own soul wisdom and purpose. They were clearer, healthier, happier and more creative than ever before. They found deep satisfaction in their own nature and truth, and were fulfilling their destinies. And as they claimed their own soul lightening process, they were similarly helping others, because they began to serve the world in positive ways.

Through the Soul Lightening process, which I will be describing in the pages ahead, we discovered that awakening arises naturally when human beings receive what they need and are supported, by themselves and others, for their own characteristics, talents and dreams, and especially for their own souls. Most of us have been so heavily conditioned by family and ancestry, and socialized by our particular culture, that waking up to *who we actually are*, and to our own soul and purpose, is usually an arduous and lengthy project. As Henry Mills, the young boy in the TV series *Once Upon a Time*, says, "They don't know who they are!"

Spiritual literature describes seekers and philosophers of the past who have spent entire lifetimes searching for their own souls, through philosophies, religions, severe practices or other rigid belief systems and disciplines. Often they had to withdraw from society altogether to pursue their own enlightenment. In the twentieth century the field of psychology was originally developed as an avenue to awaken the individual soul. As it evolved, however, focus shifted more to the mind and emotions than to the soul, and often emphasized *adjustment* to society over *soul awakening*.

After I was satisfied that the wholistic model I had developed was effective in private practice, I refined and taught the methods as *Process Acupressure*. A faculty was trained, and over the past twenty years this faculty has taught hundreds of body workers, psychologists and healthcare workers the methods that have now evolved into the broad-spectrum program we call *Soul Lightening Acupressure International*. Our mission is to teach wholistic tools and methods that help people liberate themselves and others from the web of conditioning that has virtually enslaved humans for hundreds, probably thousands, of years. We want to help lighten souls so they may return to their own true natures and purposes on the earth now, when clarity is so desperately needed.

I believe that right now our challenges and opportunities for soul growth are at a peak. I have often asked my students, "Why would you, or any soul, choose to be born in this time?" Their answers, when they contact soul wisdom, cover a wide range: to help lift consciousness in a chaotic time; to assist in generational healing; to empower people to free themselves from centuries of negative conditioning. One student said that he had participated in scientific developments in a past life that led to massive earth destruction, and he was here this time to help prevent a recurrence of that catastrophe.

An Extreme Must Turn into its Opposite

Even though it sometimes appears that we are on the brink of disaster and extinction on our planet, it is my belief that we can overcome our instinctual but misguided urges to destroy life. Though our historical negative traits seem to have reached an absolute peak of self-destructiveness, we could find solace in the Chinese medicine principle of *yin* and *yang*. This ancient teaching says that two polarities are inevitable in this world—hot and cold; black and white; top and bottom; hard and soft, and so forth—and that these polarities are always fluid and interchangeable. For example, it can be observed in nature that when either one of the qualities— yin or yang—reaches its absolute capacity, or apex, as in when destructiveness reaches its greatest extreme, it must by nature turn into its opposite: top will become bottom, emptiness will become fullness, destruction must turn into creation. In human behavior, Alcoholics Anonymous, one of the most effective approaches in the treatment of alcoholism, teaches that the alcoholics must reach rock bottom before they have the will to choose another way of living their lives.

We have just witnessed an extraordinary consciousness shift to an opposite pole in our own culture. Our history of slavery, derived from centuries of this practice on every continent, combined with second-class citizenship based on color and race, was reversed when we elected a black president to his second term. Now we have a choice to jump up to this new level of empowerment and consciousness or fall back into indignities and injustices of the past.

As we skate on the edge of disaster with weapons of war and technologies that truly threaten all life on our planet, we are waking up to the danger, and challenge, of complete annihilation. We are coming to realize that we must transform our destructive tendencies or perish.

I believe we are being offered a great creative, evolutionary opportunity in our time. As human beings we have the capacity to transform destructive urges into life-preserving and life-cherishing impulses, if we will simply wake up to our soul potentials. Enlightened individuals have demonstrated that ability throughout the ages. Right now is perhaps the only time in recorded history when there are enough people waking up, a critical mass, to transform centuries of self-destruction by returning to our inner soul wisdom that is attuned to the life-giving principle of creation itself.

Soul Lightening Acupressure fosters full human growth. It does not focus on pathology and it is not therapy according to the traditional psychological definition. Rather it is a radical departure from traditional psychology, medicine and religion even though it references the essential truths of all those fields. It is about unveiling the unlimited potential of soul wisdom and discarding the misconceptions of centuries that have kept us trapped in antiquated concepts of the human self, limited ideas of physical health and illness, and restricted ideas of how we can contact the spiritual source of life.

The mission of Soul Lightening is to share our empirical learnings to facilitate and empower souls to wake up to their true potentials and purposes on the earth at this time. The methods and skills we teach demonstrate how we can *light-en* up the soul, embrace its wisdom and power, and carry out the destiny we chose for this life. This book gives the guidelines we have discovered for soul awakening and tells you how to apply some of them in your own life now.

As You Read This Book

You will find that most chapters stand alone; they provide a sense of completion with each reading. Feel free to scan the table of contents, which will help you find subject areas you might wish to study further. Or, if you wish, simply thumb through the pages, letting your own interests guide you. As I wrote this book I realized that readers' knowledge of Soul Lightening work, or another system of healing or personal and spiritual growth, might cover a wide range, from those who are just beginning to those who are advanced practitioners. So I urge you to let your own interest and knowledge levels guide you in the pages ahead.

Lastly, while this was not intended as a how-to book in the strict sense of that term, I do trust that what I present here is detailed enough to inspire you on whatever your chosen path may be, or to call you to some of our Soul Lightening trainings.

1:
THE UNIFYING FIELD

The most essential ingredient in creating our universe is the consciousness that observes it.

~ Lynn McTaggart

In our scientific, technological age we have been introduced to the concept of a unifying Field, that is, a field of energy that enfolds everything in the universe, from the tiniest particles of matter to the vast bodies we can barely imagine, including multiple universes within universes and galaxies within galaxies. Physicists say this Field connects and holds all of creation in an indissoluble unity. In this understanding, energy precedes matter, which is then bound, within the Field.

In her groundbreaking book, *The Field: The Quest for the Secret Force of the Universe*, Lynn McTaggart explains the contemporary physics of the Field in a readable and interesting style. The book is scientifically thorough yet understandable to the layman. I strongly recommend it to anyone who wishes to understand the possibility of an expanding, awakening consciousness we are now entering in the twenty-first century. McTaggart described the Field as "a physical force between separate objects due to resonance of all-pervasive energy fields in the intervening space between the objects. Everything is connected to it; all things are known within it. It extends over all time and space."

Yet an understanding of a unified Field is as old as anything we know about. For example, the Rig Veda, one of the oldest extant spiritual texts in any Indo-European language, composed in the northwestern region of the Indian subcontinent between 1700 and 1100 B.C. described the Field this way:

> There is an endless net of threads throughout the universe. The horizontal threads are in space. The vertical threads are in time. At every crossing of the threads, there is an individual. And every individual is a crystal bead. And every crystal bead reflects not only the light from every other crystal in the net, but also every other reflection throughout the entire universe.

Throughout history, mystics and sages of the world have alluded to the Field experientially. They described their experiences by many names: cosmic bliss, Samadhi, or Divine Order. In his great classic, the *Tao Te Ching*, the ancient Chinese philosopher, Lao-Tzu, attempted to name what he said was actually "unnamable" and "beyond human comprehension."[1] He called it the Tao.

These sages and saints of the past claimed that the Field is available in consciousness to anyone, and that when people perceive that overarching unity they become aware of the benevolence within and behind the universe. They claimed that embedded within the Field is an enormous reservoir of universal truth and laws of the universe that can become available to human intelligence. This understanding implies that our human understanding can reach far beyond our personal or cultural belief systems or the religions of

---

1 Lao-Tzu, *The Tao Te Ching*, 1992. Stephen Mitchell translation. New York, HarperPerennial

our time. It points to a direct connection between the human mind and the Divine Mind.

Is there a life-promoting principle of everything within the Field? Is there a benevolent creative flow that generates, supports and preserves life, or not? I choose to believe that there is this benevolent force, the God force, which acts as an ordering principle behind everything in the universe. I would love to call it the Tao as well as the Universal Unifying Field. The universal laws within the Field are the same through everything; they flow through all of life, including you and me, and throughout investigations of all things, including science, physics, medicine, psychology, religion and whatever else is truthfully investigated.

In *The Field*, Lynne McTaggart describes not only the science of the Field but the profound effect it can have on human consciousness. One of the remarkable Field experiences she describes is that of the astronaut Edgar Mitchell, one of the first men to walk on the moon, who experienced it firsthand on the Apollo 14 voyage. McTaggart describes Mitchell's impressions:

> On their return voyage from the moon the astronauts didn't see sky anymore, as we ordinarily view it, but as an all-encompassing entity that cradles the earth from all sides. It was then, while staring out the window, that Ed Mitchell experienced the strangest feeling he would ever have: a feeling of connectedness, as if all the planets and all the people of all time were attached by some invisible web. He could hardly breathe from the majesty of the moment. There seemed to be an enormous force field here, connecting all people, their intentions and thoughts, and every animate and inanimate form of matter for all time. Anything he did or thought would influence the rest of the cosmos, and every occurrence in the cosmos would have a similar effect on him. Time was just an artificial construct. Everything he had been

taught about the universe and the separateness of people and things felt wrong. There were no accidents or individual intentions. The natural intelligence that had gone on for billions of years, that had forged the very molecules of his being, was also responsible for his own present journey. This wasn't something he was simply comprehending with his mind, but as an overwhelmingly visceral feeling, as though he were physically extending out of the window to the very furthest reaches of the universe.... It was as though in a single instant Ed Mitchell had discovered and felt The Force.[2]

Mitchell's experience had a profound impact on him. It transcended his intellect and the scientific constructs he had studied and believed in before the experience. Throughout his entire being he literally felt the connectedness of everything. This experience radically changed Mitchell's career and propelled him into a new field of research that has passionately preoccupied him ever since. He has stated that he wants to bring awareness of the Field and our unity within it to the collective consciousness throughout the world—a big but valuable mission.

Like Mitchell and so many others, I have experienced this field all my life, first in early childhood, and later in spiritual practice and in my work. When I was a child on a cattle ranch in the Sonoran Desert of Arizona I knew that vast Field through nature. On the desert there were no distractions from nature—no other children, no television, radio or even electricity. I wandered freely, exploring the nature of sky, clouds, mountains, cactus, brush and stones. My playhouse was a tiny ravine in the sandy floor of the desert. I made furniture out of brush twigs, stones and fabric scraps from

2 McTaggart, Lynn. 2008. *The Field: The Quest for the Secret Force of the Universe*. New York, Harper Collins.

my mother's sewing basket. My playmates were kangaroo rats, lizards and desert birds.

In that time of childhood wandering I first experienced the great unity of all things. Those who are familiar with my book *Soul Lightning: Awakening to Soul Consciousness* will already know this part of my story, but I will repeat part of it here because it was an integral part of the eventual development of Soul Lightening Acupressure.

During childhood, my father died in a tragic accident. The impact of his death threw my mother into a stunned state. She almost forgot about me for a while. I felt like both parents had died. I felt abandoned and alone.

One evening I wandered off barefoot into the twilight desert. Mother didn't notice. I was free and peaceful, out there in the vast silent desert. I just walked along, noticing the rocks, the afterglow of sunset on the mountains in the distance, little creatures—desert rats, chipmunks and rabbits—scurrying between scrub-brush. I walked on and on, right up what seemed like a mountain to my child's eyes, though it was simply a small ridge above the desert floor. There was nothing in my mind but a great sense of wonder.

Suddenly everything—the sky, the brush, the mountains—lit up in an intense glow. It was as if a gigantic floodlight shone out from the center of the universe, penetrating everything everywhere. The light was so bright it seemed to erase the world all around me. Mountains glowed gold, bushes turned translucent, even rocks sparkled. Everything was intensely alive. I stopped, stunned by the incandescent beauty of the light. At the same time an intense feeling of all-rightness began to envelop me.

How do I describe this feeling in words, when it was so beyond words? It was expansive, all pervasive and it filled me with comfort and love larger than anything I had ever before experienced.

Then a Great Voice spoke to me from everywhere all at once. "You are one with all of this," it said, as I looked into the sunset, over the mountains. "Your father isn't dead. He is here with you right now. I am here with you. You, he, all of this is part of one thing." And in that moment, I could feel, indeed, that my father was alive and near, protecting and caring for me.

In the same instant I knew, or perhaps remembered, many things at once: that I was a part of all this wonder surrounding me; that all of *It* was pure love; that It had never abandoned me, or anyone; that all of It was One Thing; and that It had always been right here.

After that experience I knew oneness in my body. Thus I never felt alone, even though I was the only child in my family for several years to come. I never felt that I didn't belong, because I *knew* that I belonged to all of that vast oneness that I'd experienced. I felt accompanied there, always accepted, welcomed even. After that I never felt isolated, unwanted, pushed aside, ignored, disempowered, denied or put down there on the desert, as I would feel for decades after we moved to town and I went to school after school after school.

That great light on the desert first showed me an all-encompassing, loving radiance that shines throughout the universe at all times. It showed me the unity within this world, how everything is connected and interrelated here and in the other worlds. And in that unity, everything is much more than "all right." It is wondrous, blissful and full of joy.

Of course, at the time, I couldn't possibly grasp the experience with my child's mind, nor give words to it to communicate it to others. In fact, I didn't tell anyone about it as I was growing up. Even though I couldn't integrate the light experience into ordinary life, it remained a great compelling mystery for me that has endured all my life. The Light I experienced would become a beacon behind all the tangled dramas and traumas of adult life. It gave me a first impression of the ultimate oneness and benevolence within and surrounding us. And it drove me to search for a deeper understanding of things than what was routinely offered, by my family or school.

When I read about mystical experiences in adulthood I understood what had happened to me out there on the desert. I came to realize that I was not alone in that profoundly moving experience. I read many biographies that described how such an early experience of love and unity propelled a search for truth beyond the mundane.

There were more unity experiences in adulthood. One in particular remains with me. My process partner, Laura, invited me into the water with dolphins at the Dolphin Research Center in Florida where she was working. Even though I had an intense fear of water, based on some early water traumas in my life, I lowered myself hesitantly into the water where dolphins were swimming.

In one moment I was trembling with fear on the bank, and in the next instant I was in the water with dolphins, completely free of fear and suffused by an indescribable sense of freedom, space and delight. The instantaneous transformation of consciousness almost made me dizzy. I quickly became enthralled with the dolphins as they started to swim up close to me. One sidled right up to my body so that I could touch him. A wave of joy went through me.

Although we were only in the water with the dolphins for about twenty minutes, my consciousness expanded into a pervasive realization of unity with everything around me. I saw the ocean, the sky, the dolphins and the birds as one interconnected field contained within a great flow of creative, unified movement, and enfolded by love, awe and joy. It also seemed as though that one experience in the water without fear overpowered the effects of my earlier water traumas.

Now, so many years after my initial childhood experience of the Field, I have been drawn back to live in the Sonoran Desert, in California this time. Here I once again experience vast beauty, serenity and that same oneness with nature that I first experienced as a child. All of it is enfolded in the many layers of the great rivers and oceans of life.

Only recently I had another glimpse into the bigger Field, and into other worlds, courtesy of my dear sister who had just died. Her death opened a big door, which it usually does for me when somebody goes on to the great beyond. As I followed her in consciousness I became aware of huge preparations, beyond my ability to articulate, going on in other realms, as if plans for a bi-millennial celebration were underway. As I write this I'm aware of my infantile language in trying to express what I saw and felt: *Very big activity, very big joy, very big creativity going on.* I already have another sister over there, who went on long ago, and she is really engaged in this celebration. The feelings associated with these other realms were beyond anything I'd previously imagined, feelings about how fabulous, how positive it will all be after this big wave in the universe we are now experiencing is finished.

I was shown that it's no more *business as usual*; the old rules aren't working now. For now we have to stay with the flow. Our role in the universal unifying Field is to be with it, to align more and more with the Tao, with universal law that's going on all the time. Here's the hard part, which defies all conventional wisdom: As we align more and more with ourselves and with the Field, we already have all the equipment needed for this transition within our own bodies. We were born with it. It's all here, right now, with us all the time, as we keep clearing those channels of awareness and keep empowering them, and keep going for our own truth and the truth that we hear in universal law.

In the years between the desert home of my childhood and the desert home of my adulthood, and also because of such experiences, I explored the mysticism and science of the Field.

I studied mysticism, from ancient to contemporary. I have heard spiritual teachers and shamans teach the same concept of wholeness within the Divine Order. Only recently, archeological digs have exposed ancient cultures that were not primitive, as we have thought, but were in fact highly developed. They lived in harmony with nature, were self-sufficient and cultivated reverence for all of life.

Now shamans of indigenous cultures that still endure on earth are walking out of the jungles and caves to teach us how they have survived for centuries in harmony with nature. Their teachings are even now showing up in popular retreats and growth centers.

I believe we all know the oneness of everything at an instinctual level, an intuition that is growing every year in our threatened world. Great spiritual teachers tell us that this knowing of oneness resides within each of us always. I believe this because of my experiences, and because of what I have read and been told by many clients and students. But often these experiences are so far afield, beyond our rational, ego-oriented consensus reality, that we discount them or have difficulty integrating them into our everyday lives.

Think of your own experiences of the fields and influences around you. Contrast walking into a well-tended cathedral against entering a brawling bar. Compare the experience of sitting with a loving grandmother with being scolded by a teacher after school.

Many of us have had the uplifting and expansive experience of entering the field of a great saint, sage or spiritual leader. Sometimes, just being in that field has stimulated an intense inner experience of illumination, peace or love.

In the coming week you might want to consciously tune into the field or fields around you, whether in a natural environment or around people. Can you sense a Field effect in addition to what you are seeing and feeling about the person or environment in front of you?

Fields within the Field: Regions of Physical Influence

Current physics has recognized and named a number of fundamental fields, such as gravitational and electro-magnetic fields, that influence and/or pre-date the existence of matter. Within the universal Field there are also many material, biological and informational fields. These fields hold the energy potential that can form and organize matter within specific systems. In other words, fields shape matter.

Biological Fields

Science has observed that fields of energy precede and subsequently guide the development of matter within living organisms. Recent science identifies fields that seem to define and guide the genetic evolution of an organism. Rupert Sheldrake, biochemist and plant physiologist, called them *morphogenetic fields*. These organizing fields have been called "wholes actively organizing themselves" by Joseph Needham, author of *Science and Civilization in China*.

The all-enfolding field of energy that organizes and binds all the matter of a human being as a whole is sometimes referred to as an *aura*. The same is true of all living organisms. Within a human being there are fields within and around each of the organs. Even in the last century an organizing energy field was observed that preceded spinal development in the fetus. This would be the energy field of the Great Central Flow, as we know it, one of the most important energy channels we work with in Soul Lightening.

As physics and the life sciences have identified how energy fields precede and organize matter, Rupert Sheldrake applied the concept to information. He hypothesized that patterns of energy regulate the generation and duplication of information. Information is contained in thought. Therefore thought generates or precedes energy, which generates material. A cluster of thoughts has more power than a single thought. For example, a cluster of thoughts, theory and practice patterns seems to create a template in the bigger Field. When a person has a tool (or tools) to tap into that field he can access the information held therein. Sheldrake called these patterns *morphic fields*. He further hypothesized that morphic fields are influenced and stabilized by *morphic resonance* from all previous, similar morphic units. Two examples of morphic fields are: (1) the world-is-flat morphic field that ruled science until Copernicus exploded it with additional observations, and (2) the women-carry-penis-envy morphic field that dominated psychoanalytical theory until post-Freudian research dismantled it.

Sheldrake's ideas about morphic fields ignited a jump in consciousness that allowed us to realize how a morphic field is created from organized information over time. For example, a morphic field forms around a body of information when thousands, or perhaps only hundreds, of people gather to learn that body of information.

Then this morphic field remains embedded in the universal unified Field. It is enhanced every time more people gather to learn the subject, and believe it. And it facilitates the learning and empowerment of that same information for subsequent students. For example, think of the morphic field of Christianity. After two thousand years of the teachings and beliefs about it by millions of people, it now has a morphic field that stretches over most of the earth. This makes learning about Christianity much easier for human beings now than for those living in times and in territories before that religion was accepted.

In contemporary holistic studies, Richard Bartlett, originator of Matrix Energetics, claims that the morphic field of his work has become powerful and instructive. Yet it has been taught for less than a decade now to thousands of people. Similarly, I believe now that the morphic field of Soul Lightening Acupressure is gradually building, so that future students will learn it faster and easier when we gather. Already our recent students are grasping the principles and methods more quickly than students did a decade ago. Consciousness is expanding and speeding up.

How Soul Lightening Applies Consciousness of the Field

Soul Lightening work accepts the universal unifying Field as a reality. Even while our focus is on individual growth and freedom, every session and class is grounded within our awareness of the individual, group and world Field. We have experienced time and again that beneath all layers of historical conditioning—personal, cultural and ancestral—we are all connected within the One Field of the Creative.

We know that each individual session affects that larger Field because we know that every thought and feeling we project has an effect, positive or negative, upon it. Thus we accept that in subtle ways our personal work affects the world. As we free ourselves from outmoded patterns of the past, we continually open new potentials for our individual and collective growth. We believe that our individual sanity and health facilitates the world to become more sane and whole.

We believe, as do many others who envision a new earth, that through conscious co-creation with the Field we can manifest personal and global dreams. Just like indigenous shamans, we believe that we can literally dream a new, more balanced and whole world into being.

Working to Co-Create Within the Field

In each Soul Lightening class we create a sacred working space in which we hold each other in unconditional positive respect. We do this by co-creating a pyramid over our time together, which then connects us with the greater Field (see chapter 16.) The pyramid has a tangible energy; you can feel it when you walk into the room, as it contains and graces our personal work. The respect between us supports and amplifies each person's work and the group's work. We believe our own healing and empowerment then translate out into the world Field as healing, clarifying and positive co-creative energy.

We integrate this perspective within our Soul Lightening organization. We recognize that universal law, the intelligence behind everything that is happening on earth, informs the Field. We know that the soul is pervaded by, and resonant with, the Field. Thus, by discovering the Field within our souls, we seek to reconnect with universal harmony and health. Soul to soul, when all beings on earth are in unity, there would be no rationale for destroying each other or anything in nature.

We know that the present earth field contains a *thought field* of massive pollution, not only from our own eco-destructive habits but also from centuries of ancient trash, karma and false beliefs. We inherited these qualities from the family, society, culture and belief systems we were born into. We carry them within our bodies. For example, the inherited belief that only one religion or belief system is right and all others are wrong has caused us to kill off millions of other human beings. The inherited belief that women are inferior, or at least weaker than men, has caused us to suppress women's human rights for centuries.

Soul Lightening work helps clear the body of false and useless stuff that muddies the Field, and impedes our growth and harmony with other humans and cultures. But it also helps clear the thought-field of individuals as well as the Field. The energy systems within our own bodies are directly connected to the Field of pure universal energy that flows through us. Through our energy work we stay aligned with that energy Field and unifying intelligence. My aim here is to suggest that a balance of body, mind and soul can harmonize a person with the flow of the Field (which we might just as well call Divine order or the Tao) so that he or she could walk, think and behave within its guidance.

In addition to clearing the individual field from past false beliefs, we attune with the greater Field to co-create a more life-affirming world. As we have seen, energy shapes matter. Thought shapes energy. Everybody knows (surely by now) that negative thoughts and emotions are fueled by the constant stream of negative news, and speculation about all the terrible things that will happen. What if we could replace that negativity with positive, creative thoughts, in words and images, so that the Field could become a breeding place for a new earth, as Eckhart Tolle described it?

When John Perkins, a former "corporate raider" turned indigenous peoples' advocate, asked an Indian elder what we "civilized" people could do to help in today's world, the elder counseled, "Teach your children to dream new dreams."[3]

In our work we revise the language and thought we put into the Field to correspond with a hopeful and holy vision we have for the future. When more and more individual consciousnesses are lifted

---

3 Perkins, John. 1994. *The World Is As You Dream It: Teachings from the Amazon and Andes.* Destiny Books

into that positive vision, the world Field could become the "dreaming" of a new world.

Future Prospects

By all the above means we believe Soul Lightening serves both individual growth and the evolution of the earth. We recognize that we can co-create with the universal Field. We ask: Could sane, loving individuals harmonize with the design of universal evolution? How would that impact our global problems?

We have only just begun to realize the possibilities that can open up when we work together in mutual respect and conscious co-creation with the creative flow of the universal unifying Field.

Global Implications

The ancient teaching that *all life is one* is now validated by contemporary science. The Field dictates that each of us is connected to, and in some measure unified with, all other life on this planet, as well as to the remotest star. Further, there is plenty of contemporary scientific validation for the ancient claim that there is a benevolent, organizing principle behind the Field *with which individuals can harmonize.*

The individual, social and planetary implications of this understanding may seem at times practically beyond imagination. Such an understanding, threaded through the myriad historical constructs of science, religion and politics, could literally change centuries of human knowledge and behavior patterns. It would require nothing short of a massive shift in world perspective, similar to the profound effect the Copernican theory, that the world was round and revolves around the sun, had on the flat-earth belief prior to that time. When we make this shift in consciousness most of our constructs about how life functions on the planet will be transformed.

We will awaken to the actual truth of what is held within ourselves and within the Field that supports us.

Could the world transform if we realized that there actually is no separation between us, that we are all connected, all the time? Wouldn't our relationships with one another, and to the entire world, alter profoundly if we became aware that violence to another is violence to ourselves? How would it be if we realized that our own violence radiates out into global consciousness?

Already individuals and groups are arriving at field-consciousness through many avenues. And they are applying this understanding to world solutions. For the last twenty years there has been a collective, subtle but powerful current of higher consciousness awakening. There are now many teachers and bodies of work on the planet that directly teach or foster unity consciousness, whether they explicitly refer to the unified Field or not. I believe we are already experiencing that revolution of human consciousness.

Even if a person knows nothing about quantum physics, Field-consciousness is popping up everyplace. Energy healers are working in the human aura, world healers are working consciously in the global field for world healing. Even a contemporary vitamin company advertises, "We are committed to making a positive impact on the world—a healthier planet, a healthier you." In the last few years many large groups have been convened to facilitate shifting consciousness from accelerated destruction to world healing.

Practical Applications of Field Consciousness

These teachings are joined by a growing awareness of the wisdom of indigenous cultures all over the world, many of which center around a reverence for nature and the unity of all life. For example, the indigenous Grandmothers, a group of elders who have been teaching around the world in the last few years, are directing one dramatic demonstration of world healing through the field. You may note how these teachings sound much like the ancient Rig Veda teachings I've cited. They ask the world, "Will we choose to awaken to our higher consciousness in the face of dramatic Earth changes? Will we choose life?"

The Grandmothers are urging people to adopt a one-world, unified perspective by visualizing the Field as a *Net of Light*. They teach that the Net of Light is called by different names. Web of Light, Grid of Light, Indra's Net, are a few. But all, they say, refer to the same thing. The Grandmothers tell us:

> This is the Net of Light that will hold the earth during the times of change that are now upon you. From this place on the Net of Light, cast now to those who do not know that they too are held in light, cast to those who are suffering and also to those who are disturbed by the rise of negativity on earth and want to help in some way, but who have not had a way to access the healing and love of the Net of Light. Many people have no spiritual path to follow. They cannot relate to organized religion and they have not found a way that speaks to their heart. We ask you to cast the Net of Light to them now, so the Net can take them to their path. We ask you to do this for yourself, and for everything that lives. And as you work with the Net of Light, you will become a walking blessing upon the earth.... Go forward now and take your place on the Net of Light. Somewhere where two strands come together is a place that will feel just right for you. Hold this place on the Net and let the Net hold you. You hold and you are held in light.... The Net is lit by the jewel of the heart of each person who holds it; it is held in selfless service.

There are now seventy Grandmothers groups focused on spreading their message. They are asking humans to keep visualizing this Net around the world, to heal and repair it. They say, "The energies of Yin and Yang are out of balance. Too much Yang, the energy of the masculine principle, and not enough Yin, the energy of the feminine principle, has placed the Earth in danger. Because women are the natural reservoirs of Yin for the planet, they must be empowered. It is time for this planet to return to harmony and for this, *women must lead*."

A Hopi prophecy declared, "When the wisdom of the Grandmothers is heard, the world will heal."

Can West Meet East in Agreement?

Is it possible that Western and Eastern philosophies and science can find common ground where the Field, Zero Point Field, Quantum Hologram and the Tao are understood as one thing? Could we reach a point in human evolution when our instinctual knowing of the universal Field can be made conscious? A universal evolutionary cycle seems to demand that we recognize our oneness with each other and the universe. When my twenty-two-year old grand-daughter, Lauren, who just graduated from University, read this chapter, she added here, "Before it is too late?" I took this as a signal from the contemporary generation, those wonderful young people who already understand that the present course of violence and squandering of earth resources must be replaced by conservation and sustainability.

With a unified-field perspective we could tune in to our actual, but little-tapped, human potential. If we realized how our own human thought-field affects the universal energy Field, we could take more responsibility for our own thinking and behavior. We might even learn how to set conscious intentions into the Field that would help make ourselves, and our world, a healthier place.

2:

THE PSYCHOLOGY OF WHOLENESS

*Open your eyes and see that you are far more than
you imagine. You are the world, you are the universe;
you are yourself and everyone else, too! It's all the
marvelous Play of God. Wake up, regain your humor.*

~Dan Millman

The universal Field is reflected in all human beings. Each of us is permeated and informed by the Field and thus we are potentially integrated with universal energy and information.

Each of us carries within us the intelligence of wholeness—body, mind, emotions and soul. Yet that innate wholeness has been chopped up into fragmented pieces in our consciousness so that we see ourselves as many parts, often unrelated or only vaguely related. And as we grow up, often we even lose awareness of several parts of ourselves. In Soul Lightening we want to facilitate the ability of each person to become aware of, and actualize, all parts of his or her self.

When my sister Annie was diagnosed with cancer of the optical nerve she was thirty-three years old and the mother of four small children. She was given a few months to live by her medical doctor. I loved my sister dearly and wanted to help in any way I could.

Since I was working on a graduate degree in wholistic health at the time, I wanted to apply what I was learning about healing to Annie. I didn't know much, but at least I had learned that body symptoms are often a reflection of mental, emotional and even spiritual issues in a person's life.

Naively I called Annie's doctor and asked what he would recommend regarding her wholistic needs.

"What do you mean?" he asked, rather incredulously.

"Well, what to do about other possible pressures or imbalances in her life, such as nutritional, emotional, mental or even spiritual factors that could affect her body."

"Those things are not within my realm of practice," he answered.

This was in the early 1970s, when there were almost no wholistic clinics or doctors. Deepak Chopra and Andrew Weil hadn't emerged yet, and I was making up my own degree program as I went along. At that time it was standard practice to consult medical doctors for body symptoms, psychologists or psychiatrists for emotional or mental problems, nutritionists for allergies or food imbalances, and a minister or priest for our spiritual concerns.

It is a very different landscape in health care now. In the last twenty years many major discoveries and changes in the fields of medicine, psychology, brain research, alternative care and body-work have verified or reinforced an ancient Chinese perspective that healing requires an understanding of the whole person. It is now generally understood that what affects one "part" of a person is inextricably connected to other parts. In his recent book, A Return to Healing,[4] Dr. Len Saputo explains, with brilliance and long experience, how the medical system must come to this wholistic

---

4 Saputo, Len, MD. 2009. *A Return to Healing: Radical Health Care Reform and the Future of Medicine.* Origin Press

and integrative approach in order for us to maintain health in this country.

Unfortunately, Annie didn't live long enough to benefit from most of these recent discoveries. She received chemotherapy, radiation and multiple surgeries. Her family and I tried to support and comfort her the best we could throughout the course of her treatment. Her ministers and spiritual sisters visited frequently to pray with her. I studied as fast as I could to bring her psychological or nutritional approaches that claimed to be helpful for cancer.

Annie was supported spiritually through her death process by the loving presence of her husband and family who shared her religious beliefs that heaven awaited her, and by my belief that the soul is eternal, on a wondrous growth journey through life and death. With these resources she died a peaceful death.

Fragmentation of the Whole Being

Throughout human history we have been motivated by poignant experiences, like the one with my sister Annie, to advance our knowledge and understanding. Since the "Age of Enlightenment," we have believed that the best way to gain this understanding was to split ourselves and the material universe into parts so we could analyze the pieces more closely. Since Newton's physics we have reasoned that the universe is like a machine: If we understood all of the parts we would know the whole. We intended to gain knowledge and power over human life and nature with this reasoning.

In medicine we have dissected the body into its smallest particles in order to understand how it works and how to *fix* it. Thus we believe it is necessary to consult a medical specialist to know what to do with your own body problems. With this reasoning we have given the knowledge and power of our bodies over to doctors.

In psychology we have separated out all the part of our personalities and analyzed the genetic and conditioned aspects that have made us what and who we are. By fragmenting and analyzing all these aspects of our lives, particularly those influences from childhood, we feel we have come to understand ourselves better. But this *understanding* requires a therapist. We believe we need someone else to guide our psychological development because that other person, trained in psychology and wise in the ways of dissecting all the pieces, has the answers we need to be happy. At least this is the impression we're left with.

In the 1950s science accomplished the ultimate splitting apart—fission of the atom itself. We came to the apex of that endeavor when we exploded the atom bomb over Hiroshima. We demonstrated that we could split the atom, believed to be the very basic building block of matter and life at that time. And it has taken us more than fifty years to contemplate the results of our actions and wonder if we have been on the right track. This is one of the many factors, I believe, that is leading us to a completely new phase of human evolution. We are beginning to reach beyond wanting to break everything up in order to understand. Now we want to go beyond fragmentation and find that place of fusion where we are in unity with all of life, with ourselves and with this entire planet.

In spiritual practice we also split matters into fragments. We split our closeness to God into five or six major religions, with thousands of sects. And then each sect held that it knew the one truth, the right and proper way. Of course, there can't be thousands of "one truth," so we created wars to resolve the arguments. One "true" religion would prove it had all the answers through coercion and physical force. Wars between religions further distanced us from God and our own Divine souls. We became so removed from the direct truth of Divinity that we believed we had to rely on the judgment and dogma of our teachers, priests, gurus and other authority figures to find our way.

Living from Parts of the Whole Being

Everybody knows we are made up of body and mind. Fewer are in touch with their emotions and spirit. It still isn't common awareness for people to realize they are whole, even though we are swiftly waking up to this realization.

We tend to function predominantly from one part of our being. For example, when we're ill we tend to focus on body symptoms and medical information about the body. The athlete and dancer also focus on the body and on movement. Just the opposite was true for a beautiful man I knew who was almost completely incapacitated with multiple sclerosis. When I asked him how he was doing, his response was, "Oh, I don't pay much attention to this body." I realized that his detachment from his body was completely understandable and appropriate, given his situation.

Some people necessarily live primarily in their heads. For example, an intellectual professor's life is centered on learning and transmitting information. The computer technician focuses throughout his day on digital information in the computer; he operates almost exclusively from a linear, left-brain perspective. When a bodyworker works with a person who talks or analyzes things continually as she is receiving the bodywork, the practitioner says that this person "lives in her head," signifying that the client is mostly unaware of his or her body.

Since the Age of Enlightenment western culture has cultivated this analytical mind, predominantly a linear, left-brained function. The result by now is an intellectual tunnel vision that obscures our intelligence of other parts of our being, such as heart wisdom, body knowing, and soul guidance.

By contrast, a teenager in love is immersed in emotions centered on the loved one, and their budding relationship. Her daily routine is focused on connecting with the loved one, what he feels, what she feels. She can spend hours on the telephone with him, or with her friends talking about him. Homework and housework are ignored. Her predominant verb is "feel," as in, "I feel excited," "I feel scared," "I feel ignored," or, "I feel adored."

The Hologram of Consciousness

As we learn more, in science and in studies of personal growth, we have begun to understand that we are a *hologram*, that is, a multidimensional system of the most extraordinary intelligences that work synergistically, constantly maintaining our wholeness and keeping us balanced.

We are born with this whole-being intelligence. It is embedded in our very cells. The more we explore the miracle of a whole human being, through science and meditative inquiry, the more it becomes evident that each of us carries the miraculous intelligence within us to fulfill our life's purpose.

Although whole-being intelligence is innate, it is often diminished or compromised by many outer realities, such as the conditioning we receive from our family, environment, culture, geography and education. As babies we could see and hear clearly what was going on around us, and feel emotions and sensations in our own bodies. But gradually that awareness became disconnected from our own inborn intelligence.

Waking Up

As a young woman I was heavily influenced by the philosopher-teacher G. I. Gurdjieff, who taught that all people are asleep even as they look awake and walk around. He taught that until people are awakened by psycho-spiritual work on themselves they are simply conditioned automatons. The day I was initiated into my lifelong spiritual practice I offered a silent prayer: "God, please help me to wake up fully in this life." Gurdjieff's teaching and that prayer continue to stand in the background of my work.

When I tuck my two-year-old granddaughter into bed she lays her little blond curls down on the mattress for about twenty seconds, closes her eyes and then abruptly, like a jack-in-the-box, sits up, eyes wide open and virtually shouts, with extreme vigor, "I wake up!"

To *wake up!* is exactly our goal as we teach people how to follow their own unique process, conscious and unconscious, through the labyrinthine layers of conditioning to that inviolate clear intelligence of their whole beings, particularly their own souls.

My granddaughter rejects sleeping with all her thirty-pound might. She doesn't want to nap. "No!" she cries as we tug her toward the bed. In the evening when we announce that bedtime stories are over, she starts wiggling away, searching for a toy, a cracker, the potty, and still another book—all kinds of distractions to forestall that inevitable end of day. "One more," she pleads, handing us another book. She will do anything to prevent "lights out." She wants to stay awake for every single happening.

By contrast, at the end of the day most of us grownups long for sleep and the respite of no-consciousness. We're tired out from managing adult responsibilities. We're also fatigued by endless self-talk voices: "I should have done this and that...Mother would have done better...I should be perfect...why can't I ... I should have remembered such-and-such," on and on in endless self-torture. Unlike my granddaughter who doesn't want to miss a single instant of what's happening, we're so relieved when the day draws to a close that we look forward to just letting it all turn off for a while.

When I look at my granddaughter I see the luminous brilliance of her magical child, an unaltered spirit. No *shoulds* or *should nots* yet, at least not enough to dim her light. No convoluted layers of defenses, social games, political maneuvers. I can clearly see that she is perfect just as she is.

She is my teacher. I think of her with great inspiration every time I explain the aim of Process Acupressure to new students.

I have the capacity to see that perfection, that brilliant spirit, within most adults I meet. And when I'm at my best, as a therapist, teacher, mother, friend, I focus on that brilliance and encourage it however I can. As a psychologist I have been trained to see, and label, the multiple personality layers over the soul that often result in debilitating neuroses, or simply the paralysis of too much thinking. Those layers also alter and cover over the light of the soul. Sometimes I encounter people whose coverings of familial, social and cultural conditionings are so pervasive that I forget to look beneath them for the pure intelligence and life purpose of that individual. From this perspective I see only neurotics, programmed robots, sleeping in a trance of mass hypnosis, hurting themselves and others repeatedly. When I only see personality layers I feel enormous frustration, even defeat. That world is far too limited for me. I can't live fully within it.

So my life's work has become the process of peeling away dysfunctional sheaths that cover or obscure soul intelligence. Each layer uncovered is an awakening into the magnificent landscape of spirit. And each *wake up* releases more freedom into the vast potential that we actually are.

When my granddaughter says, "I wake up!" I celebrate her. Silently I say, "Right, Lucy. Keep it up. Please don't forget, as you travel the inevitable labyrinth into adulthood, that you can stay awake, that you can remember just who you are right now. And even when you fall asleep at the wheel of conditioning, you can always jump right up like a jack-in-the-box and announce *I wake up!*"

Our aim in Soul Lightning is to wake up awareness to the hologram of being—soul, body, mind and emotions—so that each of us can reclaim as much of our innate intelligence as possible and cultivate awareness and expression in all the many facets that express our wholeness. By claiming whole-being awareness we know that we may readily access the intelligence within us, and the intelligence of the Universal Field, that can most effectively guide our individual development and realization of purpose.

The following chapters report our understandings of each part of our wholeness.

3:

THE SOUL

Our soul, our true self, is the most mysterious,
essential, and magical dimension of our being. In fact,
it is not a separate reality...but the cohesive force
that unites our body, heart, and mind. It is not a ghost
trapped somehow in the physical machinery of our
body, but the very essence of our being.

~Gabrielle Roth

Our final aim in Soul Lightening work is to uncover the guidance, power and purpose of the soul, or spiritual aspect, beneath conditioning, personality and ego. We want to help a person become aware of soul consciousness because we value the soul as the rightful director of life. Therefore I begin a whole-being view of the person by focusing on the soul, even though we usually do substantial personality and bodywork prior to gaining access to soul consciousness.

In the beginning of our work many students have asked, what is the soul? Until very recently the word "soul" had uncomfortable connotations for many people, since it was often associated with particular religious, moral or philosophical perspectives. The term has been mostly shunned by psychology, until very recently as a new interest is dawning. But I have observed over time that if I watch or question closely, almost everyone has had a direct experience of their own deep essential truth. I call that truth *soul*, though the person having that experience might not have been aware of it at the time, and probably would not have called it soul.

Webster's dictionary defines soul this way: "A person's moral or emotional nature or sense of identity, as in: *in the depths of her soul, she knew he would betray her*; the essence of something: *integrity is the soul of intellectual life*; emotional or intellectual energy or intensity, esp. as revealed in a work of art or an artistic creation."[5]

I define the soul as that eternal, inviolate aspect of every human being that carries his or her purpose and reason for being. We are all born with the soul's knowing of right direction and right action for the successful completion of our lives. The soul can be in touch with transcendent consciousness, aware of the Great Unity beyond personal ego and beyond everyday mental activity. Its intelligence is vast, its resources unlimited.

The soul is not the body, not the mind, nor is it the emotions. Yet it can animate and inhabit all of these aspects of us as instruments of its own expression. My experience is that each of us is unified with the great Creative Source of evolution and guided by it, if we allow that flow. The soul remains integrated with a body as long as that soul's purpose is served.

From Theory to Practice

In my spiritual practice I experienced soul awareness and consciousness many years ago. This presence of the soul is as tangible to me as my arms and fingers, something that has been an important

---

5 *Webster's Encyclopedic Unabridged Dictionary of the English Language*. 1989. New York, Gramercy Books

aspect of my life, long before I went to graduate school in psychology. However, as a graduate student, and as a creator of a wholistic therapy in the 1980s, I was originally shy about bringing out my own inner knowing of the soul since it was largely rejected by those in psychology, medicine and even bodywork. Nevertheless, I had a strong intuition that the souls within people could be contacted if they were intelligently introduced to that possibility.

To test this hypothesis I first experimented with close colleagues, particularly my process partner, Laura, and long-term trusting clients. I asked each to contact their own soul, or "that deepest essential part of yourself," for important guidance. While the usual mind chatter often blocked soul contact, just as it does in meditation, acupressure helped tremendously with entry to soul consciousness. Acupressure opens the flow of energy in the body, deeply relaxes, balances and allows an altered state of consciousness, similar to that revealed in hypnosis, or what occurs as we approach sleep. I was amazed at how easily almost all the colleagues and clients I worked with in this way slipped into soul consciousness. It was as if, once given permission for soul contact, they had no trouble accessing that awareness.

At first I hesitated to request soul contact with most of my regular clients. I thought they might find this weird, impossible or heretical. But before very long I was becoming increasingly confident and was asking certain of my clients to visit and access their own soul wisdom toward the end of their sessions. After they had processed whatever issues were in their minds and hearts, and while they were still in that deep state of relaxation, supported by the environment and my hands doing acupressure, their own deep knowing bubbled up quite easily. Eventually I was confident that there was enough empirical data to verify that other clients had the same capability as those people who so easily and willingly accessed their soul wisdom.

Those early, very tentative experiments were in the early 1980s. Since that time I and other therapists doing Soul Lightening work have demonstrated the fundamental truth of the soul's accessibility thousands of times. And our clients' development has shown how rapidly and healthily they progress when guided by their own inner wisdom.

I remember one middle-aged woman—I'll call her Gail—who came to us in a state of confusion and distress. She reported that she had seriously followed a spiritual teacher for many years, never questioning his authenticity. But then various events around him caused her not only to question him but also to denounce him. She felt betrayed and suddenly without a frame of reference for living. She said, "Now I feel like a fake! What I've been believing and doing all these years seems completely hollow. Inside myself I am lost."

Gail learned our work and started sifting through her life, separating what was true for her from what was false. She learned how to examine every teaching, from parents, school and church, through the matrix of her own wholistic sensing in body, mind and feelings, and especially in her soul. Through this process she began to reclaim her own power and trust her own truth. Later she said to me, "I felt like a phony when I came to you because most of what I believed was second-hand. But now I have regained my own internal *truth-gauge*. Although I can learn from an outside teacher, I don't need to rely on one for my direction in life. I feel authentic and confident now that I can be guided by my own soul truth and purpose."

One of our main tasks in Soul Lightening is to encourage that reconnection and cultivation of soul consciousness. We have found that as people regain their own inner power and truth, they are happier, more effective in their life purpose, more creative and more dedicated to a principle of unity and harmony with others.

How Soul Truth Becomes Obscured

We came into this life and body with a lighted soul, still connected to the great creative flow of ALL THAT IS. For example, in a group-supported process session one student experienced that original connection. She had already become aware of the first cells of her body in utero:

H (Client): I am very aware of four cells in utero [of her own prenatal fetus], wanting attention.

A (Aminah, beginning the acupressure protocol): Let me know when you have contact. Let yourself become conscious of the four cells and report to us what is there.

H: The soul is there.

A: So you have contact with soul consciousness, let it tell you what is useful to you right now.

H: It says, I choose to be here. I am here.

A: Allow your awareness to spread out broadly from this soul contact.

H: My soul fills all the space in the uterus.

At birth, and for several months thereafter, an infant feels the presence of its soul and can still respond from soul intelligence for his own wellbeing. The infant moves toward loving presence and touch; he pulls away from negative emotions or hurtful acts. He is free and spontaneous in behavior.

But as the soul adjusts to the constraints of a physical body and as the child learns how to adapt within the family and society, soul awareness is gradually obscured or even covered over. Approval and love from outside himself—mother, father, siblings and teachers—take precedence over his own innate soul promptings.

In ordinary development a person loses touch with this inborn spiritual guidance. After about age seven there is little awareness of soul intelligence, except as it intrudes from the unconscious, in dreams or in unexpected events such as those I described about my childhood experiences in the previous chapter.

One very significant soul communication remains in childhood. It bubbles up in dreams. It was first discovered by Carl Jung and later pursued by Arnold Mindell and myself; it has been called simply the *childhood dream*. This dream is different from others in that it makes a very strong impression on the child. Either it is a one-time indelible dream and never forgotten or it may recur several times. It is as if the soul is determined to get through the screen of ordinary consciousness. Both Jung and Mindell found that this prominent dream often gives a strong clue about the life's soul purpose.

I reported the powerful effect of my own childhood dream in my book *Soul Lightning: Awakening to Soul Consciousness.* I won't repeat all of it here, but the short version goes like this: As a five-year old child I awoke in terror from a dream of seeing my father's half-decomposed body rising out of his grave. A torrential rain swept down through the graveyard and the grave was filling up with water and mud. My father reached out to me for help. As a little girl I didn't know what to do. I loved my father and wanted to help, but at the same time I was paralyzed in fear by his hideous-looking body.

That nightmare terrified me then and thereafter, whenever I thought of it. But about forty years later it provided very useful soul purpose information when I learned how to understand it. I now urge students to search out a childhood dream that could give a blueprint, in dream shorthand, for their soul purpose.

A shaman friend reported a dream-like experience he had when he was a small child. For as long as he could recall, he had a spirit guide who always told him, "Things are not as they appear!" One day when he was around five or six, my friend found the placenta that a small animal had left behind. He did not, of course, know what it was, but his spirit guide told him that it had to do with the birth process. My friend said, "My spirit guide went on to explain that there was the fleshy part of life and then there was something more, the part that animates the flesh. He told me this in a way that made sense to me as a child, and I was moved very deeply, in fact, in some transcendent way that was more exciting than anything that I had ever previously thought or felt. But when I tried to tell my parents about this they dismissed it as a little boy's "cute story" about his "imaginary friend." Nevertheless this experience continued to be a touchstone in my spiritual life, as it is even to this day. What was perhaps most important, however, was that what my spirit guide told me that day had not been new information but a reminder of something I knew from before I was born."

Many children have experiences of this *otherworldly* kind, which they learn quickly to keep quiet about. My little sister used to have a "playmate," Johnny, whom nobody else could see. My parents told her not to lie and tell stories like that, but I believed in Johnny. I could see how much fun she had with him.

I remember talking to my dolls in the playhouse, as well as other "people" there. But when my stepfather heard that talking he told me, nicely, not to talk like that because people might think I was crazy. I never talked to my dolls or invisible friends again. But I often worried as I grew up that people might think I was crazy.

As a little girl my process partner, Laura, often had visitations from angels or dead relatives. When the hair rose on her arms she knew it was a dead person calling. Sometimes they warned her about things that would happen. Once they told her not to be sad about her grandmother's coming death. And so she wasn't sad, nor surprised, when her grandmother did die. But she quickly learned not to tell grownups about such *preternatural* experiences, just as many children do.

Most soul awareness is lost by adulthood. Yet there is substantial evidence of soul consciousness from past and present mystics who, after long and arduous spiritual practice, were able to tune in to higher states of consciousness, and to meanings and purposes beyond themselves. But they were not often able to teach others how to reach that state.

Soul Consciousness in the Present Time

In our time an awareness of soul consciousness is showing up more and more frequently. For example, when I first published *Soul Return* it was a big risk to use the word soul; now there are countless books with soul in the title and magazine articles about it.

Soul consciousness can happen abruptly in a transcendent experience, such as a near-death experience, true spiritual baptism or dramatic spiritual initiation. For example, as recently as 2012, two doctors published books on their near-death experiences, adding to the thousands of cases that already exist in that literature. But these accounts are particularly noteworthy because the authors come from scientific backgrounds and both have disciplined scientific minds.

Dr. Eben Alexander, a neurosurgeon with an extensive scientific knowledge of the brain, wrote the bestselling book *Proof of Heaven*.[6] His discovery of the soul, which he hardly believed in before his death, was unique in that his brain (the neo-cortex) was medically dead while he was in a coma for seven days. Thus he learned first-hand that consciousness is not confined to the brain. He also discovered many transcendent realms and vast knowledge, which he instantly understood, in some way far beyond his brain-based comprehension. In "heaven" Dr. Alexander was given three messages:

You are loved and cherished dearly, forever.
You have nothing to fear.
There is nothing you can do wrong.

What is most valuable to me about Dr. Alexander's book is that he explains in detail just how the brain works in ordinary consciousness, and why it can't comprehend soul consciousness.

Dr. Mary Neal, author of *To Heaven and Back*,[7] is a spine surgeon, also with years of technical scientific training and patient-experience. She described how, when she drowned in a boat accident, her soul lifted out of her broken body and soared into vast realms beyond earth, where she experienced great love and peace. She

6 Alexander, Eban. 2012. *Proof of Heaven: A Neurosurgeon's Journey into the Afterlife.* New York, Simon & Schuster Paperbacks

7 Neal, Mary C. 2012. *To Heaven and Back: A Doctor's Extraordinary Account of Her Death, Heaven, Angels, and Life Again.* Colorado Springs, CO., Waterbrook Press

dispassionately explains how her medically trained mind was fascinated as she observed just how her bones were broken while her soul was flying free. She had no pain and no regret at all about leaving life behind, even though she deeply loved her husband and four children.

Most of us will never experience a death experience from which we return to life, so these accounts help us to enlarge our understanding of the immortality of our own souls and a benevolent universe. I highly recommend both of these books that give the reader an explicit report of life after death. They add scientifically to the multitude of other near-death accounts that are now available.

Soul Lightening's Method for Eliciting Soul Truth

Soul Lightening work focuses on facilitating soul awareness as early as possible, as I've said. But true spiritual contact and guidance within an individual—outside of or in addition to religious teachings—require peeling away layers of conditioning that shroud soul consciousness. I often call that shroud the cocoon of conditioning, because it keeps us confined within the limited domain of our upbringing and educational and cultural teachings. Liberation is the experience of breaking free from that cocoon.

Therefore, before actual soul work can become predominant, our Soul Lightening program offers the perspective and tools to liberate an individual from that cocoon of conditioning—false ideas, beliefs and traumas accumulated by the personality. We never deny or bypass the necessary personality work to be done, even while we leave space open for soul wisdom.

At an appropriate time in our work—it could be very early for a spiritually-aligned person, or very late for someone who is resistant to a spiritual perspective—we might explain that each of us has a Divine immortal part, which we call soul, and which carries the blueprint for this life. It isn't necessary for a person to accept the word soul or a spiritual context in order to find his or her own inner wisdom, since we all carry that wise center within. Although we use the word soul, we make it clear that the deepest wise part within every one of us is called by many names, such as the *still small voice*, essence, center, Higher Self or Essential Self, and so forth. We explain that we can ask this part for information and guidance. It is an actual consciousness that leaves the body after death of the body and physical form, as in the cases reported in this chapter. We explain that the soul is immortal, and associated with the crown chakra.

Soul consciousness begins to naturally show up after a person has processed part of their history and become self-reflective. Soul Lightening provides tools for processing history through our process method. (See chapter 9)

After the soul has been recognized we might ask at the end of a session, "Now, please go to that deepest part of yourself, your soul (or whatever word suits the individual), and ask if it has a message or explanation about what you experienced in your session today."

After several experiences of receiving clear guidance from the soul we can even devote a whole session to soul counsel from the beginning of the session by saying, "I invite your soul now to guide this session for your highest good." Also, after soul experience, within several sessions, the person is often able to seek soul guidance on his or her own, even without the aid of bodywork.

A person can often reach directly into her own soul intelligence, to seek information, guidance and clarifications about life that extend beyond the current situation. As one student reported, "When I take my vision directly to my soul I become centered and focused. When I listen to the silence behind sounds I go to a still place in my own center. In this deep space within myself all outer senses drop away, and my path becomes clear."

When Rita came to me she looked like a hippy girl. She was living out of her van and needed help to get oriented to our town where she had recently moved from the east coast. Our beginning work was necessarily focused on her day-to-day survival needs and getting her ready to seek work. She was a fast learner and resourceful, so our work progressed easily.

After the first sessions about practical matters and after she had found work, however, we ran into rocky territory. While remembering something about her childhood she suddenly went blank; she literally went to sleep on the table. I waited through this sleep on the table for several sessions before I finally brought it to her attention. At first she was startled, unaware that she had been sleeping. But then, haltingly, she talked about some experiences in her childhood that she had felt too embarrassed to report to me. Thus began serious and prolonged processing of her childhood abuse that included physical punishment and sexual abuse. This phase was shocking (she had "forgotten" most of it) and painful for both of us. But Rita is a strong person and she was very dedicated to getting free of the past.

After we had worked together for some time, and Rita had come to truly trust me, I introduced the concept of soul. She accepted the possibility of soul consciousness quite easily and from that time forward we asked for soul guidance in almost every session. Rita rapidly gained strength in all aspects of her life, even when there were strong challenges. She experienced that she had the strength and truth within herself to endure. Eventually she became a health care professional, a mother and an author. Now she helps others come to the soul truth within and she is very successful.

Soul Awareness and the Spiritual Channel

Although it is still more common for people to be ego-directed than soul-directed, our experience in Soul Lightening has demonstrated that it is easier and faster to gain soul guidance than we have been led to believe. As consciousness is expanding and elevating in the present time, there is a growing quest for true spiritual contact. Many things are changing rapidly and will continue to do so. Our belief systems, theories and trainings are being updated regularly.

And many seekers are suddenly awakening to inner wisdom and realms of transcendent knowing. We are gradually becoming aware of higher principles and the Divine prerogative of the soul.

Soul awareness can reveal soul intelligence. We encourage the reconnection and cultivation of that intelligence. We seek to recover the original soul awareness that came with the newborn. Simultaneously we introduce the adult to the spiritual channel, a multi- and extra-sensory awareness of soul's communication. We teach students how to open their own spiritual channel to direct soul truth, and then how to keep it open for daily support.

Cultivating Soul Consciousness

Soul consciousness comes from a level beneath or beyond ordinary mind. It is a level that almost always requires a quiet and relaxed body and an altered state of consciousness. Acupressure facilitates both. When a person has reached a level of soul acceptance, and it feels appropriate at the time, we begin Process Acupressure sessions with the following invitation:

> X [name], I invite your own soul to guide this session toward your highest good. I ask my own soul to assist you. And we both invite our higher guides to assist this process.

This simple invitation signals to the soul that we actively seek its participation and direction. Thus the session is already open to a wider perspective than that of personal history and personality. It helps both the client and practitioner to expand into another dimension of wisdom.

A session can be devoted exclusively to soul work when a person already has a familiarity with soul consciousness. In this case we would set an intention for soul consultation from the beginning of the session. We would make the soul invitation and then pose a particular issue: "In this session we wish to consult the soul about [an event, relationship, issue]."

We can also set future-paced intentions, or requests for manifestation, in soul work: "We wish to devote this session to creating the conditions for abundance in [name's] life. We seek any clarification and direction about this."

The wonders of soul work are many. Each person's soul, unique in the universe, will offer something new. Messages are almost always extremely simple, but profoundly relevant to the life circumstances: Love yourself. Be kind to yourself. Love your neighbor as yourself. You are here to heal children. The list goes on.

The vibration of soul work feels clean, uplifting and nourishing. Common feelings that accompany soul work are calmness, serenity, joy, gratitude and reverence. It is deeply satisfying work, for both the client and the facilitator. The ultimate soul consciousness experience is an awakening within a person to his or her true nature and connection with the cosmos. Our soul work class helps students uncover soul consciousness and apply it in their lives.

4:

THE BODY

The human body is not an object in the world.
It is a magnificent process, a ceaseless flow,
a journey in itself.

~Norman Fischer

In Soul Lightening work the body provides the bed of raw data for life history. This includes data from the mind, emotions and even the soul. Through acupressure bodywork we collect direct experiential information that often lies beneath the reach of mind and memory. This is possible because acupressure stimulates the flow of energy in the body, which opens tissue-held memory stored in the systems and tissues of the body. (This phenomenon was only discovered in the last half of the twentieth century.) Further, as body energy is released and balanced a person's awareness is enhanced within each domain—body, mind, emotion and soul.

The human body is comprised of an estimated one hundred trillion cells, twelve systems, thousands of tissues and hundreds of functions, all of which work synergistically to maintain the miracle of life. It is curious that many of us can live within this extraordinary creation and barely know anything about it beyond its need for air, food, water and rest. Yet others can focus attention on the body, learn about it, cultivate its amazing powers and achieve mastery with it in specific ways to yield spectacular results. Think of the individual achievements of Tiger Woods, Luciano Pavarotti, Michael Jackson, Billie Jean King, Steffi Graf or Sonja Henie. We have great admiration for these peak performers. From such masters, as well as from other high achievers who became radically impaired through disease, accident or war, we know something of the body's amazing ability to survive extreme demands and still excel.

At the opposite pole from peak performance lies illness, deterioration, disease, dysfunction and death. Although we have learned from natural disasters such as earthquakes, tsunamis and volcano eruptions that humans are incredibly resilient and can survive with far less and far longer than we had originally thought, we have also seen that prolonged deprivation and illness can destroy individuals, whole cultures and whole species. Think of the indigenous tribes that are now extinct. Like our brother creatures on the earth, the life of a human body is not infinitely indestructible. It can be seriously crippled, corrupted and even extinguished. So what do we learn from all this?

An amazing record of both conditions came to us this year from an enlightening study in contrasts, *Warrior Pose*.[8] It is the memoir of a peak performer turned terminal victim of a broken body and spirit who, against all odds, reversed the swing, from broken man to transformed healer. His name is Brad Willis; his transformed name is Bhava Ram. The book tells of his successes as an NBC foreign correspondent who lived through the hells of the Middle Eastern wars only to end up with a broken back and stage IV, terminal throat cancer. On his death bed his spirit rallied. The remainder of the book recounts his healing and return to robust health through yoga. The book is one of the most inspiring soul and body

8 Willis, Brad. 2013. *Warrior Pose: How Yoga Literally Saved My Life.* Dallas, TX, Benbella Books, Inc.

stories I've ever read. Like the recent near-death records it gives us incentive for further investigation into the relationship between soul and cosmos.

Linking Body Intelligence with Body Awareness

Body intelligence lives within every cell of the body. In extremely complex ways, the cellular network within the body systems integrates and cross-communicates to promote growth, health and correction of imbalances.

The body contains its own systems for growing, balancing and healing itself, through its innate intelligence. This observation is one of the foundations of osteopathy, homeopathy and chiropractic as well as classic Chinese and Ayurvedic medicines. These systems strive to free the obstructions in the body that keep it from balancing and healing itself, rather than adding medicines or more radical procedures to treat the symptoms.

The body's intelligence is continually being explored by contemporary science. We know more and more about the parts of body and how it operates but we are only at the beginnings of understanding its miraculous capacities for body awareness, mental direction and whole-being coordination.

Although body intelligence is ever-present, it doesn't automatically enter awareness. Awareness of the body, which can link body intelligence with present consciousness, is still fairly uncommon. In general we are not trained in body awareness nor do we learn much about processing the information that comes from it.

In Soul Lightening one of our most important tasks is to enhance awareness, at all levels of the human experience. We facilitate body, mind, emotions and soul awareness through process methods. (See chapter 9.) We know that body awareness can be taught and that it can continue to expand throughout life.

People who cultivate body awareness are able to respect the earliest and most subtle signals the body provides, take them seriously and act accordingly. Thus they can avoid many common ailments that would have developed if attention and care had not been given upon recognition of the first symptoms. They can feel the sensations and signs of a cold, for example, long before it becomes symptomatic, and then take action: getting more rest, reducing stress, changing their diets, avoiding toxic environments or even changing the pattern of their breathing or movements.

This awareness is one of the reasons why, when a person arrives for a Soul Lightening session and reports some kind of distress in the body, we often ask, "What happened within the last thirty-six hours that was upsetting to you?" By tracking such events—physical, emotional or mental—we can often find the key element that started a spiral of imbalance within the body. And by addressing and resolving that event we can frequently eliminate the physical symptom or greatly reduce it. By recognizing a progression that might lead to major imbalance, we can often prevent more serious consequences.

In Soul Lightening work, healing and growth are continuously supported by energy work in the body and related process work in consciousness in order to find the roots of imbalances. As energy is released, raw data shows up in awareness. As we unravel the whole complex of symptoms and signals in the body, we usually find a root cause of a trauma, condition or belief that can then be rectified, healed or reprogrammed. Then the body, mind and emotions can return to harmony.

People who "live in their heads," as we often describe it, sometimes lose much of their body awareness because they focus so extensively on thinking, actually blocking the subtler sensations of the body. Many people have turned awareness off within the body early in life, often in order to cope with stressors in the environment, pain or shame. They are not presently aware of tension or pain within their bodies, much less the more elusive signals of tingling, muscular tension, shallow breathing, asymmetry, and so forth. It is no wonder that they often miss the early warning signals of symptoms, which, ignored, can develop into serious illness.

I once worked with an M.D. who presented with a very painful shoulder that could have been easily corrected early on with acupressure, when perhaps he had felt just a little discomfort. But the doctor had not been aware of the increasing pain until it became severe. As I worked with him I found out how numb he had become to his own body. Of course he knew anatomy and physiology very well but he seemingly didn't apply that knowledge to his own body awareness. His knowledge was all in his head.

In such cases, where the person's life has become so focused on the mind, information or impulses from the body are pushed out of awareness and hidden away in the body where they eventually cause symptoms. This is called *somatization*.

Sometimes it takes a dramatic experience to break through the shield of unawareness. Body awareness can abruptly begin when something goes wrong, such as a cold, stomach cramps or appendicitis. During or after a serious accident, awareness of the injured body parts becomes intense, as in the case of John Lilly.

John Lilly, M.D. was a successful practicing psychiatrist and graduate of Harvard Medical School. In his forties a dramatic experience catapulted his awareness and understanding of the body beyond his medical education. He thought he knew as much about the body as he would ever need to know; then a ten-minute experience changed the way he studied himself and other people from then on. And it certainly changed the way he worked. This is what happened:

Lilly was receiving Rolfing, an intense hands-on treatment method to realign body posture, when the practitioner moved a thumb deeply into the bottom of Lilly's foot. Lilly reported that at that moment he cried out a primal scream that was completely beyond his control. And at the same moment he remembered an experience that had been blocked from his mind for forty years. [9]

---

9 Lilly, John. 1973. *The Center of the Cyclone: Looking Into Inner Space.* New York, Bantam Press

He remembered that as a four-year-old child he was running barefoot behind his father through a meadow. His foot came down hard on the blade of an upturned axe, gashing into his flesh. His father rushed to him, grabbed the foot and said, "Don't cry, don't cry. Big boys don't cry." Anyone can imagine the searing pain of such a cut but he did what his father said and choked back his scream. As a little boy Lilly wanted to please his father at any cost.

The father rushed his son to the clinic where the wound was sewn up with many stitches and healed in time. However, Lilly suffered thereafter with a painful ache in that foot whenever it was exposed to any stress, such as cold, pressure or heat.

After he recovered the forgotten memory during the Rolfing session, and let the scream out of his system, the foot never bothered him again. Lily's epiphany stimulated several pieces of work where he explored his feelings for the first time. He also began to observe his medical colleagues in a new light; he realized that many of them had suppressed their feelings throughout an intensely intellectual education.

Before this experience Lilly intellectually understood a great deal about the generic human body. But as a result of recalling his four-year old's pain, and focusing awareness on the whole episode, he gained a more vast awareness in his own body, as well as about his clients' bodies. Added to the thousands of intellectual facts about the body he had stored in his mind, this awareness amplified and revolutionized the way he worked with his clients and, indeed, how he experienced his whole life.

In recent years people are realizing that physical illness is not just about the body. Many people have learned a great deal about how to stay alive and become physically healthy as a result of serious physical illness. They have written about their experiences (Brad Wallis in *Warrior Pose*, Norman Cousins in *Anatomy of an Illness*, Louise Hay in *You Can Heal Your Life* and Meir Schneider in *Self-Healing*) and helped many others to take back individual responsibility for health and wellbeing.

Epidemic diseases, such as cancer and AIDS, have made it impossible for the medical profession to continue to carry the full responsibility for our health. In learning how to take care of themselves, many people have started waking up to the early signals their bodies are sending all the time. From experiences like those of Dr. Lilly's, we see how important it can be to learn how to address the early signals of distress.

Modern society has mostly taught us how to disregard what our bodies and minds are telling us, and even how to ignore them or stoically suppress the subtler symptoms and signs so that we can "get back to work." In the chapters to come, we'll explore ways of increasing awareness of these signals to expand our vision of health and healing.

5:
ACUPRESSURE AND SOUL LIGHTENING BODYWORK

The power of life comes from within; go there; pray;
meditate. Reach for those luminous places in your self.

~Jean Shinoda Bolen

In the chapters ahead I'll be focusing attention on the mind and emotions, but before doing so I want to address the way we use acupressure to work with the whole person through the body. You'll thus have a clearer idea of how all components flow together in one session of Soul Lightening Acupressure.

First a little personal history: Bodywork was unknown to me when I first experienced Rolfing, the system of bodywork I referred to in the story about Dr. Lilly in the previous chapter. I was pregnant at the time and feared losing the baby from pernicious anemia, which I was experiencing at the time and which was not responding to medicine. A Rolfing practitioner and good friend of mine had been successful at relieving body symptoms with a series of ten

Rolfing treatments. She offered to work with me and I gratefully accepted.

After the first few treatments my blood count—which had been very low, owing to the anemia—started coming up to normal, and I was elated. Then, late in the series of treatments, a shocking thing happened. I re-experienced my own birth, complete with my own and my mother's pain. Both the practitioner and I were bewildered. What had caused this? My practitioner friend didn't know then, but I was determined to investigate until I understood what caused this very real, painful and revealing experience. Thus began years of bodywork experience and study during which I encountered many more instances of tissue-held memory, in my own and others' bodies. Through those experiences I came to understand that a true wholistic therapy had to be grounded in the body. So I would have to learn about such therapies.

But now came the matter of choosing the right bodywork to learn, one that would reveal questions that in some cases I had not yet even learned how to ask. Already, in the early 1970s, myriads of bodywork modalities were available. I didn't know enough to choose intelligently. So I appealed to higher sources. By this time I knew that my own soul was connected to transcendental dimensions. So I prayed, "Please God, bring me the right bodywork for my soul purposes."

Two weeks after that prayer I was staying overnight with a spiritual sister. This sister had been very fragile and frequently ill during all the time I had known her. But in the last few months I had observed a marked change in her health. She seemed more energized, her symptoms had subsided and she was cheerful. That night I asked her about these changes in her life.

She said, "Oh, I've been receiving and studying this Oriental type of bodywork for several months. It seems to help me a lot. Would you like to know more about it? In fact, would you like to attend classes with me?"

My soul voice said inwardly, "This is it!" So I told my friend that I would like to know more, whereupon she literally dropped an acupressure treatment manual *in my lap* before she left for a meeting.

I picked up the manual in my lap and started flipping through the pages. The charts and numbers in the manual might as well have been in Russian, for all the understanding I could get from them. Even though I couldn't make sense of any of it I kept pondering the pages. They fascinated me.

At that time I was a psychology teacher who had no healthcare or anatomy training. I didn't know a clavicle from a shoulder joint, much less anything about the energy systems of the body.

Even so, since my soul voice had been strong, when my friend returned from her meeting I told her I wanted to go to the classes.

That was the beginning of a lifetime fascination with acupressure and the classical Chinese medical model of energy in general.

Early Foundations

Those first classes, in Jin Shin Jyutsu acupressure, laid the foundation of my work. Though I studied many other forms of acupressure and acupuncture, and other Western bodywork modalities, I always retained and returned to the brilliant and compassionate Jin Shin Jyustu form developed by a contemporary Japanese master, Jiro Murai.

The beginning Jin Shin Jyutsu classes were a wonderful learning, relief and nourishment to me. At that time my life was extremely stressful, with a demanding teaching job, four adolescent children and an erratic husband. Sometimes I was so tired and over-extended that I thought I would surely collapse. In the midst of this the acupressure classes were like discovering a rich, nourishing oasis after an endless trek in the desert.

In each class, as we learned the points and procedures, we worked on each other. What a wonderful relaxation and relief that was! After each class I felt calmer, more energized and more excited about the next class—all this despite the fact that I felt completely incompetent to actually do the work. For example, in the beginning I couldn't feel the points at all. How insecure and frustrated I felt. At school I was a very competent intellectual. But there in the evening acupressure classes I felt like a dunce.

The teacher, Georgia Moody, to whom I am indebted forever, was a warm, sisterly woman who taught in a compassionate style. One evening she lay on the massage table and asked each of us to find some acupressure points on her body. When I put my hands on her she said, "Aminah, you have very good hands." That simple comment gave me the courage to persist, even though I felt so inadequate.

During the next year I continued to study acupressure and practice it on my family and friends. I had been in the habit of taking my children to a doctor regularly. But after learning acupressure, instead of rushing off to the doctor, I first did acupressure on them. The effect was two-fold: Our doctor bills were cut in half and the kids started asking me for acupressure whenever they were sick or stressed. To this day, my fifty-two-year-old son still asks for acupressure whenever I'm near him.

All the acupressure students I know have the same experience with their children. Whenever there's a real problem the kids ask for acupressure. One of our colleagues in England has taught acupressure to her three-year-old grandson. First she gave him acupressure. Then he started calling out the point names to her before she reached them on his body. Next he started giving acupressure, with running commentary, to his teddy bear!

Further Openings and Awareness

During this time another very important experience with a colleague showed me the way to proceed with my work. A teacher at the school where I taught was a good friend and confidant. She was a very intelligent woman who was often overextended with family and teaching overload. Frequently she called in sick to school.

One morning she arrived at school, obviously in great distress. She rushed up to me and said, "Aminah, I need to talk with you at the first break. I have such big problems at home I don't know what to do, and besides that I'm getting the flu again."

I took one look at her, pale and shaky, and said, "Okay, but you can't solve problems while you're sick, so meet me in the nurse's office at the lunch break and I'll give you an acupressure treatment to back off that flu."

We met. She lay on the nurse's examining table and I started the treatment. She lay still for about ten minutes. Then suddenly she started mumbling to herself, something like this: "Umm, I see.... Oh, okay. No, that couldn't be...but it must be. How odd...."

She went on like this for some time. Finally she said out loud, "All right, I know what to do!"

I didn't interrupt to try to find out what she was talking about, nor try to help her by making suggestions. I had no idea what was going on. At the end of the treatment she sat up on the table, looking very different, energized, resolved and optimistic.

"Okay," she said, "I know what to do! It all became quite clear to me during that treatment what is going on at home, who is responsible and what I need to say and do."

Just like that.

I was mystified, astounded and grateful.

My friend did indeed go home that evening and clear everything up. She had a straight talk with her husband and the troublesome teenager who were stressing the whole family. She elicited understanding and promises from those two to solve their dispute right away. Also, she didn't succumb to the flu which had been threatening to lay her low.

This experience was a great revelation to me. It was the first of many subsequent demonstrations that showed me that people hold the solutions to their own problems within them. When their own energy is flowing freely, and they are supported unconditionally, they can gain access to the wisdom within their own bodies, minds, feelings and souls. The problem isn't finding an authority to give guidance. The problem, rather, is gaining access to what is already within their own miraculous systems. Chinese energy healers have known about this phenomenon for millennia. We Western healers are now catching up, by the route of alternative medicine.

A Continuing Progression

My friends gradually found out that I was studying acupressure and began asking me if I could help with a cold, sore knee, sprain and so forth. These requests gave me plenty of opportunity to practice, and many valuable experiences.

One of the most frightening and instructive of these incidents happened one night at about eleven when there was a loud knock on my door. A spiritual sister stood there, holding her husband up because he was barely able to breathe.

"Can you please help him?" she asked. "This evening he started breathing very heavily until finally he could barely get a breath at all. He refuses to go to the hospital. I didn't know what to do until I thought of you."

My inner thoughts were, "Oh, my God, I don't know what to do about this either. It looks really serious and I'm afraid he'll die on my table!" But what could I do, in the face of the reality in front of me? So his wife and I helped him up onto my table where we propped him up with pillows because he couldn't lie flat from lack of breath.

Immediately I started the acupressure formula for respiratory relief. Gradually his breathing eased. After about thirty minutes he was breathing almost normally. Finally he climbed down from the table under his own strength and was able to walk to the door.

I advised him to consult our mutual psychologist friend about this episode because I suspected that there was some emotional factor behind it. He promised to do this. The rest of the story emerged with the psychologist. It turned out that this man had been born in a London hospital during a World War II blitzkrieg by the Germans. In a hypnotic trance session with the psychologist he saw, and re-experienced, emerging at birth in a terror-filled environment in which glass was splintering all over the delivery room, his mother and nurses were terrified and screaming, doctors were shouting orders and the blasts of the bombs were ear splitting.

This man had never remembered his birth before this, nor had he ever had asthma attacks. But just the day before his asthma attack, a gas tank in his yard had exploded. The blast of it had sounded like a bomb. That had been enough to trigger the memory of his birth experience.

No one was more astonished than I when I heard about his experience of reliving his birth. But it reaffirmed my understanding that trauma stored in the body can cause serious symptoms long after the event.

Ongoing Study and Affirmation

After many validating experiences with the effectiveness of acupressure, I began to study in earnest. My first interest was to find a way to release tension in the body and balance energy so that a person could become more whole and have access to all their faculties for natural self-regulation. But the study of acupressure led to a whole world of fascinating and healing possibilities, on all levels.

I had already learned that acupressure is the practice of applying hand or finger pressure to specific energetic or conductive points on the body, which lie on some twenty meridians, or energy pathways, of the body. A practitioner holds these points, in different sequences or "formulas" according to the condition addressed. I further learned that acupressure automatically regulates and balances the body's energy system, so it is a perfect choice for the purposes of creating a whole-being, natural therapy. Very soon I learned many of its other uses. For instance, it releases blocked energy, stale blood and lymph from the tissues, and improves circulation. Pain, tensions and toxicities in the body are released before they manifest as illness. Thus it is an excellent preventive modality.

Although acupressure certainly can't replace necessary medical care, my family's medical bills were cut in half in the first year I studied it because I learned to treat many common symptoms successfully with it. Later, I learned with clients that acupressure could address a multitude of common physical problems, such as back problems, headaches, respiratory, digestive and systemic conditions as well as colds, flu, allergies and recovery from injuries.

Then of course, acupressure provides a natural and effective means for people to receive loving, healing touch, which we know now is therapeutic in itself. In Soul Lightening we use a particular kind of touch—called "interface touch"—which I learned and borrowed from Fritz Smith's healing system, *Zero Balancing*. Interface touch assures clear energetic boundaries between practitioner and client. Our intention with interface is to diminish any psychic influences from the therapist to the client's body and vice versa.

A Short History of Acupressure

As I studied acupressure beyond the hands-on method I originally learned, I discovered that it has been a formal and defined therapeutic modality in China for more than three thousand years. And it is still widely practiced today, not only in China but also throughout Asia and in the West.

Acupressure predates acupuncture but it is impossible to learn just how long it has been used. Certainly it derives naturally from the instinctive practice of indigenous people all over the world who rubbed, held or kneaded painful places on the body for relief.

Early healers in China and Asia discovered the energy pathways, or meridians, on the body. They learned that stimulation of points, now called *acupoints*, along the meridians opened energy flow through those pathways. They found that such stimulation could assist recovery from illness and promote wellness. Over centuries of practice and experience with acupressure and acupuncture, people learned how to cure many ailments and promote greater health.

Acupressure and acupuncture have persisted in China even after Western medicine of the twentieth century was introduced to that country. Further, acupressure and acupuncture have spread throughout the world and now into the United States, where many acupuncture and acupressure schools and therapists are educating and healing thousands of people. Some medical doctors even recommend it to their patients for some conditions.

Various styles of acupressure were developed through time, such as Shiatsu, Tui Na and Amma, to name only a few. All of them rely on a basic principle of Chinese medicine, that as energy flows through the energy pathways (meridians) of the body, health of the whole person is enhanced.

Jin Shin Jyutsu is the acupressure method I first learned, and it remains the core of our present teaching. It was developed by a contemporary Japanese Master, Jiro Murai, whose contribution to healing and wellbeing was extensive, even though he is little known.

The story of Master Murai, told to me by a student of his, is a fascinating record of transformation and healing. Jiro Murai came from a traditional family of doctor-healers. As a young man he led a wild life of overindulgence until he became very ill. Disgraced and ashamed he went to the top of a mountain to die. His discomfort was so great that he held acupressure points to ease his pain. In this way he kept falling into unconsciousness and then waking up again to hold more points. Finally he made a vow to God: If he could recover through acupressure he would devote the remainder of his life to perfecting the art and healing other people with it.

Murai did recover and he kept his promise. For the rest of his life he walked up and down Japan, refining his skill and treating people for little or no payment. At one point his sister had a premature baby who wasn't expected to live. Murai went to his sister and asked if he could take the baby for healing. The mother agreed. Murai not only healed the baby but also helped her grow into a strong young woman.

After World War II, Mary Burmeister, a Japanese-American woman, was in the United States Army, which was occupying Japan at the time. She had heard of the remarkable work of a Japanese healer, Master Murai, from her father. She sought him out. She asked to study with him and was accepted. When she was transferred back to the United States, Master Murai told her, "Take Jin Shin Jyutsu back to the United States and teach it as my gift of peace to that country."

Mary did teach in the United States, and other countries, for many years. I studied with her in the early 1970s. As far as I know she taught the work, and treated people, for the rest of her life.

Another Jin Shin Jyutsu teacher I studied with was virtually the local doctor of her retirement community, in Orange County, California. I came to love, admire and respect her greatly, even though now, after forty years, I can't remember her name! She told me many fascinating stories of people who came to her with unusual symptoms, and of how they were relieved with the work. One of the stories, which impressed me greatly, was the following:

After World War II an American doctor, whose name she didn't mention, was stationed in a prisoner-of-war camp where it was impossible to medically attend to so many suffering Japanese soldiers. He noticed that a column of them was constantly streaming into a particular tent. He also noted that those who went into that tent emerged looking much better. Eventually he visited the tent himself, where he found a Japanese man treating one man after another with a "curious form of Japanese bodywork." That was Jin Shin Jyutsu. All of those men continued to get better.

When this doctor returned to regular practice in California, one of his serious heart patients happened to be a client and friend of my teacher. This patient was so fragile that the doctor told her to stay in bed and not get up for anything—in fact, to use a bedpan.

While my teacher was learning Jin Shin Jyutsu she stayed with her ailing friend, the heart patient, and treated her with whichever acupressure formula she had learned that day. After a few weeks the fragile patient looked and felt so much better that she got out of bed and went to see her doctor. Her doctor said to her, "What are you doing here?! I told you to stay in bed."

"Well, I have been receiving this Japanese bodywork and I'm much better."

"Do you mean that curious form of Japanese bodywork called Jin Shin Jyutsu?" he asked. When she said that it was, his response, surprisingly, was, "Get all of that you can!"

And that is when he told her the story of the prisoner of war camp. He was the doctor who had witnessed the results of this "curious form of Japanese bodywork."

Through the years of my own practice I have also witnessed many remarkable recoveries from various maladies with this acupressure alone.

Contemporary Progressions of Acupressure

There have been several contemporary American progressions of Jin Shin Jyutsu. Among them are Jin Shin Do, developed by Iona Marsaa Teeguarden, which combines Reichian release principles with acupressure; Jin Shin acupressure, taught by Michael Gach, founder of the Acupressure Institute in Berkeley, California; and Process Acupressure, described later in this book, which I developed, combining psychological and spiritual work in consciousness with acupressure.

The consciousness work of Process Acupressure is deeply supported by acupressure, which automatically integrates and balances a person. It is an appropriate approach for anyone who wishes to learn more about her or his own development and participate consciously in it.

Through the years, my colleagues, students and I have also found many other practical applications for acupressure. Now in Soul Lightening work we teach a complete track of acupressure alone, as *Clinical Acupressure*, separate from Process Acupressure, to address hundreds of body problems. At present it is becoming quite well known through the tireless efforts of our Soul Lightening president, Cathy Miller, and other teachers she has trained.

Following are some of the most successful uses of this form of acupressure.

Balancing, Nourishing and Recharging

In our goal-oriented society we are not attentive enough to the need for relaxation, rest and recharging. Health practitioners especially suffer on the edge of burnout much of the time. I have found through the years that healthcare workers sensibly urge their clients to get what the practitioners themselves need, including vacations, even as they push themselves into exhaustion.

Acupressure provides a deeply nourishing state for letting go of tensions and taking a break in the most fundamental parts of us, namely, the mind and the nervous, muscular and energy systems. In fact, the wholistic state of peace, wellbeing and calm that generally ensues through acupressure is virtually unknown through other means. I find it impossible to adequately describe in words. It has to be experienced to be believed.

For example, I first worked on my grandmother when she was ninety years old. I noticed how very tense her whole body was. I asked her to relax. She said, "Honey, I don't know how," and to my amazement I realized this was true. She had no doubt lived most of those ninety years within a tense body. The effect of acupressure for her was akin to cosmic bliss. She would close her eyes and gradually the most sublime expression would come over her face. She would be calm and peaceful, and deeply with herself for several days afterward.

Working with Body Symptoms and Healing

Clients typically arrive with a particular complaint or body symptom. Problems can range from simple headaches or colds to major illness, such as arthritis or diabetes. Although acupressure will seldom cure serious disease, it can greatly diminish the discomfort of it, and can support the effectiveness of medical or other treatment. We teach many specific formulas to address various symptoms, with the aim of relaxation and relief. Most symptoms are eased. And all these formulas increase the body's ability to strengthen and heal itself.

A principle within Chinese medicine says that wherever energy is flowing freely and in balance, disease cannot manifest. In working with healing over many years I have found that whenever greater balance is brought into the body, physical distresses and symptoms are reduced and the natural healing process is hastened.

We receive reports every week from colleagues and students who have helped others to heal, more swiftly and with greater ease. The following note to me from another bodyworker is an excellent example of this.

> I just want to pass on thanks from my friend. She had surgery to remove a cyst from her spine last Wednesday. I visited her on Sunday, and I noticed how she could not stand up straight, had a lot of pain and a generally poor outlook. I sat on the edge of the sofa with her and offered SEVA [described in chapter 17], with extra attention to the very hunched shoulders and back points.

> The change was noticeable and immediate! By the end, her back was resting against the sofa back, she stood up straighter and her shoulders were even and more on the back, and of course she was happier. She thanked me profusely...so please accept those thanks, as I did.

Bringing More Awareness to the Condition and Its Remedy

Acupressure is particularly valuable in exposing and clarifying whatever is bothering a person, with either body or psychological issues. As more energetic balance is brought into the body the presenting problem will take on different perspectives. The person may begin to understand the mechanisms of the problem in a deeper way, as my colleague did. She or he will experience each session at deeper emotional and physical levels, beyond thinking.

Healing messages and feelings can also be brought into the session. For example, if a person has been emotionally wounded by a cutting remark from a friend, the negative effect is particularly strong because of the openness and trust toward the friend. A strong positive antidote is needed to override the emotional wound. The relaxed, open state brought on by acupressure promotes the imprint of new messages and brings a clearer, stronger field through the event.

Aiming for Specific Outcomes

The session can be directed toward a particular intention or outcome. The acupressure therapist and client can decide this at the beginning of the session. By simply and clearly stating an intention, and placing it "in the field," as we say, we can encourage its manifestation through greater energetic balance in the body and understanding in the mind.

Once I worked with a young woman who was intensely agitated because the lease on her home had been cancelled and she hadn't been able to find a suitable place to move. She was very distraught and was using all her session on upset and negative expectation, such as, "I'll never find someplace as good as we have now!"

I suggested that we could more productively use the session by putting into the Universal Field a clear, specific statement of her needs and then asking that it be met within the week. She agreed, and constructed a detailed request, something to the effect of, "within this week I will find the perfect home for us that has enough space and attractive surroundings. Oh, and we can afford it!"

I asked her to state her request and then simply relax into that statement for the remainder of the session. She calmed down. The next day she called me with great excitement:

"Aminah! We found the perfect place," she exclaimed. "After I got back from our session I looked in the newspaper ads again, even though I had already scanned them, and there was a house I hadn't noticed that seemed possible. I called. The landlord said I would have to come right over because someone else was interested. We drove there immediately. It was perfect and we rented it on the spot. I can't believe this miracle!"

We have experienced many such examples of the effect of conscious intention placed into the Universal Field. I don't understand the physics that makes this Field phenomenon possible, but I am fully convinced, by experience, that there is some natural mechanism that makes it work.

Working on Yourself

I have recommended self-work to students for years because I learned through working on myself that I could relieve tension, promote and strengthen health and stimulate insight.

Many students have been amazed to experience the results of working on their own points, casually or seriously. Often deep insight about certain body or emotional conditions arises during acupressure. For example, one movement therapist who was very knowledgeable about the body, and who had received a lot of bodywork on her own body before studying with me, told me that after a year of doing this work on herself alone she noticed a gigantic improvement in her health and awareness.

I advise students to give time and appropriate space to work on themselves whenever possible. Working the points can quickly be helpful, even in less than ideal situations, for example while sitting for extended periods of time surrounded by other people, such as on a plane, in a car or at a noisy dinner party.

Soft rubber balls in a sock can be used for points that are not easily reached, such as points on the back. The balls press into the body while a person lies or sits down against something. This method prevents arm and shoulder strain. With a little practice and knowledge of the points, ease of stimulating them becomes automatic. Acupressure has a cumulative effect, so each session increases overall health and wellbeing.

Clinical Acupressure Work In the World

Now that we have been teaching Clinical Acupressure widely for some years, we have experience of its effectiveness in schools, hospitals and communities. As medical professionals began to learn our work they started using it in their regular medical practice as first aid, for recovery and for personal comfort. One of our nurses reported the following experience during a medical procedure.

A patient was having anxiety with a procedure. I did acupressure points instead of ordering pain medications. The patient's anxiety decreased quickly. This intervention was more time effective than requesting orders, having the unit coordinator take the orders, then having the prescription prepared at the pharmacy, and the medications delivered to the patient and then waiting for them to take effect. This saved time and empowered the patient. I see how it can play into the hospital framework, while saving time and resources, eliminating steps and empowering patients. I had a discussion with the nurse manager about the possibility of an integrated unit where acupressure could be used. She requested a proposal to be submitted.

Another nurse practitioner had set up a study for her nurses to use acupressure in the hospital. She reported:

> Five nurses, who were trained in Clinical Acupressure, have been keeping track of their in-patient treatments. The results astounded me. Acupressure was more effective than medication for pain, nausea or constipation. In fact, the need for meds was obliterated. Treatments generally consisted of using just a few points or SEVA. Almost all patients that received treatments reported satisfaction. One treatment ended up reducing length of stay in the hospital by two days. Patients were sleeping better, smiling, releasing traumatic memories, and gaining insight into their medical conditions. Only one patient out of 40 reported no effect.
>
> These effects are improving care and satisfaction and reducing direct costs to the hospital and the nurses are happy and excited to offer the treatments and are teaching the patients how to care for themselves. Doctors are tracking nurses down to thank them for this additional care provided as patients speak out.
>
> We are writing these records into a proposal to convert an eight-bed unit in the hospital to an integrative medicine unit staffed by these nurses to provide care alongside conventional care. Treatments will be tracked. Even if we can categorize 200 patient treatments, this would be a worthy publication.
>
> In a year I hope we will be ready to start to receive a crowd of nurses for Hospital Based Acupressure

Training. Our unit can be up and running as a living model. We need to prove that this intervention is cost-effective (not a problem). Even in our short survey, we could probably assign money and prove that in those 40 treatments we saved the hospital DIRECT costs of $5000 AND improved patient satisfaction. Hospitals would not have to wait more than a few weeks (or less) to recoup their costs of training.

Our hope and our plans are that this kind of service in hospitals can be instituted to speed healing, ease patient discomfort and reduce hospital costs.

The work has been used in hospices where it delivers much comfort to dying patients. Due to Cathy Miller's efforts, Clinical Acupressure was delivered to caregivers at the wounded soldiers ward at Walter Reed Army Hospital in Baltimore, Maryland, where it received praise from grateful and tired workers. We hope to have the opportunity to offer the work to returning soldiers, because one of our practitioners has had success helping clients who were soldiers suffering from PTSD.

From my perspective, as a mother, teacher and therapist, I think every household could benefit from at least one person, if not the whole family, knowing acupressure.

6:

THE MIND

The human mind will not be confined to any limits.

~Johann Wolfgang von Goethe

Webster's Encyclopedic Unabridged Dictionary defines the mind as "the element of a person that enables them to be aware of the world and their experiences, to think, and to feel; the faculty of consciousness and thought; a person's mental processes contrasted with physical action; a person's intellect, memory or intellectual faculties; a person's attention."

Our definition of mind in Soul Lightening is both specific and expansive. We see the mind as a brilliant instrument of consciousness, which uses a vast array of functions from the conscious and unconscious minds, left-brain, right brain and the less-understood paranormal faculties, to perceive phenomena. These many interactive functions govern mental awareness, thinking, understanding, knowing, clairvoyance and clairaudience.

We know more about the human mind now than at any other time in history, although it is still more complex than our science or psychology have yet adequately described. We know, for instance, that we are born with two sides (or hemispheres) of the brain, left and right, and that each side tends to specialize in directing certain functions. We know that part of the mind is conscious, that is, aware of itself working. And that another part of the mind, called the unconscious, is often hidden from our awareness. In Western cultures we tend to assign the mind, and thinking, to the brain. We are a thinking culture. Our attention is primarily consumed with thoughts, words and intellectual presentations.

Left- and Right-Brain Effects on Consciousness

Contemporary research on the brain posits that the two different hemispheres of the brain tend to control two different modes of thinking. It also suggests that each of us prefers one mode over the other, although a small percentage of people apparently take a whole-brained approach, drawing from both sides of the brain more or less equally.

The longitudinal fissure separates the left and right brains, with each side being approximately the same size. Although the two hemispheres of the brain look anatomically like mirror images of one another, their functions vary greatly. They each characterize different styles of thinking and even different personality traits.

The Left Brain

The left brain directs verbal and mathematical skills and memory. Thus it processes information either visually or auditorily and sequentially. It is the analytical part of the brain, processing information logically and rationally. For example, it can take each part or piece of information and process it linearly and sequentially in a systematic manner, in order to solve a problem or come to a particular conclusion. Left-brained people make decisions based on logic or established facts and detailed analysis of information. They would call this "rational" thinking. They may tend to shy away from material that is emotional, creative or intuitive, or that requires complex spatial, that is, holographic or three-dimensional, organization.

The left brain processes symbols, such as letters, words and mathematical notations, in a logical way. It bases conclusions on "reality," that is, on the phenomenological world, what we seem to perceive with our five senses, things as they are, rather than unrealistic imaginations. The left brain usually follows established rules, or rules that it creates, such as A leads to B leads to C, and so forth. In the absence of rules it tends to make up its own set. And a fascinating recent scientific discovery demonstrated that when the left brain can't remember an event, it makes up a story about it that fits a logical pattern.

In Western culture, we have been dominated by left-brain functioning since the Age of Enlightenment. At that time tremendous credit and power were assigned to the intellect. It was predicted that we would be able to satisfy human needs and control nature through the analytical function of observing and manipulating facts. We worked from a model of the universe as a giant machine, consistent with Newtonian physics, that is, that the entire universe was governed by laws or rules that we would ultimately, through investigation by the rational mind, be able to discover and control. Several centuries later we are living with the results of that perspective: massive technological advancements, much more ease in the performance of routine tasks, environmental disasters, burgeoning diseases that originate from the pollution caused by our own devices or their production. Hundreds of books have been written that reflect on the failure of this pervasive left-brain approach. Yet modern civilization still predominantly proceeds from those assumptions, despite the new quantum physics that replaces Newtonian ideas.

When we turned predominantly to reason and mechanical logic to solve our problems and guide our development, we tuned out some very valuable input that could assist our health, our feelings of wellbeing and our connection with other forms of life, human and otherwise. When we gave precedence to the left, analytically-based brain, and veered away from the right brain and heart intelligence, we sidetracked much of the valuable wisdom of the heart and emotions. Just look around at the world today. Our actual survival as one species among millions of life forms may depend on reconnecting with our sense of wholeness with all of life, as we recognize our complete interdependence.

In the East, the intellect, or "rational mind," is often referred to as the "monkey mind," to characterize its continuous and often superficial chatter. Eastern adepts locate the intellect in the third chakra, at a primitive position in human evolutionary development.

The Right Brain

The right brain governs aesthetics, emotions, feeling, intuition, sensations and creativity. In recent decades we are beginning to reclaim the value of the right-brain functions. These are considered to be associated with heart intelligence, transcendent knowing, a sense of wonder and respect for all of life, and connection to the web of the universal unifying Field.

While left-brain conditioning urges us to adopt a realistic, practical and logical approach toward a problem, our right brain is the center of creativity and emotions. Its intuitive function contributes valuable insights beyond simple facts and manmade systems or constructs. The right brain contributes meaning and inspiration to linear thought patterns. For a fascinating and inspiring record of a "takeover" by the right brain after a stroke, read Jill Bolte Taylor's *My Stroke of Insight*.[10]

In reality, the two hemispheres of the brain complement one another, constantly exchanging and intermingling data. We simply cannot do without one or the other. It is the right brain that makes us think in a different way in order to develop new ideas or

---

10 Taylor, Jill Bolte. 2009. *My Stroke of Insight,* New York, Penguin Books,

to innovate. In his book *A Whole New Mind: Why Right-Brainers Will Rule the Future,* [11] Daniel Pink makes a very strong case for how our future must be led by the right brain. He says that the days of "a certain kind of person with a certain kind of mind...like lawyers who could craft contracts and MBAs who could crunch numbers are coming to a close. The future belongs to a very different kind of a person with a very different kind of mind—creators and empathizers, pattern recognizers, and meaning makers."

The Thinking Function

So how do we evaluate our thinking? If we pay attention, we notice that our thoughts go on continuously. Our brains never stop. Even highly practiced meditators find it impossible to completely stop thinking. Why do we call this ongoing mental activity "chatter" or "monkey mind?" Is continuous thinking a liability or an asset? What makes thinking a liability and how could thinking be an ally? Soul Lightening work explores these aspects of thinking through our process methods.

Recent advances in bodywork have verified what has been known in some Eastern cultures for centuries, namely that the mind exists throughout the body. It isn't merely that three-pound mass of gray matter caged inside our skulls, a protein-based computer that we carry around on the top of our necks. We have learned that body tissues, and virtually all the cells of our body, store memories, particularly traumatic ones, as we learned in John Lilly's story of his injured foot. These memories can be recaptured directly from the body, without intellectual analysis.

The discovery of soft tissue memory was one of the many reasons I chose to approach the whole being through the body with acupressure that would open the body's energy as well as reveal its

---

11 Pink, Daniel. 2005. *A Whole New Mind: Why Right-Brainers Will Rule the Future.* New York, Riverhead Books, .

history. The raw information that comes directly from the body is usually more trustworthy than labels or theories we might create with our left brains. When we are not confined to the brain that is already conditioned through family, society and education, we can receive vast stores of information—from the universal Field and from energetic, emotional, cellular and transpersonal sources—that can transform our understanding.

Transformation and Whole Body Awareness

Sheila arrived at my office as an unhappy and ill young woman. Despite her high intelligence, privileged background and considerable physical attractiveness she was truly suffering. She was the perfect example at that time of a thinking type; she was a walking, talking, thinking machine. Blessed with a very astute mind, she had learned, through school and eleven years of psychoanalysis, to think her way through every event, problem, encounter and relationship. At the drop of a hat she could analyze any situation for me, without missing a single detail.

Sheila had come to me because she was blocked as an artist, which was her chosen field, sick in her body and unable to find a stable relationship, for which she longed.

Even as I was doing the basic acupressure protocol on her body she was pouring out a constant monologue about her problems, frustrations, symptoms and past diagnoses, with her own analyses of all of these mixed in. She was utterly convinced that she could think her way to what she wanted—a loving partnership, a productive career as an artist and happiness. And she believed that she already knew everything she needed to know to achieve her goals.

But she just couldn't manifest those goals.

The principal problem at first was that she couldn't think herself out of the fibromyalgia that was seemingly preventing her from carrying out all these objectives. After she learned how to attune to her own body signals, sensations and movements, she began to notice how they corresponded to her painful physical symptoms. She noticed, for example, that when she overloaded herself with projects—which, of course, she planned and tackled with her thinking mind—she became anxious; her stomach would then start aching and eventually she collapsed in fatigue. By putting all these signs and observations together and learning how to coordinate her workload with what her body needed and would tolerate, her symptoms began to abate and finally disappeared. Eventually Sheila learned how to coordinate her strong thinking mind with the needs and capacities of her body, emotions and soul.

Sheila's mental awareness was highly developed before I ever met her. Because of her astute intelligence she had been an excellent student in school. Her visual and auditory faculties were so refined that she could picture or describe anything that came to her mind. She had eyes like a hawk and a huge vocabulary and she could string all those words together in a logical, convincing sequence. She used her mind very well. In short, she was a terrific thinker.

Yet it was as if Sheila's mind was separate from her body, emotions and spirit. Intellectually she had learned anatomy and studied various spiritual philosophies, but this word-based knowledge didn't translate to actual awareness of her own body or inspiration of the spirit. While she could talk about these subjects extensively she couldn't seem to apply much of that knowledge to her own life.

The focus of our work together was on her body and on her emotional and spiritual awareness. As we worked she gradually connected her body sensations and feelings with her understanding of her physical symptoms and relationship problems. As she did so, she began to experience more ease in her body and more success with relationships.

Self-Knowledge and Healing

Working with Sheila took me into familiar territory, reminiscent of my own journey toward wholeness. Here's the background: Very early in my own spiritual practice I observed that my mind was full of what I would now call trash—useless, irrelevant wanderings of the mind that led me nowhere. So I began a direct psycho-spiritual meditative exploration to better understand it. I came to realize that there were beliefs, mental habits and ideas in my thinking that were far outdated. I remember thinking, "I need to clean up my mind. It's still got too much trash in it, even after all these years of working on myself and studying." I started an ongoing practice of paying more careful attention to the constant thoughts in my mind and how they related to emotions.

Fortunately, in our time, there are many methods for exploring the mind even apart from psychotherapy. The Buddhists are masters of mind mastery and they are teaching their methods extensively in the West now. Biofeedback, neurofeedback and hypnosis are other methods for investigating the mind. I studied a number of them in my quest to "clean up" my mind.

One of them was the process called "The Work," developed by Byron Katie, who is the author of several bestselling books, including, *Loving What Is: Four Questions that Can Change Your Life*.[12] I studied The Work and found it a valuable tool for finding out just what goes on in the mind.

Byron Katie had a spiritual awakening during which she received a simple, straightforward method for cleaning up the thinking mind. Her method simply involves four questions and a "turnaround," which calls for the original thought to be transformed into its opposite.

Here's how this method works. You choose a troublesome thought and ask the following four questions:

1. Is it true? (Yes or no. If no, move to 3.)
2. Can I absolutely know that it's true? (Yes or no.)
3. How do I react, what happens, when I believe that thought?
4. Who would I be without the thought?

---

12 Katie, Byron Katie. 2002. *Loving What Is*. New York, Three Rivers Press

Then, turn that thought around, e.g. find the opposite of it. And find at least three specific, genuine examples of how each turn-around is true for you in that situation.

Katie, as she prefers to be called, used the method intensely on herself for about three years before she shared it with others. In her books she tells how she was a terrible person, neurotic and mean to her children and everyone around her, before she discovered and applied the four questions. It must have worked because when I first met her I experienced her as a loving and very clear, honest and straightforward person.

Katie has been teaching The Work nonstop for at least twenty years now. I once asked her what her purpose is in this life. Her answer: "To deliver the four questions to as many people as possible." (You can learn more about Katie and The Work at www.thework.com.)

In my first experience with the four questions during a weekend seminar, I was so startled by the unexpected twists I found in my thinking that I decided to pursue the method further. I enrolled in Katie's ten-day intensive. During that ten-day period I weeded through my own thinking relentlessly, throwing out bushels of trash that served no useful purpose. I was astounded to find roots of the child's experience that were still feeding and distorting my thinking and growth in the present.

I experienced firsthand the thinking component of what I was teaching all the time, that early core imprints shape our whole life. And I was learning how to clear out the child's thinking that kept those imprints in place. I also gained even more compassion for the limits in the ability of any child's mind to make sense of what was going on around her.

Simultaneously I was seeing much more clearly how a mature, adult mind functioned. During the training with Byron Katie I watched a psychiatrist gasp in wonder as he witnessed the quick effects of Katie's four questions and the turnaround to unravel what usually took months or years in therapy.

The effect Katie's work had on me has been profound. I knew I would understand clients' and students' internal mental architecture better than I ever had before. Although I grew up in this thinking culture, am fairly well educated and have always thought of myself as a thinking person, I was amazed at the global effects of clearing my thinking of all the useless, outdated and even destructive trash it had accumulated. I gained a sense of a "clear mind."

I realized why Buddhist meditators seek this state they call the *clear mind*. Long before I met Katie I understood that the ordinary mind is only really useful when it is at least somewhat free of *neurosis*, that is, not restricted by the thoughts, fears or beliefs that hold us back from satisfying social interactions or make it almost impossible to fulfill our personal gifts or chosen goals. We need minds that can be used as clear, clean instruments to figure things out freely in the present.

I was already after freedom of mind and soul, and had used many methods, with therapists and on myself alone, to gain that freedom through energy, body and emotional releases. Now Katie's work showed me another simple way of freeing the thinking from outmoded dogmas, beliefs, false ideas and traumas of the past. Beneath all of our conditioned, obsolete ways of experiencing the world lies the clear adult mind. How fabulous it will be when we teach our children how to think clearly. In fact, children can actually learn to use Katie's four questions quickly and easily, with only a tiny bit of coaching.

Knowledge, Understanding and the Tyranny of Information

We have been accumulating information for centuries. Libraries, schools and now the internet are full of it, moving faster than even the most powerful computers can keep up with. Yet with several centuries of information gathering and the Information Age under our belts, or rather, in our heads, it is clear that raw, head-centered information alone is not enough. Has our knowledge-driven approach provided what we need to live healthy, happy lives and solve our severe global problems? Apparently not. We are out of balance with ourselves, with life and with evolution.

What about penetrating understanding that goes beyond data, to bring it all together into concepts, overviews, solutions to problems? What about wisdom? We normally think of the mind as the instrument of understanding. Certainly the brain in our heads helps us collect knowledge, which in turn can help us understand our experience. So what have we been missing in the equation for health and happiness that is *not* contained in the brain?

Part of what we have left out so far is the undervalued right brain. In *A Whole New Mind,* Daniel Pink (see Bibliography) explains very well how much we now need the right-brain qualities of inventiveness, empathy, joyfulness, intuition and holism to balance out the analytical, sequential, knowledge-gathering dominance of the left brain we have lived with.

The Unconscious Mind

There is another gigantic aspect of mind that is undervalued in traditional education—the *unconscious mind.* I first learned of the unconscious mind in Psychology 101 at the university. As presented, the unconscious seemed like a dark, unpredictable force that could trip you up if you weren't careful. I concluded that the unconscious was an enemy, and I treated it accordingly.

But over the years, and with further study, particularly the works of C.J. Jung, and with exploration of my own unconscious and those of clients, I came to an opposite view. I learned through dreams, "unconscious" slips of the tongue, Process Work and through recognizing synchronous events, the profound importance of exploring the unconscious directly and bypassing theoretical or speculative interpretations of experiences. I found that the unconscious is a seemingly unlimited treasure trove of current and ancient knowledge. Sometimes it even extends into the future through pre-cognitive dreams and visions. As Jung discovered, the unconscious houses the archetypes or primal symbols of the historic human experience.

Now I have come to the utmost respect, even adoration, for the beauty and power of the unconscious mind. Several times a day I say, "Oh, unconscious, thank you, I love you so much." This evolution in my thinking came about because I discovered years ago that my unconscious remembers everything; where I have mislaid a book, which fork in the road leads to my destination, when I first encountered a particular place or thing, and so much more.

As my conscious, short-term memory weakened and became less trustworthy, I learned that I could ask the unconscious for a piece of information and it would respond within minutes. Curiously, its response came through the body, not the ordinary mind. For example, if I ask my unconscious where I have put my glasses, I need only let go of conscious mental speculation entirely and allow my body to move to the glasses. Many times these are places or things that would seem quite unlikely to my conscious mind.

Now I regard my unconscious as a most precious ally. The reach of it is actually quite miraculous. It is a huge repository of all that I have experienced in this life and others but have forgotten consciously. And when the conscious mind can't fathom a subject, the unconscious will produce a dream that addresses it.

My unconscious is much smarter than my conscious mind. It has become a loyal friend that I can always depend on. I talk to it regularly, ask questions of it and respect the answers. I eventually learned to say, "Darling unconscious, show me where x is." This makes it easier to release any mental ideas I might have about the thing I've lost or have forgotten, and to follow the wisdom of my body.

Metaphysicians, personal growth and transformation teachers and even abundance and business consultants have taught how to use the unconscious as the powerful manifestor that it is. For example, Napoleon Hill, the author of *Think and Grow Rich*, mentored many along the path of unconscious manifestation.

Joe Vitale is one of his students who teaches now how to use the unconscious. Jerry Hicks, of the Abraham teachings, was first tutored by Napoleon Hill. L. Ron Hubbard, Scientology founder, was a student of the same teachings, which came originally from Eastern Masters who kept it secret. The "new thought" Christian churches, like Christian Science, teach it. I think it is a gift that the cat is now out of the bag, so to speak, and that information is available to anyone who wants it. For a good summary of the foundation and proliferation of this method of enlisting the unconscious as the giant it is, go to http://www.originalteaching.com/accessingthesubconscious.html

Exactly where is the unconscious located? At present nobody seems to know. In fact, by all measures of logic and science, it can't possibly even exist. As far as we can tell, it may not even be contained in the brain. Some have claimed, including Jung, that the body is the unconscious. It's true that when we work with the body unconscious information often arises. As we learn more about neurology, energetics and the Universal Field there will probably be many more explanations about the origin of the unconscious. But for now we can accept that it is a pervasive, powerful potential ally that is a hardly-used part of our total consciousness.

I strongly recommend to anyone who is pursuing deeper knowledge about consciousness to make friends with the unconscious; it will serve you in many ways. The first step is to acknowledge it and greet it as a friend. Then find out how it operates; ask it simple questions or ask it to find something for you. Let go of the analytical mind, relax your body and simply let it move on its own volition. Study this process for a while until you are closely tuned in to your own unconscious.

Working With the Whole Mind

In Soul Lightening work we view the mind as a valuable instrument of our wholeness and mental power. So we work with the entire mind—intellect, right brain, left brain, intuition and unconscious. When all of these components work together we have everything we need to assemble the various data we can perceive and then bring it together to form functional and usable strategies, concepts, theories and solutions. We know that the mind can also reach into a broad range of feelings, sensations, visions, sounds—signals from many sources—to provide a wholistic comprehension of what is going on.

Thus we teach how to gather information directly, as accurately as possible, through waked-up awareness, from raw data and experience. We are after a clear mind that can think effectively, freely and extensively in present time, untethered by the cocoon conditioning of the past. Therefore, we don't analyze, theorize or categorize. Instead, we pay attention in the moment to the signals that arise naturally from all parts of ourselves.

Creating with the Mind

We are creating with our minds all the time, through the words we speak and the thoughts we project into the Field. Imagine the following monologues:

> If I only had the money I would take a cruise to Tahiti but of course that will never happen because I don't have the money and besides even if somebody just gave me the money probably there wouldn't be any cruises to Tahiti anymore by then....

This could happen out loud or quietly occur in the mind, almost without you noticing it. Do you hear how this mind has cancelled out or placed obstacles in the way of achieving this dream at every turn? There is no possible way this person can ever get to Tahiti from that frame of mind.

Now sense this mind:

> When the money arrives I'm going on a cruise to Tahiti. Boy, is that a wonderful trip! Everywhere I go I'm seeing posters of Tahiti and hearing people talk about their wonderful trips to Tahiti. I'm loving it!

Get the difference? Even if this second person doesn't have the money now, you can be quite confident that she will have the money before long. Biographies are full of real accounts of how they grew from homeless (think Joe Vitale or Neale Donald Walsch) to comfortably abundant living.

At first it seems unbelievable that we are actually creating our reality day by day with our thoughts, our words and our beliefs. This concept needs validating by the actual daily experience of constant thought monitoring. Simply be attentive to your thoughts and your words and ask yourself where they are likely to lead you. Use Byron Katie's four questions, which we explored a few pages back; they will help tremendously.

Although I had heard and read this concept of how our words and thoughts affect our lives several times, it took a gracious colleague—I'll call her Clara—to teach it to me firsthand. She was a soft spoken, compassionate, person. When I commented on these lovely qualities of hers she said, "I wasn't always that way. I used to be very negative and angry."

I was shocked by this apparent contradiction. I asked her how she had changed that.

"One thought at a time, hard work," she replied.

Then Clara told me the longer story. All in one year her beloved husband had died; she had been diagnosed with Crohn's disease and had three-quarters of her colon surgically removed.

"I was so angry and bitter I could spit tacks," she said. "I hated all doctors. But when I went to a homeopath he told me that unless I changed my thought patterns I was going to die. So that's when I started reversing every single negative thought into its opposite, or at least compassion. It was terribly hard work, but I'm still alive."

That advice from her homeopath had come years before I met Clara. When I knew her, she was so loving, understanding and compassionate, it was impossible to imagine her as a negative, bitter person.

When I have a rush of negative thoughts I have to STOP and think of her.

Higher Mind or Soul Consciousness

There is another domain of consciousness that is not associated with the brain; it reaches into transcendental realms, the higher mind or *soul consciousness*, which I've alluded to previously. This mind does not originate in the brain but is associated with the crown chakra. Nevertheless, it is accessible in meditation.

Metaphysicians, meditators, "new thought" practitioners and many other philosophers that derive their thinking from metaphysics claim they can co-create their reality through conscious cooperation with higher intelligence and their own disciplined use of mind and emotion. Louise Hay (*You Can Heal Your Life*) created a happy, prosperous life of service from those principles.

7:

AWAKENING TO EMOTIONS

*If your emotional abilities aren't in hand, if you don't
have self-awareness, if you are not able to manage
your distressing emotions, if you can't have empathy
and have effective relationships, then no matter how
smart you are, you are not going to get very far.*

~Daniel Goleman

As a young woman and educated American, I had a particular mental orientation to life, to people, events and social situations, focusing very much on externals and whether or not I would be accepted. For example, I tended to ask questions such as: What does she look like? Does what he says make sense? Am I smart enough? Do I know enough? Do I fit in here? What are the rules of this game?

So imagine my shock when, during a visit in Indonesia for the first time, when one of my Indonesian hostesses invited me—but not my male traveling companion—to dinner. I didn't know how to respond. According to my perception at the time, my companion was the star of our relationship. I reeled through the facts in my mind. My companion was so much more impressive than me.

He was smart. He was a physicist. He had helped engineer the first Apollo flight. He had hobnobbed with the big guys in Washington and he sprinkled his sentences with names of famous people and the acronyms of an insider, such as DOD (Department of Defense), DOE (Department of Energy), and so on. He took charge of most conversations with a superior grasp of any subject while others listened in mute admiration. It was the '60s. He had all the right credentials for success in our American culture of the time.

Why would my hostess want me but reject him? I had no clue. So I sneaked away to that dinner, had a lovely evening, albeit burdened with guilt for leaving my companion behind, as I observed new behaviors and ways of speaking. There was human warmth, a lot of smiling, touching, super politeness, and gentle voices talking about sweet subjects. What to do? I wondered. So I didn't tell my partner about the evening, nor that he hadn't been invited.

I started thinking through the particulars of what I'd experienced that evening. It was true that my partner was aggressive, even explosive at times, and that he was quick to disregard or destroy a conflicting opinion. He was not even averse to out-and-out put downs; in fact he seemed delighted to put over a particularly clever one. But this all seemed like normal behavior to me in the society of scientists and intellectuals. I had learned to adapt to it fairly well. Sometimes I even tried to emulate it to keep up...with little success, I might add.

I also started to observe, and *feel*, how Indonesians behaved. I noticed that they talked less and listened more than most Westerners. Their voices were gentle, musical, and what they said was always polite. They seemed to feel out a situation and then respond accordingly. I saw that they went to all lengths to avoid hurting someone's feelings. They went to similar lengths to assure that my feelings were well cared for around them. They were embarrassed, even shamed, in the presence of outright conflict or confrontation. They smiled. They stepped back to allow another to pass first. They were always offering something—tea, flowers and a batik shawl as a present.

This was my first dramatic introduction to a *feeling culture*, distinct from a Western intellect-dominated perspective. I quickly learned that if I intended to stay in Indonesia I would have to re-discover my feeling sense. I would have to reconnect with the wide range of natural emotions, aside from my analytical mind. And I would need to attune to my heart, find its softness and its wisdom. This early introduction to the world of feelings led me later to an extensive study of the heart, emotions and feeling awareness.

In Soul Lightening work we pay close attention to emotions. We know, as I learned in Indonesia, that our emotions are a very impor-tant ingredient of our humanness; they are a natural expression of the human condition.

From the first startle and cry response of a frightened baby, through the anger or grief that are common during the end of life, we all experience *feeling responses* to life's events, whether we are aware of them or not. Feelings are felt within the body first. They often alert us to danger or love, peace or war, safety or threat, long before we can put words to a situation or analyze it. Even though emotional feelings register in the body, they are not the same as the "feelings" we associate with tactile sensations or movements that we also experience in the body. Emotions have a tone and meaning that reach a different part of the brain, the limbic system, than do tactile sensations or movements that we also often call feelings. *Not all body feelings are emotional, although all emotional feelings can be located in the body.* Thus, bodywork can give us more immediate access to our emotional feelings than talking alone does because talking is already three steps removed from the actual feeling. First a feeling impulse travels to the brain, where it is converted into a mental construct and then further translated into words for talking.

Emotions have a natural cycle, a wave effect in the body: They rise up, are expressed, and then they taper off, in just about thir-ty seconds, to return to homeostasis. Natural emotions, such as those experienced by young children, have a pure expression and response. Someone takes a toy from the child and he may become immediately angry. He grabs for the toy, trying to get it back, or he screams because he's lost it. The emotion is direct: It is felt, expressed and quickly fades away.

This early flow of emotions reflects a natural energetic, biochemical response within the body. A stimulus (grouchy face) evokes a startle or fear response within the body, which translates into feelings that bring about a natural response (tears, pulling away, and so forth). The biochemical processes within the body rise to a peak and then taper off until the physiological effects return to normal. The child's response of fear or startle also tapers off and is soon forgotten.

When we grow up within a healthy family situation, where our natural emotional expressions are allowed, supported, respected and gently guided toward appropriateness, we learn and grow.

I have a vivid memory of a scene with my son, his wife and four-year-old granddaughter, Lauren. We were walking to the beach. My granddaughter, utterly adorable, brilliant and headstrong, asked for something the parents didn't think was appropriate to give just then. She threw herself down on the sidewalk in a tantrum, kicking, screeching and in general writhing around on the cement. I felt intimidated and fairly helpless in the face of her rage power. The parents (one a doctor and the other a psychotherapist) stood calmly over her, making sure she didn't physically hurt herself but simply observing the tantrum and letting it run its course, which happened within a few minutes. I was very impressed. When I was a child such a scene would have brought on an immediate serious spanking and scolding.

A wonderful follow-up to this story occurred during a recent family reunion. Lauren, the granddaughter in the above story, is now twenty-two. Another granddaughter, Lucy, is just five. They share many of the same characteristics—brilliance, beauty and a strong will. Both are the apples of their fathers' eyes. Little Lucy's daddy had promised her a swim in the pool, and she was waiting there for him to return from a business meeting. But mother arrived and said Lucy was too tired and had to go home for a nap. Rerun!

Lucy threw herself down next to the pool, kicking and screaming, "I want Daddy! I want Daddy!" Cry, cry, cry. A few crocodile tears seeped down her darling cheeks. Mother, who knew Lucy was way overtired and needed a nap, picked her up bodily and carted her off to the van and home.

Lauren turned to me, a sense of wonder on her face, and asked: "Did I ever do that as a child?"

I laughed hard for several minutes. Then I told her the story of her own tantrum, which hadn't left a trace in her consciousness. She wasn't in denial, nor was she repressing the memory. Her tantrum, so skillfully handled by her parents that day, was simply a healthy expression of her feelings in the moment, expressed openly in the present and quickly forgotten.

When emotions are not allowed to run their natural course, they can leave an energetic and biochemical residue within the body, and that residue could later cause trouble. An unfinished emotional cycle can sit in the tissue for a long time, disturbing natural balance and possibly laying the foundation for future misinterpretation of an event. For example, post-traumatic stress disorder (PTSD) shows the tangible effects of such suppression. Emotional "illiteracy" occurs when a person has had to deny her own feelings, become numb to her own signals and stuff old unexpressed emotions.

When emotions are suppressed, held back and not allowed to be expressed naturally, they can leave a record of unspent feelings in the body, which may show up at another time in completely inappropriate ways. Think of times when you have burst into tears, or shouted out in anger when the situation in front of you didn't seem to warrant that response.

On the other hand, if an emotion continues expressing itself beyond its natural cycle, or is even repeated or held on to, it can similarly set up a biochemical and energetic imbalance that restimulates that same emotion within the person's being, again and again. Think of the perpetually angry or grief- stricken person whose recurring feelings seem to persist long after the events that evoked them have passed or ended. Or, imagine what would have happened if the parents had urged Lauren to go on tantrumming after the natural cycle was finished.

As children we continually learn about emotions by observing and feeling the adults around us. In a healthy family we learn how to navigate our natural expressions and then, as we mature, how to moderate them according to what works for us in the present environment.

In an unhealthy family, or even at school, at the work place or within our culture, we can learn and mimic distortions of emotion. And different cultures have their own mode of dealing with emotion, as I have noted in the story at the beginning of this chapter. We may learn to suppress or exaggerate emotions, according to the prevailing habits of the environment we're in. For example, a rageaholic father shows his children, by example, that extended, overtly expressed anger is an effective way of manipulating most people and will bring certain rewards. The child may imitate that strategy well into adulthood, expressing his anger without reservation and intimidating those around him. Over time he isolates himself from congenial society because most people prefer not to be around him. This form of behavior will imprison the unfortunate son of a rageaholic.

When emotions are repeatedly expressed in this exaggerated way they push the body beyond its natural biochemical and energetic response, setting up a continual biochemical and energetic imbalance. The ancient Chinese model of wholistic health teaches that the under- or over-expression of any emotion causes imbalances in the energy, organs and attitudes of a person.

But just how do we learn to moderate our family-inherited emotions? Certainly not in school. The only courses for emotional maturity are within advanced psychology curricula and even then, they are more theoretical than practical. Many people get their emotional education through movies, television or novels, which is, of course, terribly limiting at best. The truth is most of us learn through the "college of hard knocks."

And the emotional maturity of our world is at about age fifteen at best. It's further known that people who become dependent on alcohol, drugs or other substances or behaviors stopped maturing emotionally at the age where they began that behavior, often as young as ten or twelve.

Despite the state of one's present familial, cultural and spiritual environment, our emotional body *can* change, be educated and develop greater maturity. We know more now about neurology, biochemistry and childhood developmental stages than ever before in human history. No matter what the makeup of the family of origin, no one has to be imprisoned forever in the conditioning of the original family. The unfortunate son of a rageaholic is not permanently shackled to this learned anger-centered behavior. In adulthood the son can become aware of its untoward effects, *choose* to modify it and learn new emotional expressions.

Emotional "literacy" develops when one is able to feel the emotion that is happening in the moment and stay with it in awareness (without necessarily acting it out) until its cycle is completed. Such flowing awareness often results in an insight or understanding that the emotion is offering us a gift. And we can continue to learn new emotional responses to challenges beyond the family patterns.

Yes, emotional patterns can be changed in adulthood, resulting in more satisfying relationships and greater health. Professional help might be needed, as well as one's own investment in the form of self-reflection, awareness and some neuro-reprogramming, but the payoff can be profound.

Types of Emotion

It was fascinating and very helpful for me as a therapist to learn the five principle emotions of the ancient Chinese five-element wholistic health model. It gave me a deeper, more extensive understanding of the power and purpose of emotions than I had in my psychology studies.

Ancient Chinese medicine viewed a person wholistically. They saw the body, emotions, mind and spirit as a synergistic whole that required all parts working together for health. They worked out the energetic, physical, emotional, mental and spiritual components of wholeness, which allowed them to therapeutically address any conditions that arose within the parts.

In this model there are five basic polar emotions: joy/sadness, sympathy/self-absorption, surrender/grief, courage/fear, creative assertion/anger, with all other emotions being expressed as some variation of one or more of these. (For a more detailed account of the five elements, see my book *Soul Return*.)[13]

Five-element acupuncturists work very effectively from this model to help their clients balance emotions energetically. For me the five-element approach was more complete than simply talking about an emotion, or even expressing it again and again. As I studied the model I learned how to help regulate and balance emotions directly, through energetic acupressure interventions in the body, as well as through overt expression. I found that when conscious, skillful means of expression were combined with energetic balancing, there were rapid and satisfying results. This is one of the approaches we use in Soul Lightening Acupressure to work with emotions.

Broadening Our Understanding of Love

In the West there is a long tradition of championing love as the apex of human feeling. Writers in all genres, especially poets, have glorified it as the treasured prize at the end of a long quest. In the West we think of love as a heart-centered experience, but upon closer reflection it is easy to experience how many other emotions wrap around it.

---

13 Raheem, Aminah. 1990. *Soul Return: Integrating Body, Psyche and Spirit, 2nd ed.* West Palm Besch, Fla. Upledger Institute,

For example, we love someone possessively, which implies the factor we know as jealousy. We love another but embedded in that love is the fear that we will lose him. If we are unfaithful to someone we love, we feel the guilt of betrayal. We love another for what she can give, mean or stabilize for us. We even say that we love money.

In the Chinese five-element model, love is regarded as a complex feeling that includes aspects of all five emotions. The heart is understood as the central supervisor of all the emotions. It was known as the "Empress," or "Emperor," who ruled over the emotions to keep them aligned with the spirit and destiny of the person. The heart's own specific emotion was joy, the expanded, contented feeling that comes with being in alignment with the soul and its life purpose.

8:

HEART, LOVE AND
INTELLIGENCE

Destroy the temples
And the mosques
Do not break the human heart for God resides there.

~Rumi

During the first meeting of a Soul Lightening seminar we ask students to attune to their hearts. We emphasize cultivating an attitude of compassion and unconditional respect, for ourselves and each other. We know from experience that when attention is moved from the analytical mind, where it is directed in most formal education, to an open heart, a nonjudgmental attitude of support begins to greatly enhance healing and growth.

Every individual session of Soul Lightening addresses the heart center, with attention and touch. Every class includes the energy of heart love and intelligence until finally a heart field of unconditional respect is securely established. Over time students begin to expect that field and relax into it to feel its support. Within it they find a safe place for healing and their own growth process. They also commit to each others' growth.

Historical Understanding of the Heart

Some of the earliest recorded civilizations, including the Egyptians, Greeks, Mesopotamians and Babylonians, wrote of the heart as the seat of wisdom. For the Egyptians the value of a life was measured at death on the scale of the heart. For millennia indigenous cultures around the world sought intelligence and wisdom from the heart rather than the brain. Many still do.

The ancient Chinese saw the heart as the regulator and coordinator of other emotions, as I mentioned in the last chapter. In Soul Lightening we are strongly influenced by this point of view, that the heart centralizes the individual Spirit, called in Chinese medicine the Emperor or Empress. The heart is thus the seat of individual wisdom or intelligence, intuition and Spirit vitality. Some people find their soul consciousness in the heart center. Although I find my soul consciousness in the crown center, I completely honor each person's experience of his or her own spiritual wisdom.

When one is centered within her essential spirit (heart) her life and behavior are animated by the most vital and pure energy. Her own essential intelligence is coordinated with life purpose and action. She is happy, has inner joy and is content because she follows her own Spirit. When the Spirit is curbed or denied, that essential vitality gradually erodes. A person becomes less animated, more mechanical, dry and finally brittle. Heart damage (as in heart attack) can result. Unless a breakthrough back into essential Spirit happens, a gradual decline into deterioration of Spirit, motivation and life energy will occur. In Soul Lightening work we see the soul and individual spirit as twin aspects of individuation.

For many centuries in the West the heart was seen as simply the reliable pumper of blood. Little scientific attention was paid beyond that. But now contemporary science is beginning to support more of the ancient perspectives.

Contemporary Scientific Exploration of the Heart

Contemporary science reveals that the heart possesses more intelligence than we could ever have imagined. Although our training in this culture is still predominantly geared for the mind or intellect, logic and rationality, this is beginning to change. Researchers such as Doc Childre of the HeartMath Institute; David Hawkins with his consciousness work; and Richard Bartlett, creator of Matrix Energetics are just a few of the innovators who are identifying the vast intelligence capacity of the heart. Scientists are discovering what the heart really does besides pump blood. We now know that heart intelligence is multi-dimensional, transpersonal, and trans-time/space. It knows in many directions and shapes simultaneously, unlike the intellect's linear A-B-C style. It knows in ways that seem miraculous (or imaginary, or wrong) to the mind that has been captured in a two-dimensional reality. Some healers and scientists believe that the love/intelligence/compassion/unity of the heart has been greatly neglected.

Dr. David Hawkins, a long-term practicing psychiatrist and contemporary spiritual teacher, author of *Power Versus Force*,[14] claims that collective consciousness operates far below actual human capacity. He created a range-of-consciousness scale that begins at the most base level (violence and war) and ascends beyond even enlightenment to oneness with Divinity. He says that the state of consciousness achieved through the heart and true love is higher and greater than that realized by the intellect. He describes the state of heart consciousness:

---

14 Hawkins, David, 1995. M.D. *Power Versus Force*. Carlsbad, California, Hay House.

The 500 level [of consciousness, reached by only 4% of the world's population] is characterized by the development of a Love that is unconditional, unchanging, and permanent. It doesn't fluctuate—its source isn't dependent on external factors. Loving is a state of being. It's a forgiving, nurturing, and supportive way of relating to the world. Love isn't intellectual and doesn't proceed from the mind; Love emanates from the heart. It has the capacity to lift others and accomplish great feats because of its purity of motive.

At this level of development, the capacity to discern essence becomes predominant; the core of an issue becomes the center of focus. As reason is bypassed, there arises the capacity for instantaneous recognition of the totality of a problem.... Reason deals only with particulars, whereas Love deals with entireties....

Love takes no position, and thus is global, rising above separation. It's then possible to be 'one with another,' for there are no longer barriers. Love is therefore inclusive and expands the sense of self progressively. Love focuses on the goodness of life in all its expressions and augments that which is positive—it dissolves negativity by re-contextualizing it, rather than attacking it. This is the level of true happiness.

Bert Hellinger, a German psychiatrist, the author of more than sixty books including *Love's Hidden Symmetry: What Makes Love Work in Relationships,* and the originator of Constellation Ancestral Work, claims that the only thing that keeps people stuck in old hurtful and dysfunctional family patterns is when the "chain of love" between members has been broken.

Doc Childre, founder of the Institute of HeartMath® in Boulder Creek, California, has produced scientific evidence to back up an "intelligent heart" theory. Scientists at HeartMath have focused their research on the emotions, heart intelligence and how to create coherence and resilience for the purpose of improving people's lives at home, school, work and play. HeartMath understands the link between the heart, learning and emotions. Its self-regulation techniques promote emotional balance, academic excellence and resilience. Corporations such as Hewlett-Packard and Motorola, and all four branches of the U.S. Military, are now using HeartMath techniques to teach employees how to become more mentally and emotionally balanced, and provide for individual and organizational transformation. In addition, educators have found that school children can better manage their behavior, and improve their ability to absorb academic information, by using the techniques pioneered by Doc Childre and the HeartMath institute.

The core of the HeartMath philosophy is that the heart, physically and metaphorically, is the key to tapping into an intelligence that can provide us with fulfillment. Science has shown that the heart communicates with the body and brain on a variety of different levels:

- The heart sends neurological information to the brain and the rest of the body.
- Through the pulse, the heart sends energy in the form of a blood pressure wave. Researchers have seen that changes in the electrical activity of brain cells occur in relation to the changes in the blood pressure wave. (This information is particularly relevant to Soul Lightening acupressure, since we connect directly with blood pulse in every session, to balance the energy flow.)
- The heart communicates on a biochemical level, releasing atrial peptide, a hormone that inhibits the release of other stress hormones.

- The heart communicates electromagnetically. An EKG measured in the doctor's office is actually an electrical signal produced by the heart. This signal can be picked up anywhere on the body, and permeates the space around us.

HeartMath has translated this information into simple tools that focus on teaching people how to listen to, and follow, the intuitive information of the heart. An extensive examination of these techniques, including scientific data, can be found in the book *The HeartMath Solution*, by Doc Childre and Howard Martin. Anyone who is seriously interested in using these tools will find a wealth of knowledge there.[15]

The Next Stage of Evolution

In western education we have been conditioned into a left-brained, analytical, thinking, mechanistic, Newtonian mindset for centuries. Human evolution has swirled in that eddy for a long time. That perspective is now causing stagnation, disease, distortion, and deformation. When we gave precedence to the left analytical brain, and veered away from the right brain and heart intelligence, we sidetracked much valuable wisdom of feelings. As I've mentioned in previous chapters, we turned predominantly to "reason" to solve our problems and guide our development and thereby tuned out some valuable heart input that could have assisted our health and wellbeing.

Now the flow of universal evolution pushes up against that one-sided approach. Fortunately, that mind-fix is being dislodged. It will be augmented one day by the more advanced wisdom of the heart as we evolve into the heart center.

---

15 Childre, Doc, et al. 2001. *The HeartMath Solution: The Institute of HeartMath's Revolutionary Program for Engaging the Power of the Heart's Intelligence.* New York, HarperCollins,

Heart intelligence can bring together the fundamental intellectual function of the left brain with more advanced faculties of the right brain and integrate both with its own awareness, which is vast. Thus, it is the transformative coordinator between feelings and thinking.

I believe we are at the beginning of such fascinating and useful heart and right-brain research, and that all of this exploration and experience will help humanity leap across the abyss of destruction we are facing now to claim an evolutionary jump into a more enlightened age.

The Heart and Love

In Soul Lightening work we accept the heart's love as actual because we can feel it, in the energy of the Field, with our hands as well as between one person and another. We work as much as possible from love and heart intelligence, for ourselves and others. The compassionate heart can support and nourish life with unconditional love and acceptance. We are always cultivating these heart qualities with every acupressure protocol because the heart, of both giver and receiver, is being nourished and awakened with each one.

Love originates in the physical heart; from there its healing and restorative properties can travel to the entire body, to the emotions and the mind. The central matrix of the heart energy is located in the chest. The heart's energy pathways (meridians) make up the delivery system of its essential spirit and intelligence, which is pulsed out into the world with each heartbeat, through blood and energy, to all the systems. In particular, the heart's energy radiates down through the arms and into the hands. Thus love can come directly from the heart into the hands for healing.

Yet another complex network of heart energy is concentrated through several internal pathways in the body. One travels across the chest through the heart; another travels from the heart straight down the midline into the belly; and another travels from the heart up through the throat, eventually ending in the eyes. Thus the center of individual spirit is radiating throughout the body—into the torso, head and arms, and eyes—continuously informing the whole being of its essential nature and purpose. No other organ or energy system informs the body as completely as does the heart.

When we send love from the heart center it comes from the whole of our being, more than from a thought or a wish. It is suffused with love energy, soothing but potent. The heart is both a receiver and transmitter of love. It can radiate its healing, loving and joyful vibration, a soothing balm, to others, from one heart to another, across the entire world. This has been demonstrated concretely through prayer broadcasts.

Love energy alone can heal, as has been proven by countless hands-on healers who had no other instruments besides their hands. Think of Jesus. Alaya Chikly, originator of Heart-Centered Therapy said, "I've witnessed that every trauma can be healed with willingness, loving guidance and an open heart. That understanding is the foundation of Heart-Centered Therapy." Alaya shares our belief and experience that each of us carries healing within ourselves.

Universal Love and the Oneness of All Life

Heart love and intelligence connect with universal love and the oneness of all life. An open heart can connect with the unconditional love of the universe or Divinity. It is the unconditional love of a true mother. It is caring, nourishing and unconditionally accepting. It promotes life, rather than destroying it. It is aligned with the feminine qualities of loving that have been suppressed for centuries and which have now become a more active part of human evolution. Of course, this loving quality is not restricted to gender.

• Note: Chikly, Alaya. Heart-Centered Therapy, taught through the Upledger Institute, West Palm Beach, Florida.

In contemporary life, when families often require both parents to work away from home, many men have taken on the function of the loving, nurturing mother.

Heart intelligence extends far into the universal Field, the Tao, and fuses with it, where it can access information and power far beyond any individual. It flows with the vitality and rhythm of the Field and thus is congruent with universal evolution. The connected heart can send love out to others. Great spiritual healers connect with love in the Field.

A dear friend of mine told me the story of experiencing his heart *resynching* with the universal Field after a series of major surgeries, including triple by-pass surgery. He said that he felt very disoriented for weeks after the surgery, even long after all the anesthetics, which cause their own form of disorientation, had left his body. Finally he realized that during the surgery the doctors stop and then restart the heart arbitrarily. After weeks of being disoriented, he had an epiphany; he recalled that the cells of the heart are the first to take on a pulse soon after the fertilized egg begins to develop into separate organ systems. At the time he had this thought he was sitting on his deck at home. He found himself asking, "But where does this pulse come from? How does it begin?" He gazed out at the stars, the infinite universe. "Of course," he thought, "the pulse comes from there!" He immediately felt a shock of recognition that this had to be true. Furthermore, it occurred to him that following his surgery his heart had been restarted *arbitrarily*. "Could it be," he asked himself, "that this medical procedure, as necessary as it was, could be the cause of this sense of disorientation? And will my pulse eventually come back into sync with the larger order or rhythm?"

For several days after that, he meditated at night under the stars, feeling what he could only describe as the larger universal life rhythm, or pulse. He then began to feel a resonance with that pulse once again. He thought of his heart like a radio being tuned into the "broadcasting" station, which was, in effect, the energy of the universe, or, as he put it, *All That Is*. Over time, he felt that this universal transmission was coming in sharper and sharper; all the sounds that were being transmitted by the universal field were coming in loud and clear. As this was occurring his sense of disorientation was diminishing. His heart felt more vital and connected to the whole than he had ever before experienced. His sense of disorientation quickly vanished entirely and never returned.

"Now I know that we are all totally immersed in the rhythms of the universe, or God," he explained. "The basic rhythms of our hearts are just part of the whole. The flesh and blood parts are just manifestations of form within that infinite rhythm of the universe or God or All That Is. It seems impossible to express with words because the words instantly create an illusion of separation, regardless of what I try to do with them."

As I listened to his story I had the feeling that my friend had discovered first-hand a precious mystery of the relationship of our heart to the whole of creation, a mystery that few of us will ever experience.

Soul Lightening Methods for Expanding Heart Intelligence

In our classes we use various methods to expand our heart intelligence and reconnect the stream of love. Some of these are:

The Acupressure Heart Protocol

The heart acupressure protocol is one of the many hands-on acupressure protocols we use in our work. This one focuses on the chest and the heart pathways that travel from the chest down through the arms and into the hands. We first prepare for a session with the receiver by creating a sacred working space around us. Since we work in consciousness while we simultaneously do the bodywork, we then discuss topics the client may be ready to explore to help nourish and expand heart consciousness, such as the ability to give and receive love, or obstructions to it; forgiveness, of self and others; compassion, for self or others, or obstructions to it; or joy, or obstructions to it.

Forgiveness Meditation in the Group

We often say the Forgiveness Meditation, an adaptation of a Buddhist method, in class together. It is a very useful tool in many different situations and is good world work. We say it as follows:

> I ask for forgiveness from all those people, living or dead whom I have knowingly or unknowingly hurt, demeaned or otherwise disrespected through intentional action, ignorance or clumsiness of thought, deed or action. Even though they may not condone what I have done, I ask for their forgiveness to the best of their ability.
>
> I offer forgiveness to all those people, living or dead who have knowingly or unknowingly hurt, demeaned or otherwise disrespected me through intentional action, ignorance or clumsiness of thought, deed or action. Even though I may not condone their action, I offer forgiveness to the best of my ability:
>
> I ask and accept forgiveness for all the ways in which I have knowingly or unknowingly hurt, demeaned or otherwise disrespected myself through intentional action, ignorance or clumsiness of thought, deed or action. Even if I don't condone my action, I ask and accept forgiveness for myself, to the best of my ability.
>
> For any forgiveness I am unable to give or receive I ask God for help.

The Miracle of *Ho'oponopono*

Love can shift perspective instantly. This magical effect, together with the extensive power of love, was demonstrated recently by a psychiatrist in Hawaii who used an ancient Hawaiian method of healing to treat inmates in a hospital for the criminally insane.

This fascinating phenomenon has been reported around the world through the internet. You can look it up there, under "Ho'oponopono," or "Hew Len." Or, read *Zero Limits,* by Joe Vitale[16], which tells the fully researched story in a very readable way. The story is hard to believe until you practice the method. I didn't believe it when I first read the story on the internet. Neither did Vitale until he went to Hawaii, worked with the doctor and practiced the method.

Basically, Dr. Hew Len was hired to direct a hospital criminal psychiatric ward that was failing in all categories: Inmates weren't rehabilitated, and there was a frequent turnover of the staff. Dr. Len arrived at the hospital, asked for all the files of inmates and then closed himself in his office with them. He didn't come out for a long time. He only saw inmates as he walked through the grounds to and from work.

The whole tenor of the prison began changing. Inmates started to recover. Staff members not only stayed but also were eager to come to work. Finally the hospital was closed when the work was done.

I read about Dr. Len's work and the practice of the Ho'oponopono (roughly translated as "making right") ceremony, and how it is employed for making peace between individuals, families and even warring neighbors. Many Hawaiian elders also teach forgiveness, which is at the heart of Ho'oponopono. Of course, many spiritual systems advise forgiveness because it is a core spiritual principle since there is no possibility for change without it.

---

16 Vitale, Joe. 2007. *Zero Limits*, New York, John Wiley & Sons, Inc..

After practicing it myself, I began using Ho'oponopono in my teaching. Early on I taught it to one of my friends. I had given him several other strategies as well, to help him in caring for his wife, who was dying with Alzheimer's. Of all the strategies I'd given him, he said of Ho'oponopono, "I think this is the most helpful one."

This method is perhaps the most effective one I have ever encountered to apply the power of love. Several of my friends, as well as Fritz, my husband, and I, did the forgiveness prayer for a while. My students and I have all experienced literally miraculous effects in our lives—subtle but dramatic.

The method in its most basic form is very simple. You do all the work on yourself alone, no matter what the event, situation or person you have a problem with or want to transform. It goes like this:

> You locate the *problematic* topic within yourself.
> You then say to yourself about that problem:
> I'm sorry.
> Please forgive me.
> I love you.
> Thank you.

For me, Ho'oponopono verifies how love can travel and transform things within the Universal Unifying Field. In fact, the intentional use of love allows us to enter the realm of miracles. (Other demonstrable modalities of the miraculous effects of forgiveness are *The Course in Miracles,* Alcoholics Anonymous. Matrix Energetics and our own Pyramid.)

Prayer in the Pyramid

The Pyramid (See chapter 16, "Working Within Sacred Space,") is a fundamental part of our work in class, in our therapy spaces and in our own lives. The practice consists of the group, individually and collectively, visualizing the entire seminar surrounded in a giant pyramid of energy. Within the pyramid our classes have become chambers of healing, growth and love.

Despite the fact that we process very difficult problems and issues, we rarely encounter conflict, violence or any really negative emotions that don't quickly dissolve in the spirit of "unconditional positive regard" and the mutual commitment to growth that we all share. We may not like everyone in each and every class but we accept their right to grow with us. This unconditional acceptance is not due to denial or suppression either, because we are also committed to processing as much secondary material as a person is ready and able to handle. I believe it is principally because of a consistent higher vibration that is maintained through the pyramid and the consistent recurring memory of that vibration in the brains of all the students.

This pyramid vibration can be projected over great distances, to be employed for distance healing. One or several of us place prayers for healing or strength in the pyramid at the same time for another person. For example, several of us agreed to pray at the same time for one of ours who was undergoing a rigorous chemotherapy regime in Switzerland. She later reported that she felt such great comfort and strength at that very time when we were praying. She also recovered. We have used such prayers to good effect many times, sometimes for healing, sometimes for visions we wish to manifest in the world.

The Heart Song of a World Teacher

I have to tell the story of Mattie Stepanek here because of his heart song and because I saw and felt his power as a world teacher while he was alive. You may have seen him on Larry King Live while he was living. His message was peace and his philosophy was, "Think gently, speak gently, live gently." He wanted to be remembered as "a poet, a peacemaker, and a philosopher who played."

Mattie had discovered a secret that enabled him to be a world teacher during and after his death. The secret was simple and deep. Mattie said, "Everyone has a heart song. When you discover and live from your heart song you are happy."

In his very short life he delivered his own heart song, like a meteor across the earth's sky.

One day Larry King asked him, "So what is your heart song, Mattie?"

"Oh!" he said. "To tell as many people as possible that we should all live in peace in the world together and love one another." I can still easily see his beautiful face in my mind's eye. And it's easy to remember his heart song.

In his short thirteen-year life his message was broadcast throughout the world, on television and in his five books of poetry. During his lifetime, he appeared with Oprah Winfrey, President Carter and Larry King, who all endorsed and supported him. From his wheelchair Mattie taught his mother, priests of the Catholic Church and countless others about universal brotherhood, love and peace.

Mattie's life was very difficult. He was born with a rare, incurable form of muscular dystrophy that resulted in his death a month before his fourteenth birthday. His mother saved his life with CPR just after his birth, before he ever left the hospital. He had many near-death encounters, suffered in great pain, was in hospitals hundreds of times, confined to a wheel chair at about age five, and lived on a respirator the last years of his life.

Yet he delivered his message with love and cheerfulness wherever he went. I saw him on television every chance I got because his beautiful, cheerful face and resounding powerful voice were so uplifting. Larry King would look at him with wonder each time he appeared.

When Mattie died, his funeral was held on June 28, 2004, at Saint Catherine Laboure Roman Catholic Church in Wheaton, Maryland. Nearly 1,350 people attended, including Oprah Winfrey.

President Jimmy Carter said, "We have known kings and queens, and we've known presidents and prime ministers, but the most extraordinary person whom I have ever known in my life is Mattie Stepanek." After he died Mattie's mother, a truly remarkable and brave woman, wrote a book about him and recorded it. It's called *Messenger: The Legacy of Mattie J.T. Stepanek and Heartsongs.*[17]

---

17 Stepanek, Jeni. 2009. *Messenger: The Legacy of Mattie J.T. Stepanek and Heartsongs.* New York, Penguin Books,

9:
THE PROCESS METHOD OF
SOUL LIGHTENING

He who knows others is wise;
He who knows himself is enlightened.

~Lao-tzu

Process Acupressure is the Soul Lightening method for working with body, mind, emotions and soul simultaneously. It differs markedly from traditional psychological methods since it includes direct body and soul work. Rather than intellectually *talking through*, analyzing and interpreting problems, personal history and future goals during a seated interchange between client and therapist, we use bodywork and process methods to respond to and process what is happening within the person. We assume from the outset that he or she already has the truth of who she is within. Our job is to help that truth become apparent to him or her. As we work on the body with acupressure, the body becomes the reference field of all processes.

In all stages of Process Acupressure we work with a method derived from Process Work, as formulated by Arnold Mindell, Ph.D. Dr. Mindell is a contemporary psychology genius who developed Process Oriented Psychology (now more commonly called Process Work) in Zurich, Switzerland. His work bridges psychology and bodywork in a revolutionary way.

When I was led to Process Work I realized it was the perfect method for working naturally with the impressions and information that arose from the body during an acupressure session. I gravitated to it immediately and studied it for more than ten years with Dr. Mindell, in Zurich as well as in the States.

Dr. Mindell's background is significant in that he arrived in Zurich as an M.I.T. physics graduate, led there by a dream. Once in Zurich, he discovered and attended the Jungian Institute where he became a Jungian analyst and trainer. When he became dissatisfied with interpreting, analyzing, or imposing preconceived concepts of health, balance or sanity on his patients, he began to formulate his own method. Beginning with Taoism, physics and Jungian psychology, he worked first with himself, his small children and a few select students, to develop a way to facilitate a person's natural growth process. He discovered that by following the person's actual unfolding process, he and the client were led to unravel psychological truths that led to the evolution of each person's natural growth. In this way, Process Work helps to reveal the whole person's unique growth path, in body, mind and emotions, in the present.

Mindell established the Process Oriented Psychology Institute in Zurich, and later, another center in Portland, Oregon, where it remains today. He expanded process work to include quantum theory and *deep democracy*, a deeper form of democracy that applied to all states of consciousness for individuals and groups. Now Process Work applies to individual therapy, body problems, coma and near death experiences, as well as to large group and organizational change management.

I studied with Dr. Mindell while Process Work was spreading around the world. Arny's (as we all call him) work continues to expand the scope of traditional therapy, as well as educational and organizational psychology. He has written twenty books and influenced every field of human behavior or growth. He is leaving an imprint on this century at least as large as Freud or Jung did in the twentieth century. I was very blessed to study with him, and continue to study with him whenever I can because he is certainly the most brilliant therapist I have ever observed.

Since I was already developing a wholistic therapy with a foundation in acupressure, Arny asked me to prepare and teach Process Acupressure at the first Process Work Intensive in Zurich in 1986. I was both thrilled and terrified. I fantasized that the Swiss students of Process Work, and people from other countries who had moved to Switzerland to study with Arny, would resent this new upstart from California (me) coming to teach a Process Work class. Partly my fantasy was justified. My method of working directly through the body was not the same as the method they had been using. Although my class was not heavily attended, those who did come were pleased and had good results.

Now, after twenty-seven years, Process Acupressure has proved itself through lasting, excellent results and healthier, happier, more soul-aligned students and clients. And Arny and Amy Mindell have been my dear friends all these years.

Process Defined

Process Work is hard to describe in words because it is so wholistic, involving movement, speaking, or sounding and visualizing everything at once. It almost has to be experienced first to comprehend its brilliance.

The "process" of a person, as defined in Process Work, is the fluid movement of information that emanates from a person through all the pathways (which we call "channels") of perception and expression. Process is the sum total of what that person is living and expressing at any given moment. It includes all that the person is aware of now, which we call *primary process* (conscious awareness). It also adds what is beneath conscious awareness, the unconscious, which we call *secondary process*. Past history, the usual subject of psychotherapy, shows up in a person's process as it impinges on the present. In reality we are emitting from our bodies and fields what and who we actually are all the time. Naturally, heightened awareness is a prerequisite for Process Work.

The whole being we work with in Process Acupressure is conceived of as an ever fluctuating complex of body, mind, emotions and also soul. As we process material that arises from the body we are paying attention to both conscious awareness of the person (primary process) and the unconscious (secondary process) signals that are also showing up.

We study and follow the natural unfolding process of a person. During a session, we encourage the person to just flow with what happens. We watch what exactly is happening in a person and what wants to happen next. A person is awakened to more of herself and her own growth patterns as we facilitate awareness of her own process. We constantly encourage more awareness, self-expression and self-directed growth.

In Soul Lightening work we use process methods to reveal the personality formed from personal history. We don't analyze or label the personality. Each person is unique, though he or she may share characteristics with others. We support the individual's process as she discovers the various components that make up her unique personality. We watch for congruence in all parts of being as the process unfolds.

In Process Acupressure the body is seen as the *bed of process*. The process itself arises in the form of images, feelings, sensations, insights or energy movement. The body doesn't lie, as one therapist put it. As acupressure opens energy through the body and mind, the flow of process is supported as new information or perspectives arise. Signals emerge for the next growth steps. By following and facilitating those signals, we can support a process as it unfolds toward healing, growth or completion.

In Process Acupressure we trust each individual's growth pattern as it unfolds naturally. We trust that the individual pattern will be shown by signals that arise naturally from the body in the person's process. Therefore we never push nor require specific conditions or outcomes.

By paying attention to what is actually happening naturally in the present, and following and encouraging what is trying to happen next, the helper supports all aspects of the whole person *as they are.* The helper becomes an assistant for the safe and most congruent next steps of the client's development.

We don't try to "fix" a particular symptom, condition, attitude or idea the person may have. We don't attempt to bring about some pre-determined personality trait or structure. Rather we facilitate the client's own unique awareness and understanding about the roots and causes of conditions. We seek to reveal the whole person to herself. By supporting a person's unique styles of learning, growth and responsibility for health and wellbeing, we become an advocate for their true nature and their deepest truth.

The Growing Edge

Long ago the psychologist Carl Rogers discovered that people have a *lead growth shoot,* just as trees do. As the name implies, a lead growth shoot precedes and leads the way toward new growth within a person. In Process Work terms, a lead growth shoot would show up as an *edge,* the point where a person is cautious or downright frightened to move forward, even though forward motion points toward a new growth possibility.

Our final aim, of course, in Soul Lightening work is to uncover the guidance, power and purpose of the soul, or spiritual aspect. We believe that beneath all the conditioning of life there is a brilliant, complete soul blueprint for the right purpose of the individual's life. Therefore we value the soul as the rightful director of life. Thus, long before personality work is finished, we introduce the concept of soul.

At the end of each session, after deep relaxation, energetic balance and an altered state of consciousness are realized, we usually ask if there are any soul messages. It is surprising how often insights or directions are given. They have a strong affirming effect on the individual that goes beneath ego. At the end of one student's process the soul showed up as a bright light. I report part of that session here. The client, H, had been talking about fear and stress in her life:

A: How does this fear and stress affect the soul?

H: The soul goes out and away. Then cells [in the body] feel abandoned by the soul. Fear, aloneness, sadness.

A: Follow the soul out, can you find it?

H: Like a shooting star going out. Horse flying with wings.

A: How is it there, where you're flying free?

H: Peaceful, no stress, no concerns. Light. Soul is watching the cells

A: What about bringing that light back with you? Trail that light, like a falling star.

H: sobbing.

A: Let yourself feel it all the way.

H: I waited for so long for this to happen.

A: Has the physical self been without the soul all this time?

H: I first felt my soul at a Process Acupressure 1 class. I knew she was there but not accessible. It wasn't completely disconnected but inaccessible. Far away.

A: Feel right now how that is for the physical form.

H: Flower...like life force that was gone...is back. Colors. Not alone anymore. I don't feel abandoned, no stress now.

A: What do you feel instead?
H: Residual sadness. But I feel peace, quiet. My soul is taking good care of my being.

After this session H was able to bring a higher perspective to her normal life stresses. She also felt much more confident about contacting her own soul consciousness.

Cultivating the Unconscious or Secondary Process

In Process Work the unconscious part of ourselves is called "secondary process," because it is that part of our process, and ourselves, which we are not yet aware of. The unconscious contains the deepest layers of our psyche—those experiences, far back in our history that have either been forgotten or repressed.

The unconscious lies beyond the *edge*. It is all the unknown layers underneath the conscious mind that nevertheless exert tremendous influence over us. Much, perhaps most, of our growth comes up from the unconscious or secondary process. Therefore, it is very important for us to develop a strong awareness of secondary signals. Events that seem to just "happen" to us—rather than those that are within our own conscious awareness or control—indicate that unconscious secondary process is at work.

Jung called the body the *unconscious*. Certainly we are in very close contact with the unconscious all the time we are touching the body. Since unconscious material often bubbles to the surface during bodywork, we have a chance to process and reprogram it, and thus release a person from old burdens of the past. For example, it is my experience that when an unconscious is full of negative imprinting it requires a certain amount of conscious processing, with bodywork, to release and reframe its content.

I seriously doubt that a negatively burdened unconscious could ever be adequately released through either bodywork or talking alone. The more unconscious negative material we process and re-lease, the more free an individual becomes to recognize and begin to follow his own inner wisdom and direction.

At the same time that we are burdened by unconscious con-tent, we carry untold treasures of talents, strengths and memories within the unconscious, some of which will never be tapped in one lifetime. The unconscious carries many of the seeds of our growth. Unused potential can be discovered within it. As secondary process is brought to consciousness, more charge is released for positive change and we can occupy more of who we actually are. In fact, we can greatly enhance a person's growth by eliciting only a tiny amount of the unconscious.

Becoming Aware of the Channels of Perception and Awareness

To reveal what is actually happening, and *trying* to happen for an individual, we encourage enhanced whole-being awareness. For example, what is happening in the present moment? What do you feel in the body? What do you see? Hear? What thoughts are hap-pening right now? Therefore part of our process method is aware-ness training, in which we stress all the channels of perception and expression.

The most essential instruments of human awareness are the senses, which feed information to the brain. As the senses pick up impressions (which we call signals) from the environment they feed them into the brain, which sorts, organizes and interprets them. While we are usually born with sight, hearing, sensation and move-ment in the body, we may not have conscious awareness in all of these. Our awareness training in Soul Lightening is to wake up all our senses to conscious awareness, which will eventually promote whole-being awareness.

In Process Work, conscious awareness was defined by "chan-nels of awareness" in order to clearly differentiate them from one another. (These channels are shown in the chart on the next page.)

In our work we teach the channels of awareness in body, mind, emotions and soul. Each channel has an external aspect, representing the person's awareness of things outside himself, and an internal aspect, representing the person's awareness of things going on within him. One person may have a highly developed and awake mental/visual channel while his body/sensation is hardly developed or awake at all.

The channels are also agents of expression. For example, we can be aware of things we hear (through our ears, the auditory channel) and we can also express ourselves auditorily, by verbalizing, or making a sound, or making some other gesture in response to what we hear.

The channels of perception and expression are shown as follows:

- *Energy:* General Sensing of energy flow in the "field" or body
- *Visual or Auditory:* Mental channels of seeing and hearing
- *Sensation & Movement:* Body channels of sensation or sense of movement
- *Emotion:* Emotion as it arises throughout the body
- *Spiritual:* A higher level of the other channels, in combination or as a composite, including clairvoyance, clairaudience, clairsentience, etc.
- *Relationship:* Connections that arise between two people
- *World:* Awareness of environment, in groups, cities, with global conditions, etc.

As our senses pick up signals (impressions or signs) from the channels, we learn how to identify them as visual, auditory, sensory and so forth. A whole-being awareness begins to evolve. With practice we are able to follow signals from all the channels at once.

As we work with acupressure on the body, signals from one or several channels arise more easily than in a verbal dialogue or talking situation. As the signals from these channels arise in the session, we urge the person to notice them. What comes up might be in the form of imagery, or a voice in the mind. It might be an emotion felt in the body, a body sensation such as tingling, pain, heat or cold, or even a gesture such as an arm raising or a finger lifting or some other body movement. We ask the person to encourage that sign to reveal more and to remain aware of its progression. We notice and encourage this unfolding through various means, such as making the signal stronger, repeating it, talking to it or even strongly resisting it.

Awareness increases with practice, of course. As a person's awareness grows he can become more facile at picking up signals and allowing them to unfold, expressing themselves more and more fully. A growing interest, excitement and facility in staying with a process develops.

For example, what first came up as a tensing of muscles is encouraged to express more fully, and eventually that small movement could become a full, graceful gesture of the whole arm or even a dance. Through this process of greater awareness and expression the person gains more understanding and greater personal freedom to express what are essential parts of his being. As processes progress, growth happens. Even when some processes are psychologically painful, like remembering an embarrassing moment or an abuse, a person knows there is always resolution and growth as the process unfolds.

Process work is like the flow of a river; it rushes and ebbs, slows down and goes through rapids, but there is always a current up ahead, beyond what is happening now. Process has its own timing, according to the unfolding growth of the individual.

Personal history, personality patterns, present obstructions and current aspirations are revealed as we process what comes up naturally. A person experiences that the journey never ends, and that it becomes ever more interesting as new insights, understanding and strengths develop. Awareness continues to expand, not only within the individual but within his relationships and world understanding. A person is more present in the now, can enjoy more, give more and receive more. In Soul Lightening we are not after any preconceived model of what an ideal individual should be like, but rather we assist a person to uncover his true nature to him. Of course, the therapist is simply an ally for the client as process reveals himself to himself, regardless of what the therapist might think or feel.

Channels of Awareness in the Body: Sensation and Movement

In Soul Lightening work we teach students and clients how to notice body signals and then how to process the information within them. By waking up to body awareness we can notice the present signals that alert us to imbalances. We can also access the raw data of history stored in body tissues. In our work we have also repeatedly found that information for healing a symptom is often embedded right in the body process *around* the symptom.

Students who cultivate body awareness can attune to body intelligence and preserve their health better than people who are not body aware. They are able to respect the signals the body provides, take them seriously and thus avoid many common ailments that would have developed if attention and care had not been given upon early recognition of the first tiny symptoms. I've previously noted the example of how a body aware person can feel the sensations and signs of a cold coming on, through awareness such as a little bit of tightening in the throat or nasal passages, a slight tension in a particular muscle in the neck (these signs vary greatly for each person) long before it becomes an actual pathology that really gets them down. By recognizing these early signs of an illness the person may make lifestyle changes that give their bodies an opportunity to heal before further symptoms develop.

Body awareness shows up as *bodily sensations and movement*. Sensation and movements are obtained via nerve receptors throughout the body. Nerve impulses then feed into the brain where they are either registered in our awareness or not.

A body-aware person can consciously locate many sensation signals that arise from the body, such as tingling, pain, pressure, hot or cold, in any given moment when attention is focused on the body. In fact I have known bodyworkers who can follow the energy pathways (meridians) in the body, or locate a particular vertebra that is misaligned, through their awareness alone.

We have found that many students do not have ready awareness of either sensation or movement in their bodies. Yet there is often much valuable information stored in one or both. Certain professions require body awareness and knowledge, such as dance therapy, occupational therapy, athletics, some kinds of bodywork, and so forth. But for the most part, in mainstream contemporary culture, we "live in our heads" until some very insistent physical condition comes to our attention or interferes with our ability to function. For example, after a broken leg, a massive hives breakout or a serious illness, we start noticing our bodies more: how they work, what they need, and so forth. I once read an account of a nun who reported that until she contracted cancer she had almost no contact with her body. After surviving cancer, however, she developed what she described as a "holy connection" with it.

Awareness of Movement

Movement that arises naturally from the body provides different impressions and information (kinesthetic awareness) than tactile sensations of hot and cold, scratchy, prickly, and so forth. Each time we gesture, walk, dance or change positions within a chair, we have feelings within the body that are subtly different from the sensations. These movements often carry rich information about what is going on with a person.

I worked with a college professor once who pretty much lived in his head. He was disconnected from his body as well as in his relationships. Toward the end of a session with him I noticed that one foot made a very subtle kicking motion. I called his attention to that foot. At first he was completely unaware of it. I asked him to focus attention on it anyway. Gradually I could see that he was locating the foot. Then I asked him to exaggerate that kicking motion, and repeat it. He complied but it took several kicks before he suddenly exclaimed, "Oh! I get it! I'm kicking off the constraints I feel in my department where I'm stereotyped as the remote intellect who can't relate to anyone!"

After that session he started to notice how his body reacted *in the moment* as he was talking with a colleague. This awareness led to an ability to open up to others that he hadn't experienced before.

Dancers and movement therapists are often, though not always, intensely aware of the slightest movement within their own or another's body. Most people, however, are not usually aware of subtle movements they make, such as scratching, doodling, hand gestures, and so forth. Such subtle movements often carry significant information for the unfolding process.

Spontaneous movement often arises at the edge of consciousness. It may signal a hidden motivation or an important growth shoot. For example, I worked with a promising young college student who said he was stuck in his forward motion. He had lost interest in school but he had no motivation for any other pursuit. He said he was lethargic and bored. As he verbalized these symptoms I noticed a very subtle movement of his tongue along his lips.

I said, "What an interesting movement you're making with your tongue right now."

He looked surprised and said, "What?"

I asked him to bring attention to his tongue and then to let it move naturally as it had been doing, without altering the movement at all. He did this several times.

Suddenly he smiled broadly and exclaimed, "Wow! I haven't remembered that in a long time." When I asked him what he remembered exactly, he said, "I was the youngest of seven children. Sometimes the only way I could get attention was to make some kind of noticeable mischief. And I remember now that I made this movement with my tongue as I was figuring out how to do that."

I asked him how this insight might help in his present school boredom or his relationships.

He said, "I think I need to make more mischievous actions or remarks in my life at school. Maybe mischief would ignite my creativity or spur more interest for me. And who knows? Maybe for others, too."

One good way of exploring your own movement is to allow yourself to get all the way into spontaneous movement while paying attention to what else you are feeling, seeing, hearing. In this way you can often discover valuable messages within your movements that were formerly unconscious.

A person who has body awareness is therefore able to respect and attune to his body intelligence. Many dysfunctions of the body can be avoided or changed so that they even become assets. I know a really busy and accomplished psychiatrist who turned his diagnosis of ADD (Attention Deficit Disorder) into an asset by accepting that he could do many things virtually at the same time, in different locations. He is a master multi-tasker. By honoring and following the body's intelligence that person can learn how to stay in harmony with his or her own growth process, and destiny, while maintaining health.

Channels of Mental Awareness: Visual and Auditory

Since we are working on and through the body in Soul Lightening we pay attention to what a person reports that they are seeing (visual channel) and hearing in their heads (auditory channel) as the work proceeds. When a person says she "sees" something we know the mind is engaged. Similarly, if he "hears" something we know he is thinking in some manner. We encourage clients and students to notice clearly what they see and hear in the environment as well as inside their minds. We also urge them to increase their awareness of their unique mind style. For example, do they primarily think in pictures (visual) or in words (auditory), or a combination of both? We encourage students to notice their particular thoughts and thought streams as the process unfolds. We have been trained in school primarily through words, in lectures or reading, so we tend to place more emphasis on verbal understanding in our culture.

In our work we seek to bring more light of consciousness into an individual's mental functions. This means being conscious of as many aspects of the mind as possible—thoughts and thought streams, signals from the body that turn into thoughts and signals from the unconscious. And all along we encourage integrating mental awareness with the other centers of intelligence, such as emotion, movement or sensations in the body.

Positive or Negative Thought: Creative or Destructive Mind

Thought is one of the most powerful agents of change and creation. In this time of transformation we are learning more and more, from science and spiritual practice, how greatly thought influences our lives. In fact, this is one of the frontiers of modern consciousness work.

I have already mentioned how metaphysical thought has seeped into modern new thought religions, new psychology, entrepreneurships and business. One of the contributions of that body of knowledge is an emphasis on creating whatever you want by positive thoughts. Louise Hay's book *You Can Heal Your Life* has sold five hundred million copies around the world. It has literally changed consciousness globally. The ancillary concept is that negative thoughts and emotions can make you sick and miserable and stop creation. I already told about the woman who explained that she had reversed her physical illness and negative and bitter outlook on life by changing her thoughts one at a time. And then of course the language we speak reflects our positive or negative thoughts. The growing popularity of the *law of attraction*, first taught by Abraham and featured in the film and book titled *The Secret*, is only one of the numerous approaches to transform thought and therefore health, prosperity and creativity. Brad Willis, the author of *Warrior Pose*, changed a "skeptical, negative and bitter" outlook on life to become a compassionate teacher and healer. All these people and methods demonstrate that negative thought can be changed to its opposite. Results of mind transformation range from pleasant to miraculous.

Emotions Are Felt Through the Body

In Soul Lightening work we encourage awareness and expression of all emotions, both positive and negative. We may say, "Go on and feel what you are feeling and bring your awareness to it." Then a person can claim a direct contact with feelings in their body and allow awareness to go deeper than it has before. For example, we not only encourage a particular emotional expression, but sometimes we even ask a person to exaggerate that emotion, within the safe container of a session.

In this way a person can become familiar with her own emotional nature. She will learn how emotions can bring out a deeper understanding of a situation. She can notice which emotions bring a feeling of wellbeing and which seem destructive, like prolonged fear. If she follows the fear in the moment she is much more apt to locate and understand the roots or causes of it, and learn how to release the fear safely.

A person can learn to notice an emotion arising in the body and make a conscious choice whether to express it within a particular environment. For example, it can be very therapeutic for a man to rage at his boss in the safety and privacy of a session, although it would be unacceptable, and probably disastrous, for him to rage in this way at the office. But in expressing it and processing it through, in the safely of a session, he can find the underlying truth that the emotion is trying to reveal.

Clearing Obstructions to Soul Consciousness

The past conditioning that forms the personality, such as family dynamics, can often obstruct soul work. We process obstructions as they arise, one by one, until the personality is more or less cleared and current. Soul work is particularly valuable after most of the processing (in a given session) has completed.

One student, Paula Macali, reported how she had come to her "essence" and cleared up personal history through our work:

> Soul Lightening Acupressure awakened me to my essence and set me free to be me. It was the fastest track to liberating the parts of myself caught by conditioning; it brought light to the places I had been unwilling to accept. There are no limits to where Soul Lightening Acupressure can take you. It is truly one of the greatest modalities to free beings from their limited selves and take them through the stages of liberation with grace and ease. I think it is one of the most elegant systems of mind-body-spirit work in the world today.

> When I first studied Soul Lightening in the late 80s I was quite amazed to realize that this modality was far superior to all the psychotherapy sessions I had in the past. It released restrictions from my body that directly related to my past history. It would have taken me years to release both the body restrictions and the old habits that no longer served me had I just received bodywork or talk therapy. My life took on new dimensions and moved me into the work and path that most suited my soul's evolution. I cannot imagine what life would have been like if I had not connected with this most authentic healing modality which has carried me to the deepest core of my being and connection with the Divine.

After clearing obstructions from the past that no longer serve a person we work directly with the personality, as it is right now. At that time we can take the data of personality processing to the wise counsel of the deeper soul consciousness and ask for guidance. Then it is often possible to reach beneath any conditioned patterns and beliefs to soul truth. For example, we might say, "Now let's take this deeper, to your soul. What would your soul say about this?"

The Soul Is Contacted through the Spiritual Channel

Soul awareness reveals soul intelligence. We teach students how to open their own *spiritual channel*, a multi-and extra-sensory awareness in touch with soul truth. The spiritual channel is an altered state of consciousness that can, and often does, use aspects of the other channels. For example one might *see* a vision of some transcendental truth and *hear* a voice with it at the same time. Within the spiritual channel one *feels* vibrant, even electrified, "tingling all over." A person could have an inner vision, as mystics do; could hear voices as Joan of Arc did; could feel the presence of dead people, as my process partner did as a child. Or a person could have a cosmic consciousness experience that included all the senses at an elevated level at once, as Edgar Mitchell did on the Apollo mission to the moon.

The spiritual channel can take us into extra-worldly realms besides our ordinary, daily life state, to communicate with other beings, such as ancestors, spiritual guides or deities; or with other worlds; or through extended sight into the known world and beyond, to stars and galaxies. It can even penetrate into the tiniest factors, as in the case of vision into bodies with the ability to see into blood, bone, organs or molecules.

The spiritual channel involves a higher frequency or vibration of each regular channel. For example, *clairvoyance*, seated in the brow chakra, corresponds with the ordinary visual channel but it enables a person to see what is not seen with ordinary eyes, such as visions of colors, symbols and figures that are not visible to most people.

Clairaudience corresponds with the auditory channel. It is centered in the throat chakra and allows a person to "hear" voices, higher guidance, animals or plants speaking or otherworldly music. It has been written that Beethoven, who was stone deaf in the last years of his life, could "hear" music as he composed it.

Clairsentience is the counterpart of sensation. It is usually located around the second and third chakras. It enables a person to "feel" sensations within another's body. A clairsentient bodyworker, for example, often *feels* the stomach or headache of her client or friend. This feeling is different from the overall body tingling, champagne-like enlivening, that can accompany an opening of the spiritual channel.

Movements that arise naturally and congruently in the body, such as a hand waving in the air, eyes moving or a foot twitching, seemingly of their own accord, can be expressions of the spiritual channel as well. They are different from normal movement in that they seem to have no objective references in the environment. And a voice or vision, or both, may accompany them.

The emotions that prevail within the spiritual channel are joy, contentment, bliss, love, appreciation and gratitude, sometimes all together. In relationships there is a sense of union and un-possessive love.

How We Work with the Spiritual Channel

To access the spiritual channel, the soul almost always requires a relaxed body and an altered state of consciousness. Such a state is facilitated by acupressure. We need to be patient and quiet while a person accesses their own soul consciousness, which is absolutely unique to that individual. Analysis, labels or diagnoses from the practitioner will inhibit the "still, small voice" of the soul, since soul consciousness comes from beneath or beyond ordinary mind. We allow the chattering of the "monkey mind," the ups and downs of emotion, and the thinking analytical mind to settle down before we can approach it. Soul awareness develops over time as we ask for soul messages at the end of sessions

When a client has reached a soul level we might ask her, "Would you like to ask if your soul has a message for you today, or about this particular issue?" The answer will not necessarily come in words. (Notice the silence in the process session coming up.) The soul is not chatty, nor analytical. When you do encounter this chattiness or analytical voice you can know that you haven't reached soul consciousness. Feelings, images or a symbol may appear instead of words, but these will convey a meaningful message. It is only necessary for the facilitator to notice what happens after asking the client if she wants to access the soul, and then wait respectfully for her to receive a response in her own way. In fact, often a person will remain quite still and silent and only later report to the facilitator what happened. Soul consciousness is often sensed in the Field as a *stillness* and a kind of *reverence* that comes in. Some have called it grace.

While almost everyone might have brief glimpses or messages from the soul, it can take a while for a person to experience soul consciousness for any extended period of time. Soul awareness develops over time as we ask for soul messages at the end of sessions. When we think a client is at this stage in her understanding, and when it feels appropriate, we begin Process Acupressure sessions with the following invitation: "X [name], I invite your own soul to guide this session for your highest good. I ask my own soul to assist you. And we invite both our higher guides to assist this process."

The following soul processing session was begun with that invitation. It happened during a class. The session illustrates the unique and curious way a soul can show up and how the spiritual channel flows through all the others. I call the session "Flowing into Pure Being." As a point of information, the following client, Dawn Robbins, had been working with her father and grandmother in a previous session:

A: What is the resolution with father and grand-mother from the previous session?

D: No words, it's a very deep place. [Hands move down, making a container with them.] The well-spring of my own soul. I'm in a still place from where it bubbles up.

A: Explore your soul in this deep well.

D: Beneath this life of personal history, I sense a huge expansion of water. There's movement there but no disturbance on the surface. [Hands moving.] It's a natural flow, doesn't empty, rise and fall, ebb and flow. Held in a chalice or valley, vessel grows. Natural expansion and contraction. The fluids of my body are responding to this natural flow. I am in a bowl; on the rim are the ancestors and Indians around the rim. I'm watching. I see the reflection of my being in the water. [Hands exploring outwards, as if touching or reaching for something.] It's a natural rise and fall.

A: What is rising and falling like?

D: Like yin and yang, coming and going. Expanding out of that, lots of light. [Arms over head.] Up above, light streaming into a valley. Beyond and above it. [Arms wide open.] Still place. No coming and going.

A: What does this experience say to you?

D: Only to be it.

A: It?

D: Silence. [Hands move down the body, over belly.]

A: What is your relation to this field of beingness?

D: I am it. This is edgy. But the wrath of heaven didn't descend on me when I said that. Disturbs wa-ter a little to digest that I am it. The ancestors' reflec-tions were disturbed, but as it settles their reflections are clearer. How much we can serve by just being.

A: Would it be right for Dawn to just *be it* right now?

D: Yes.

A: Dawn, check out how it is for everyone else in the room when you are just being it.

A: [With her arms and hands, Dawn streams energy in front, up and above. She smiles.]

D: Big heart field. Walk into Divine field. Lots of love.

A: [To the group] Let's all open to the love field in the heart.

A: [To Dawn] What can you say about this?

D: More expansive in heart chakra. I sense more resonance in group and world.

A: [Touches heart acupoints to spread heart energy.]

D: Waves of love. Can't find the difference between out and in. [Laughs.] I hear angels singing, new opening in auditory channel. There is a resonant quality. [Hands explore space around her.] Vast space again.

A: Is there a soul Message for you? Or for others?

D: [Smiles.] Okay. So do you get it? In this moment in time? [Dawn turns her head toward the group. She apparently trusts that the resonant energy of the Field is felt by everyone. She starts laughing.]

D. Now I'm seeing a little cartoon of the WHATS? characters leaving, running off into the desert with all the other WHATS. [From a previous session we knew that the WHATS were negative emotions, internalized voices and beliefs of others, saying, what do you think you are doing? WHAT? What now? What if? What will they think? and so forth.] They can't reside here anymore. They cannot survive in the higher frequency in this field. This leaves me a little naked, to see a clear reflection of my totality. An empty still place. The WHATS are watching from a distance, curious. I recognize I need to continue to be conscious with this process, so as not to fall back into old patterns of behavior, thinking, etc. Because the WHATS are more than willing to come and reside with me again.

A: Stream beingness down throughout your whole body, so that all parts of you know this. Beingness has all the richness you will ever need right now.

D: I want to lie and rest for a while.

The next day Dawn reported that during the evening following the above session, she saw a snowy owl that circled close overhead. (She is a shaman, so such an occurrence had special meaning to her, especially here in the desert where we almost never see snowy owls). And in Chakra Tai Chi the next day she asked what her growth shoot was now, and received, "Be That, Be That, even in your persona."

Cultivating Soul Consciousness

One can facilitate a client's ability to reach a soul level by asking a few well-placed questions, one or two at most, during a session. Below are questions or comments that can help further soul consciousness.

Soul Questions

- Ask your soul to show itself to you. Wait patiently for whatever image, color, feeling, symbol or words it may present. Then simply be with those impressions, letting it fill and inform you.

- Shall we go deeper now and ask for your soul's guidance about this?
- Would you like to consult your soul about this [problem, event, feeling]?
- What would your soul say about this?
- How would your soul respond to this? Ask your soul if there is [was] an important learning in this difficult event [situation, relationship].
- What does your soul need now?
- Ask your soul to view this [situation, event, trauma] from its perspective. Does it have a comment or guidance?

A session may be devoted exclusively to soul work when a person already has a familiarity with soul consciousness. In this case we would set an intention for soul consultation from the beginning of the session. We would make the soul invitation and then pose a particular issue. For example, "In this session we wish to consult the soul about [an event, relationship, issue]."

We can also set future-paced intentions, or requests for manifestation, in soul work. Example: "We wish to devote this session to creating the conditions for abundance in [name] life. We seek any clarification and direction about this."

The wonders of soul work are many. Each person's soul, unique in the universe, will offer something new. The ultimate soul consciousness experience is an awakening within a person to his or her true nature and connection with the cosmos.

The Relationship Channel

The relationship channel involves the reciprocal interaction between two or more people. In other words, when there is an energy or communication exchange between people we say that the relationship channel is open. But when a person is closed to that interaction, then the channel is not open. The person might not communicate; he might refuse to look at another, not want to be touched, not respond to another or decline communication in some other way.

The World Channel

The world channel awareness is a person's awareness of what is happening outside himself; this might be awareness of a group, city, country, the world, the universe and so forth. We say that a person has an open world channel when he is attuned to what is happening in his own world, whether that world of his perception is his present group, his town, his country or the whole global world. That person might be very involved in current world news or perhaps what is happening in his city or neighborhood. On the other hand, we may say that a hermit, who has isolated himself from all contact with other people, has almost no world channel available.

Working with Awareness of Whole-Being Intelligence

As we have explored in chapter 2, and elsewhere in this book, we are born with whole-being intelligence. How do we access that intelligence with our present awareness? We begin by waking up to it, and by following signals that arise from any or several parts of the body, mind or emotions. We access whole being intelligence by following what comes naturally, instinctively, from all parts of our own being, penetrating to the core of who we are—the soul itself.

Although whole being intelligence is innate, whether or not we can learn to be aware of it depends on many outer realities, such as the conditioning of family, environment, culture, geography and education. In addition, the full flowering of an individual's intelligence will depend on his or her use of will, work and opportunity.

Whole-being intelligence brings us back home to our own truth, to what is happening right now as well as what is trying to emerge within our own growth shoots. As one Swiss psychologist [Vivienne Rauber-Decoppet] said, "When I got to know Aminah Raheem and Process Acupressure in 1986 it felt like 'COMING HOME.' It was that synthesis of spirituality, psychology and energy work that I had not yet found in my psychology studies and the many therapy forms I had come to know."

Through Soul Lightening we teach each person to respect the raw data of her own experience, rather than seeking outside expertise to interpret or tell her how to understand herself.

By noticing and depending on the body's signals we can maintain physical balance. When body signals alert us to impending imbalance or symptoms we can correct what is off, and usually prevent a symptom or serious illness before it progresses. We can realize the deep intrinsic wisdom that the body holds for promoting our growth, maintaining our health and keeping us strong.

When we attune to our natural feelings we can stay current with our own honest response to ourselves, others and the environment. We become more human. We recognize our humanity with others who have the same kinds of feelings, needs and awareness. We are more sensitive to both the pain and joy of others, and thus can be a resonating friend. Compassion increases for the human condition.

By paying attention to our own thoughts and thinking strategies we can make greater use of our present mental capacities. We can readily differentiate our own thinking from that of others. We can honor our own unique way of arriving at mental constructs and learn how to cultivate our own mental abilities for their maximum use. And we can also realize the limits of mental analysis.

Allowing awareness in all parts of our being enables us to respond to life from our wholeness, to stay awake and be present to what is happening. When we add soul consciousness to the combined awarenesses of mind, body and emotions, we can tap into the essential meaning of our spiritual blueprint and guidance for our unique destiny. The soul becomes the guide, supported by the full awareness and intelligence of the whole being.

The State of Awakening

Awakening is a term and concept that originated in the Eastern world, particularly India, where achieving higher consciousness and enlightenment have been a part of spiritual values for centuries. A wave of consciousness occurred during the 1960s when throngs of young people traveled to India and came back transformed, bringing a new brand of spirituality with them. Their stories began to filter through Western consciousness. Ram Dass, born Richard Alpert, is a prime example: From Harvard professor of psychology he morphed into a spiritual teacher and author of the bestselling book *Be Here Now.*

Since that time a great many teachers of spiritual awakening have written books about the state of consciousness referred to as "awakened." The mind, or knowing, becomes holographic rather than two- or even three-dimensional; it extends into the universal Field and simultaneously is in contact with many dimensions, times and other bodies of knowledge. In the awakened state we seem to know anything we want to know...in a flash. Some call this "access to Universal Mind." Richard Maurice Bucke, in his book *Cosmic Consciousness*, coined the term "cosmic consciousness." In the book he described cosmic consciousness states of Descarte, Tesla, Einstein and Edison as beyond the brain and mind in which they had their original creative insights or visions. Most people who have had near-death experiences describe this cosmic, unifying state. It is known by seekers of enlightenment as liberation, meaning release from the cocoon of conditioning.

The more awareness we have, the closer we come to awakening to our true nature and to those connections with the cosmos that go beyond the individual self, beyond the realms of personality, ego and the everyday reality that we all live in. Released from the past, a person sees into a much vaster, more promising vista of possibilities; all things seem connected in the universal Field, which is filled with light; often there is a feeling of love for everything.

This state of consciousness is so different from normal consciousness that sometimes people in the midst of it are locked up by those who are not aware of this state. I mean that literally! For example, some years ago I had a client, a wonderful, highly intelligent doctor, who had such an awakening. She had experienced a state of union with ALL THAT IS, a state of love for everything and everyone. When she tried to tell her colleagues about it, they referred her for psychiatric treatment. She told me that when doctors in the psychiatric ward questioned her, she gave them the answers she knew they were looking for, describing her experience to them in a way that they would judge her as being rational and healthy. She said that even as she was deliberately conforming to what they would accept, she could actually see the auras and inner character of those doctors, while they questioned her. In that way, she avoided hospitalization.

When I worked with her she was balancing two worldviews at once: the medical world of her professional education and the awakened awareness of her direct experience. In this way she was able to function as expected in her profession while continuing her awakened state. I would love to know where and who she is now.

An integral condition of this state of openness is that we have both soul consciousness, described above, and cosmic consciousness, which implies direct contact with the greater Spirit. We don't need interpreters of spirituality, or intermediaries, to put us in touch with Spirit. In fact, some experiencers of it claim that they become aware of being a part of God in this state.

Tertiary Process

A fascinating development can occur when the individual mind moves beyond the primary process of his conscious mind, beneath the secondary process of the individual unconscious mind, and finally into a transcendent flow of union with the universal

Field or All That Is. I call this the *tertiary process*. This is the third depth of consciousness in which individual and cosmic consciousness merge and flow with the creative unfolding of Source, or the Tao. In tertiary process one would feel at one with the Source of creation, and his consciousness and action would flow with the Tao. Synchronicities happen. In that state you *know* things you don't ordinarily know. That state was described by Lao Tzu in the *Tao Te Ching*:

Something undifferentiated but complete was
Born before heaven and earth,
Silent and formless, standing alone and unchanging,
Moving in an endless cycle
It is mother to the world.
I do not know its name,
So I call it the Tao.
The great Tao is everywhere, flowing right or left.
All things depend on it for growth in life.
It does not refuse them.
It does its work with humility.
Its accomplishments fulfilled, it does not dwell on them.
It lovingly nourishes all things but does not control them.
As it has no desire or aim, it can be called small.
All things are embraced by it without being dominated.
In this way it is called great.
Because it does not consider itself great,
It can accomplish what is great.[18]

Will the Mind of the Future Be Awakened?

Genius innovators of the past have often been called mad by their contemporaries, whereas later developments and reflections have

---

18 Lao-Tzu, *The Tao Te Ching*, 1988. Stephen Mitchell translation. New York, HarperPerennial

proven them not to be mad at all but, on the contrary, to be able to reach beyond the rules, limitations and perceptions of their time.

In his book *The Spiritual Gift of Madness*,[19] Seth Farber claims that a professional diagnosis of madness in our time has more to do with social control than therapy. He says that "mad" people can be the catalysts for social change and that their right roles are as prophets of spiritual and cultural revitalization. He believes they can seed new visions for the future. Certainly some mystics, like Swedenborg, Tesla, Galileo and Joan of Arc, were called mad by contemporaries. More circumspect observers, sometimes hundreds of years later, would discover they were anything but. Of course, it should be noted that not all "mad" people are prophets, nor do they always have anything constructive to offer in terms of insights for living. Think of Hitler, Charlie Manson and various proponents of terrorism.

Some awakenings into higher consciousness can be volatile, dramatic and unsettling. Most descriptions of the process include perceptions and behaviors that consensus reality would classify as crazy. Some persons may even become radically imbalanced for a period of time and not be able to function well in terms of taking care of themselves in their daily lives. Many mystics of the past have reported periods of intense disequilibrium, punctuated by visions, voices, bliss or terror, and a sense of being in other worlds.

One person of our community had a very difficult period that was diagnosed as schizophrenia. Although she took the prescribed drugs and followed all instructions she simultaneously used Process Acupressure, by herself and with others, to process the demons that plagued her. She has made a full recovery and was advised by her psychiatrist that she could stop all antipsychotic medications.

A few of us in my spiritual practice have had a disruptive experience that lasted from several days to a few weeks, which was

---

19 Farber, Seth. *The Spiritual Gift of Madness: The Failure of Modern Psychiatry.* Rochester, Vermont, Inner Traditions, 2012.

called a "spiritual crisis." In fact, some people were even given a medical diagnosis. Fortunately, no treatment, such as medication or hospitalization, was administered in those cases. During those episodes we saw visions, had premonitions, couldn't really be responsible for ourselves, and usually felt entirely blissful. We were disinterested in the activities and requirements of "Earth life," as if some part of us had already died, similar to the near-death experiences reported by many people.

Perhaps when we understand altered states and higher consciousness better, such experiences could be called an inflow of grace, during which the person should be cared for in a supportive environment. For example, Alcoholics Anonymous provides safe-houses for recovering alcoholics when they are coming off alcohol. The psychiatrist J.D. Lang created such an environment for his schizophrenic patients. During their stays in the facility Lang demonstrated that love, safety and encouragement could help patients heal. In *Warrior Pose*, Brad Willis described a pain center on Coronado Island where he received all the initial help he needed to discontinue drugs, heal his broken back and throat cancer, after years of failed medical help. Unfortunately for the patients, both these facilities were eventually discontinued for lack of funding. Nevertheless, in the future we can hopefully learn from these innovators how to better care for people in crisis recovery. Alternative medicine is making inroads in many conventional clinics.

There is an explosion of consciousness technologies in our time. More people, in all walks of life, are waking up to much greater awareness and development potential. My thought is, wouldn't it be wonderful if our obsession with the material side of life morphed into a serious search for health and illumination. When we begin to realize the dead-end of material accumulation will the person of the future be more apt to seek true awakening rather than power, celebrity and material wealth?

10:
PERSONALITY DEVELOPMENT AND SOUL ACTUALIZATION

Just keep coming home to yourself.
You are the one you've been waiting for.

~Byron Katie

As a formal discipline, psychology has helped us understand the development and structure of personality, or character, since the 1870s, though for centuries before that it was recognized as part of philosophy. We now know a great deal about how our personal identity, our behavior, our thinking and our emotional styles form in our lives. Many personality types and dysfunctions have been named and defined by scientists and people in the medical professions. The *Diagnostic and Statistical Manual of Mental Disorders: DSM-5*, prepared and published by the American Psychiatric Association (APA), is a thick catalog of categories such as these. The book includes definitions, symptoms, diagnostic protocols and therapeutic approaches for each pathology or psychological dysfunction recognized by the APA.

In our work we are focused on defining and finding wholistic health, wellbeing and freedom to follow our soul's destiny. We don't label personality types.

Personality Defined

Soul Lightening defines personality as the sum total of the physical, mental, emotional and social characteristics of an individual. Psychology studies the mental, emotional and social aspects. In Soul Lightening we also include soul and body aspects of personality.

Social Adjustment or Individuation

Through psychotherapy, the therapeutic branch of psychology, an individual may discover ways to shed dysfunctional personality traits or behavioral patterns and replace them with more useful and "appropriate" ones. The aim of most psychotherapy is to facilitate clients' self-understanding—their own behavior and perceptions— so that they may better recognize and fulfill their innate abilities and goals, and thus function more comfortably within the context of their existing culture or social milieu. However, the ultimate goal of depth psychotherapy is individuation, that is, a growth process whereby an individual evolves from a culturally conditioned or co-dependent person into her own distinct individuality.

Soul Lightening's Approach to Personality

In Soul Lightening we regard the personality as a vehicle for the soul to accomplish its purpose in the present life. Understanding the personality and facilitating its development to a useful function is a necessary part of our work. After all, the personality is the interface between the soul's purpose and its accomplishments in the world. We want to free individual consciousness from enslavement to the past so that it can be fully present in the now. Individuation is a useful phase of development, in that it frees us to operate from our own core characteristics, as opposed to conforming to cultural norms or another person's prescription for how we should live our life.

But the soul holds a perspective beyond the present world, family or culture. At birth the soul brings with it a blueprint for its own development, derived from multiple lives over centuries and from a soul intention. For example, there may have been great accomplishments in the past that the soul wishes to devote to present world evolution. Or there could have been talents developed over several past lifetimes that the soul wishes to bring together to serve in the world. For example, a student remembered that he had been a prominent scientist in an advanced culture of the past that was eventually brought to destruction by its advanced technology. He is now trying to discover how to cultivate his considerable technological talents so that he can apply them in our world, in a life-serving, rather than life-destroying, way, because without massive change our world seems headed to a similar demise. There could also have been great mistakes, such as murder or betrayal that the soul wants to atone for in the present life. Buddhists call this concept of payment for past mistakes "karma."

So why does Soul Lightening concern itself with personality work at all, if its principal purpose is to facilitate soul realization? Why not go straight to soul work and bypass the personality? The answer is that personality wounds, entanglements and misperceptions in past history can block soul truth and inhibit soul inquiry in the present.

As I've mentioned before, usually a fair amount of personality clearing and reprogramming are required before a person can even see the light of the soul or hear its subtle promptings. As one student said to me, "I can't find my soul. Maybe I don't have one!" And that was not an uncommon response to our introduction to soul.

An intellectual explanation of soul is not good enough in our time, when rationality, scientific investigation and skepticism are normal, and the concept of a soul is commonly considered leftover medieval fallacy, or only a religious concept. However, since the turn of the twenty-first century, there has been a wide recognition of the soul in New Age literature. Even so, for the soul to be recognized as a real entity now, a person must experience its energy, truth and power. In Soul Lightening we affirm those qualities as soon as possible.

Personality development and adjustment to society are not our final aims. Even as we process personality, we recognize that soul truth can pop through at any time. When it does we emphasize its value and urge a person to recognize its place in the evolution of his or her whole being.

Personality Processing

We work with the personality through the process method described in chapter 9. Rather than identifying, labeling, categorizing and analyzing the personality, we use process methods to help reveal personality history and structure as it expresses itself in the present. Though each personality is unique, each of us usually shares at least some characteristics with others. We support the individual's process as she discovers the various components that make up her unique personality. We facilitate consolidation and integration of those components by grounding them energetically through body and mind consciously.

Our objectives in processing personality material are twofold: 1) to open the person's awareness into the present, so that her consciousness is free from the bonds of the past, and 2) to support natural growth of the whole person.

We don't try to shape, or "fix" some pre-determined personality structure. We facilitate the client's awareness and understanding about the roots and causes of the personality structure. We seek to reveal the person to herself so that her own unique personality type serves her learning, freedom and growth.

Layers of the Personality

Most of us are familiar with the metaphor of the personality as an onion, and therapy, or the process of self-discovery, like peeling away its outer layers. The deep inner core of the personality is formed very early in life, beginning at birth, and continuing to around five years of age. Subsequent influences—environmental, familial and cultural—form layer upon layer around the core as an individual is conditioned and grows.

In the beginning years of life we are highly influenced by our parents or other "grownup people" and external influences around us, and will behave to please or resist them. Often we will identify most strongly with one parent or the other and seek his or her attention and approval. Later, school and other social influences add to and alter the core patterns formed by our relationships with our parents.

By our early twenties, our personality is usually fairly set and stabilized. There may be small adjustments as we mature and age, but normally we will continue to be recognizable by the most distinctive features of the original, core personality. I remember attending a high school reunion in my late sixties. In my early twenties I had moved away from the town where I'd spent my teen years, and had not returned until this particular reunion. Going back decades later I could recognize my old classmates more from their personality traits than by their physical features. One person, who had been the class clown, was still a comedian. Another who was very religious in high school still strictly followed a very straight-laced religion.

There can be major exceptions to this personality stability in the case of persons who take on some kind of intentional transformation, such as the commitment to a strenuous physical or spiritual practice, such as having a military career, becoming a professional athlete, joining the priesthood or spending many years at an ashram. A personality can also be dramatically altered as a result of a severe illness, accident or trauma.

The Core of Personality

The center, or core, of personality is shaped in the first five years of our lives, as Sigmund Freud first observed, and which has been verified repeatedly in our work. Freud and his followers believed that early behaviors, such as thumb sucking or nursing, and experiences like rigid potty training could leave a disproportional imprint on the person's later development. He proposed five stages of development associated with the young child's sources of pleasure, and named them accordingly: *oral, anal, phallic, latency* and *genital.* Freud believed that, at any given stage of development, a person could become fixated on that specific source of pleasure, which would affect how they experienced themselves and the world around them thereafter. For example, a person who got stuck in the *oral stage* might grow up overly dependent on others and be obsessed with the mouth, as in eating, smoking, talking, and so forth. A person stuck in the *anal stage* might become obsessed with cleanliness and orderliness—or just the opposite. The *phallic fixation* might result in focusing attention on sexual pleasure. If fixated on the *latency* period one would mostly relate to others of his own sex. And in *genital* development, the person focuses on sexual pleasures with the opposite sex.

Of course Freud's theories have been progressed and even replaced in our time with more research and failed Freudian therapy. For example, the core of personality is called the *metaprogram* in the language of neurolinguistic programming (NLP), a recently developed method for clearing personality patterns. Metaprogram seems an appropriate term because it implies the most formative and powerful beliefs that we ingest from ancestry and the nuclear family. And I use it in our work.

The best depth psychotherapy often penetrates to this level to reveal how those programs drive so much of our normal behavior. Recently, in his book *The Biology of Belief*, Bruce Lipton[20], a prominent biochemist, described how our early metaprogram beliefs can actually affect our biochemistry.

In Soul Lightening we recognize the power of our early imprints and influences. Therefore our Inner Child Healing class (See chapter 13) is the foundation work for the personality. We have discovered that inner child healing is one of the most powerful methods to free a person into his true self and release him from destructive core conditioning. In the class we teach about different stages of development and their attendant behavioral characteristics. We explain the power of early traumas and offer whole-being interventions to heal them. This kind of reforming of the early personality can bring about present change.

We also recognize the impact that ancestral and environmental influences have during the first years of life. We learn how to process ancestral effects in an Ancestral Healing class. (See chapter 14, in which these principles are explained.) We process the very early energetic and environmental effects on personality formation in our Soul Lightening 1 class, "The Awakening Human—Stabilizing the Base." In that class we demonstrate how the play of the twelve organ meridians and chakras affect whole-being development.

Subsequent Levels Are Laid Around the Core

As we grow, the personality becomes more complex, with additional layers of conditioning forming around the core. Formal education, traumatic experiences and intense physical, mental or spiritual trainings beyond the standard educational curriculum can alter the basic personality structure. Our Soul Lightening 2 class, "The

---

20 Lipton, Bruce. *The Biology of Belief*, Carlsbad, Calif, Hay House, 2007.

Awakening Human—Entering Higher Consciousness," deals with these layers, principally through the chakra system.

The Persona

By adolescence we become quite concerned about how others, particularly our peers, see us. As we begin to pay attention to the impressions we make on others, we may try to compose ourselves accordingly. We may try to assert ourselves by taking charge of our own development. Usually we start to design a surface layer of personality, called the *persona* in psychology. This is a public part of us that we want others and the world to see. It is a social role that we play. We want to be like our peers and fit into the prevailing culture. For example a boy might want to be seen as tough or macho according to the standards set in his surroundings. He might cultivate a certain way of dressing or certain habits, a particular way of walking or a physical attitude and voice to suit that image. Or a girl might want to be seen as a flirt and attractive to boys. Accordingly, she might dress, behave and cultivate seductive relationships with boys to fill out that particular image.

As we mature, we modify our persona to fit the prevailing culture where we want to be successful. For example, a businessman will dress, speak and accumulate suitable possessions (the right clothes, the right car, the right house, perhaps a boat) to present the right impression for achieving his goals at work or within a particular social milieu. A woman who wants to fit into the "right" neighborhood might cultivate the characteristics of a "housewife" (cooking, cleaning, being at home) even when her own interests and talents lie in other areas, such as art, music, business, and so forth.

A good example of a well-crafted persona was demonstrated by the actor Peter Sellers. For each character he portrayed he constructed a different persona to fit that character. One interviewer said of him. "He [Sellers] was a vessel into which characters, personalities ran like phantoms. But once that particular character was stripped away, there seemed to be no one inside." Sellers said of himself, "I don't really have any personality of my own, there used to be a me behind the mask, but I had it surgically removed. If I didn't have characters like Clouseau, I don't know who I'd be." Although such a talent contributed greatly to Sellers' acting career, one has to wonder how much it detracted from his development as a whole person.

Processing Personality

Personality is processed in all phases of our energy and bodywork, through Process Acupressure One and Two, and Soul Lightening 1 and 2. Personality material, in structure and themes, is constantly related to corresponding body and energy patterns. For example, hunched shoulders may relate to an early loss of self-esteem, derived from an overcritical mother and a corresponding slumping of the upper body to protect inhibition. Or the same physical condition might relate to a lack of heart love and withdrawal from others. Rather than interpret such a condition, and label it according to some preconceived set of standards, we rely on the person's direct expression and process that part of the body to reveal the underlying reason and resolution. Throughout, we encourage more personality awareness and inquiry, and the updating of those influences that no longer serve each individual.

In Process Acupressure 2, we examine the multiple parts of a personality, especially as they relate to parts of the body and stages of development. For example, the head could relate to an intellectual part whose analytical assessment of events precludes heart and body involvement. Or the head could just as easily relate to a dreamer part of that person, someone who resists grounding, or actualizing his or her dreams. The pelvis can express sexual themes or perhaps aggression. The legs can relate to the ability to be "realistic" and to ground plans. Hands can be associated with one's chosen work, such as playing music or sculpting clay. A spoiled child part can be trapped in the era of over-indulgent parents and expect adult companions to treat him like his parents did. On the other hand, an abused child part will expect to be abused in adult relationships.

The origins, configurations and purposes of parts are unlimited. Only individual processing can reveal exactly how parts were developed and how they serve, or limit, a particular person. The right resolution or updating of parts to serve in the present can be shown through the individual's process. We teach a person how to process parts for his or her own benefit and how to integrate them into a functional whole that will serve that person's present growth and fulfillment.

Personality work can extend over a lifetime, since there are always deeper layers for exploration. Our principal aim in personality work, however, is to teach the process skills that will enable each person to continue to do the mental, emotional and physical work that can facilitate functional wellbeing in the present and continue to support soul actualization.

Bridging Personality and Soul Work

In addition to updating and reprogramming dysfunctional personality patterns in the present, we also inquire about the teachings or strengths beneath those patterns. For example, we might ask, "How did this particular trauma or false teaching affect the current personality? Did some traumatic events actually *serve* that soul's evolution?" When possible, we ask for the soul purpose(s) of such experiences.

As our name, Soul Lightening, implies, we wish to lighten, enlighten, or uncover souls to their own unique power and purpose in this current lifetime. It is my belief that if only a small percentage of currently living souls could engage in their true missions (like Mattie Stepanek) we would experience a world transforming for the better. We urge students to seek deeper truths beneath personality so that the soul can be known. Since the soul has an eternal perspective that started before and continues beyond our present lifetime, it frequently holds answers or guidance that are quite different from personality adjustment. For example, in personality work we can see an abused child as a victim who requires lengthy healing and nourishment in order to function optimally. From a soul perspective, however, those same abuses can be understood as the catalyst for spiritual growth and expansion and our deepening understanding of abuse on our planet.

I was astounded to read only yesterday, in Brad Willis' fine book *Warrior Pose*, that he asked his *soul* to tell him what to do about the lingering cancer in his throat. Here's the answer he received:

> You've been in avoidance of the cancer rather than acceptance, in fear rather than faith. Healing must now be your utmost priority. You must embrace and thank the cancer, just as you have your back pain. Take your practice to a deeper level. Purify yourself in every way possible. Take it all the way.[21]

Willis thanked his soul for this guidance and then, of course, being a spiritual warrior, he followed that advice. He took up a radical purification process, prescribed by ancient yogic texts, which seemed almost beyond endurance. But in the end he was rewarded with freedom from throat cancer, verified by his oncologist.

In the past, soul actualization was a rare occurrence. Examples of actualized souls are Gandhi, Martin Luther King and the Dalai Lama. But now we live in a time of greater awakening, as I mentioned in the previous chapter. Many individuals have experienced an awakening, which resulted in a subsequent commitment to teaching others how to "wake up." Examples are Amaji, the Indian teacher who has dedicated her life to fostering love between all

---

21 Willis, Brad. *Warrior Pose: How Yoga Literally Saved My Life*. Dallas Texas, BenBella Books, 2013.

beings; Mother Meera, another Indian teacher who stimulates the light of soul in those who visit her; Ram Das, the former Harvard professor who awakened and now teaches higher consciousness and love to all who come to him; Adyashanti, an awakened teacher of higher consciousness; Byron Katie, who teaches how to clear the mind of ideas and beliefs that obscure a person's true nature; Eckhart Tolle, who teaches about the profound illumination in the present moment, or *now*, as he calls it. And right now I'm adding Brad Willis, for surely he is, or will be, a fine teacher from his experiences.

These are only a sampling of individuals now living who dedicate their lives to help the rest of us wake up, through what they say and by their presence. Some of these teachers, like Amaji and Mother Meera, seem to have discarded the personality altogether. Others, such as Ram Das, use a well-cultivated and stable personality to accomplish their soul purposes of awakening people. We might note that he has even been able to do so after suffering a major stroke that has limited his physical movement. We can learn by listening to these teachers, or reading their books. We can also be partially awakened by simply sitting in their presence because their auras expand out from them and far into the Field. Even proximity to an awakened being can evoke greater energy and consciousness.

In the past, soul actualization was a long and arduous process that often required abandoning a regular life in the world. But now, some mysterious shift in human evolution seems to have opened doors to soul realization that had been closed heretofore. And often those openings occur in a dramatic event or time in which heightened energy and consciousness impact a person in one burst, or in short order. As I've noted elsewhere, such openings can happen through initiation with a spiritual teacher, a near-death experience or other high impact event, and visits to holy places. The purpose of initiation is to build a higher, stronger charge of energy and consciousness that will break through the cocoon of conditioning.

It now seems that when a person makes the intention of awakening, the resources and opportunities for accomplishing that awakening arrive. In Soul Lightening we seek to provide those resources, as well as support the methods of awakened teachers.

Reinforcing Central Alignment

We humans are connected to both soul and Source through a continuous flow of energy, called the Great Central Channel, which runs through the center of the body. When this Central Channel is open and flowing we call this our "alignment between heaven and earth." That alignment opens the spiritual channel, which is the avenue for soul messages. It also connects the soul directly with the Field. Thus we emphasize this energetic alignment in almost every session. Energy work in the body continuously supports the individual's growth process. For example, as we support the Great Central Channel through bodywork, the strengths and possible obstructions in the seven central chakras are uncovered. (We teach about these progressions in our class, "Soul Lightening 2: Entering Higher Consciousness.")

In our Soul Work classes we ask for soul contact from the beginning. Any obstacles to soul awareness are processed and resolved. If soul messages emerge from beneath those obstacles we accept and integrate them into the evolving whole-being work. For example, if the soul offers a vision of a task or suggestions about the work a person is already doing, then the mind is put to work making a plan for that task or work. The emotions are supported to call up the passion to go forward. The body is similarly informed or strengthened to prepare for that work.

Soul Lightening work is a constant interweaving of soul guidance and personality adjustment. Old obstructive patterns may arise as this work progresses. When they do, we process them and harvest whatever lessons may be embedded in them to further clear and uncover the soul's purpose.

Gradually, individual characteristics of the personality are modified, changing in order to better fit the soul's purpose. Eventually the soul's direction and purpose are foremost in attention, that is, the person may begin to consciously create a soul-aware personality, with body, mind and emotions more fully integrated to serve soul purpose consciously.

Soul actualization requires a fully present awareness of, and commitment to, the soul. As that awareness develops it will eventually evolve into a dedication to soul guidance and realization of purpose. Equally important, continual support of the spiritual process is required to keep soul consciousness active. This may include: meditation; pilgrimages; focused awareness on the spiritual channel; seeking impressions of higher art; and listening to the soul, which is always nudging us from beneath the cocoon of conditioning into directions that are expansive and destiny-fulfilling. (Remember that I have defined soul destiny in the beginning as *fulfillment of the soul's original intention* when it entered life.)

Soul Lightening is about lightening or "enlightening" souls that have been partially or more fully asleep, so that they may accomplish what they came to earth to do in this current lifetime. It is my belief that soul-directed individuals, energetically aligned with Source, would contribute to the highest good of their communities and the world.

11:
WHOLE HUMAN DEVELOPMENT—STABILIZING THE BASE

*What is more important for us, at an elemental level,
than the control, the owning and operation of our own
physical selves?*

~Oliver Sacks

What is whole and mature human development? Psychology seems to define a mature human being as a "grown up" who can accept adult responsibilities, has a healthy ego and has adjusted to, and is thriving in, contemporary society. But what about the misfits, rebels and innovators whose theories and creations have moved humanity forward in a positive way, like Albert Einstein, Steve Jobs or Martin Luther King? Shall we call their resistance to the status quo immature? Or is it even more mature than adaptation? Does human potential offer us expansion beyond adjusting to the way things are?

Ancient Eastern (Chinese and Indian) traditions take us a step beyond individual development and adjustment to society, offering guidelines for the evolution of consciousness, all the way to enlightenment.

From my own perspective, a complete human life is measured by how well individual destiny is fulfilled. For example, at the end of a life the soul could conclude that it had completed the purpose or destiny it arrived with at birth. From this perspective each life would have to be evaluated exclusively by its own standard. How could anyone else know the individual's complete potentials, genetic inheritances, karmas from past lives and primary soul intention? I will never forget the evening we were ending a class, sharing our personal aspirations for life, when Fritz said, "At the end of this life I want to be able to say, "it was *a life well lived.*"

From a developmental point of view, the most complete and reliable guide I have discovered for tracking a human being's development and maturity is the ancient Indian chakra system, from root to crown. It is a system that has endured in practice for more than two thousand years in India (reflected in China and Japan), and is the only template for complete human evolution I have ever encountered. It addresses all phases of human development, from physical survival to spiritual health and enlightenment, irrespective of culture, history or religion, and it is rooted in physiological fact.

The chakra system is comprised of seven major swirling energy centers, which together make up the energy body that corresponds to the physical body. The seven chakras are located along the midline of the body. Each one affects the part of the body where it is located. All seven chakra energies exist in the physical body from birth. But each chakra is more fully activated at a certain age.

In their book, *The Body Electric,*[22] Robert O. Becker, M.D., and Gary Selden explained the bioelectric structure of the body. They

---

22 Becker, Robert O., M.D., Gary Selden. *The Body Electric.* New York, William Morrow & Company, 1985.

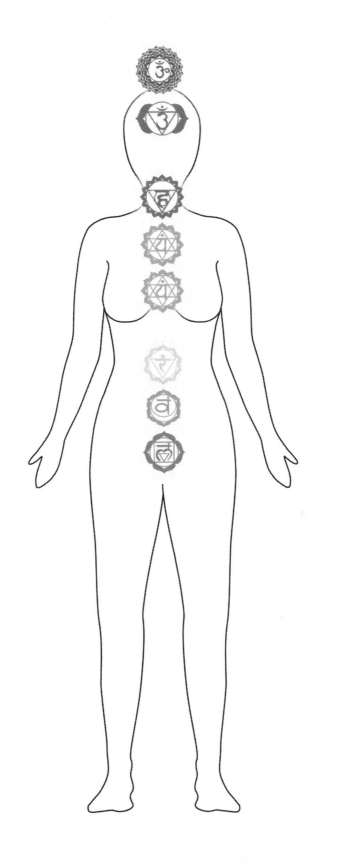

claim that a person's health could be determined by the vibrational frequencies of his body. Energetically the chakra system establishes a progression of frequencies from root to crown that corresponds to the tone scale.

In the West we are only at the very beginning of understanding how vibratory frequencies affect health and wholeness, but we can *experience* this effect when we work directly with the chakras, as we do in Soul Lightening. Strength, balance and evolution of consciousness increase as we progress through the chakras into higher energetic frequencies.

Soul Lightening work uses the chakra model, together with Eastern and Western understandings of the progression of consciousness. In this chapter I compare contemporary Western psychological understandings of the stages of development with chakra progressions.

Psychologists discovered that as we master one set of life skills, we are prepared to learn the next set, until we are equipped to handle life with confidence. To some this means that if we do not master the appropriate skill in a certain stage we will be handicapped by the lack of it, or its negative aspect, all through life. This lack diminishes our overall confidence and competence. Fortunately these skills can be learned during a later stage of our lives, through conscious work on ourselves, or psychological training. It helps to know about these stages and their strengths. If we find one of the strengths underdeveloped or missing we can focus on learning it.

Some lives can progress through all these stages successfully. Then the adult is well equipped to guide his own life and relate well with others. But when a person seems to get stuck in, or keeps cycling around, a particular stage, we say that he is arrested in that stage. He stops learning and growing psychologically.

It is also true that a person can skip the skills of a particular stage, jump over them and go to the next stage and keep learning. However, until the gap in development, which the person missed by that stage, is filled in, his future skills and learning will be slowed or impaired.

The Base Chakras Guide Early Development

The foundation of human development can be defined in the body by the first three chakras. The development of chakras one through three is generally understood to predominate between birth and seven years of age. The psychosocial developments of this stage of development were observed and then defined by the noted psychologist, Erik Erickson. He described the necessary learning, or *conflict*, as he termed it, during each of the early developmental stages. I apply them here in each case because I have tested his findings with clients and students of this time and found them reliable for discerning necessary skills.

The strengths (or lack of them) developed in the first three stages of life also form our core beliefs about ourselves and the world and these often persist throughout life. What we know now, from recent neurological and biochemical research, is that core beliefs, almost always unconscious, drive our behavior throughout life unless and until they are changed or expanded. For example, a child who didn't receive adequate encouragement for his own skills and power early in life, and who thus did not develop adequate self-esteem, may develop the belief that there is something wrong with him, and keep that belief throughout life until it is uncovered and reprogrammed.

Root Chakra, Birth and Infancy

The root chakra, located at the base of the spine, in the *coccygeal plexus*, usually opens at birth and comes into predominance in infancy. From the base of the energetic body and nervous system, the root chakra protects physical survival in a body. It is anchored to the earth through the legs and feet, and its element is earth. It keeps us aware of survival needs and alerts us to the need for physical protection. A person with a stable root chakra can be attuned to the practicalities of physical life on the earth.

The root governs development until well into the first year, during which time physical survival is supported by the mother or others. As a person grows up the root chakra will continue to signal the need for physical survival by alerting the person to danger or threat.

The basic instinct for fight or flight is seated in the root and usually endures throughout life. Fight can manifest in self-defense or outright aggression and violence. Fear can warn us of actual threat, or become constant anxiety about perceived threats. When a person's development is stuck at this level he can be shackled by those emotions. He will automatically fear or fight physical threats.

As development progresses through higher chakras a person will retain root strength by claiming a sense of his own physical needs, and be able to eventually assume the responsibility for covering them. In our culture in this time, money symbolizes this level of physical survival.

The Root Chakra and Birth

In psychology, birth is considered to be the first life trauma. Imagine the physical struggle, for both mother and baby, as a large mass, from five to twelve pounds, is pushed down through a narrow birth canal. Until recently a great deal of physical pain was experienced by both mother and child. For the mother there may be fears and thoughts of death, to herself or the baby, because of the enormous pressures happening in her body.

The most basic instincts for survival are triggered during birth, such as struggles for space or breath. Sometimes lifetime patterns of fear and flight behavior are established in the individual's nervous system. The following case report, by Paula Macali, shows how birth trauma can affect life:

> I had a difficult birth experience, when my mother almost died during the procedures. My soul just

wanted to flee this earth and connect with the ethers. I didn't want to be trapped in a body or be a part of all the suffering here on Earth. This pattern manifested in many ways through my life until I discovered Soul Lightening Acupressure. With it I learned the tools to come back to earth safely and fully embodied to play in this Divine ground where we can experience heaven on earth. Each day is another opportunity to deepen into that embodiment. May the benefits received from this most sacred and blessed work be the cause for all beings to awaken to their souls' divine purpose.

Paula Macali, yoga instructor, USA

Childbirth has been almost completely changed medically since my first birthing experience. There is much more understanding now of the whole process and more preparation of the mother. It is undertaken with compassion, comfort for the mother and baby and more continuous support.

For the baby, physical life is a contraction of the soul into a body. Birth is the physical shock that catapults consciousness into the body and usually erases the soul memory of the infant. In my observation, parents' awareness of just how close the soul is within a newborn is just beginning to show up. When my granddaughter Lauren was born she looked like a Tibetan; her eyes would drill straight through you, as if she were seeing through to your very soul. Sometimes I see other newborns who have that soul glow about them.

Infancy

Since a young child is helpless to keep itself alive, it instinctively depends on others for nourishment, safety and comfort. Her support, in the form of nourishment, affection and holding, will form a strong bonding between the infant and her caregiver. That bond, known in psychology as *attachment,* is a very important foundation for the later ability to relate to others.

Erickson described the necessary learning during infancy as *trust versus mistrust.* If the child is safely cared for and receives his basic needs, such as shelter, oxygen, food, water, rest and elimination, all of which are vital, he will develop trust that the world will support his life.

The infant who can trust the original environment and the providers can also more easily come to eventually trust that the world will support him. He will also more easily trust himself and his own strength. Later in life, a person will be able to count on his own root energetic and physical strength, as well as instinctive intelligence, to preserve his physical survival.

On the other hand, if an infant is not cared for, or especially if he is abused, he will develop mistrust of the world and the people close to him. And of course this mistrust would be preverbal and lodged in the unconscious. Thus it would be almost impossible to access by ordinary means, as in intellectual analysis.

Later Root Chakra Strengths

Root chakra survival strengths are needed for all of life, right up to death when the soul departs the body. A strong foundation, starting from infancy, includes survival instincts, reflected in sensation awareness at the base of the spine, lower abdomen, legs and feet. Adults who have this available awareness will be instinctively moved to nurture and protect the body. On the other hand, if infancy needs are not fully met, the drive and skill for survival will be diminished at an unconscious psychological level. The extreme of this condition can manifest as an unconscious death wish (not wanting to live in this world). However, remedial psychophysical work with the root can correct this weakness later on.

Instinctual awareness and physical strength associated with the root chakra often shows up in emergencies. An almost super-human power can emerge from the root when a person, or a loved one, is under serious threat.

A strong root chakra and psychophysical grounding help a person assume responsibility for his own survival, security and eventually wellbeing. A well-grounded person usually knows how to "take care of himself." Conversely, an excess emphasis in the root chakra can develop into hoarding, possessiveness and money obsession. Some of my European friends think our country is stuck in the root chakra, with a money mania.

Without such strength in the base, a person usually has trouble attuning to reality on the ground. She may unconsciously want someone else to take care of her and assure her survival. Money can become a problem because she may not connect survival with the need for money in the world.

How Soul Lightening Works with the Root Chakra

In our work we acknowledge and support the root chakra, by strengthening the lower back, hips, legs and feet. We emphasize grounding, which includes not only physical strength in the base but also awareness of the psychological needs associated with it. We work to release any limiting traumas from the past that are lodged there.

Second Chakra Development Begins in Early Childhood

The second chakra is located in the lower abdomen, below the navel. It is associated with the genitals and lower back, and the element water. It begins to develop principally from age one to three years.

From the second chakra we derive the sensation of pleasure; a person is drawn toward what feels good and pulls away from what feels bad. There is often a drive for self-gratification. Emotional identity and emotional flow originate in the second chakra. Movement and flow are supported by it.

Erickson called this stage of development *early childhood.* He said that the required learning is *autonomy versus doubt and shame.* This learning starts when the child begins to separate her own identity from the mother. She wants to experience pleasure and explore and discover on her own, without mother's helping hand. Yet if mother is too far away from her physically she will quickly seek the security of mother's presence.

If a child is constantly stopped, or shamed, during explorations she will learn to doubt her own sensory information or perceptions. Certainly if the child is abused at this stage she will feel shame; she hasn't the cognitive skills yet to place responsibility with the abuser and often considers herself at fault. An adult client told me that she discovered during processing that she had always carried a dark psychic band around her lower abdomen since early childhood abuse. In her child's mind she was afraid for anyone to touch her in that part of her body lest they be hurt!

The child learns to *feel* things, both emotionally and in the physical sensation of pleasure. She will seek personal gratification, for her body and her emotions. She starts to learn her own sensory abilities. If she is encouraged to explore and test she will start developing a rudimentary sense of self and her own abilities. By experiencing pleasure she is opening her body to later, more complicated pleasures, such as sex. On the other hand, a child who is deprived or over indulged during this stage could become an over-emotional adult.

During this period children usually discover their own, or another child's, genitals. They can become fascinated by them and want to explore. This is the rudimentary beginning of later sexuality. Since Freud, traditional psychology has claimed that healthy sexuality, or libido, is a very important part of adult development.

Without that vital aspect, it was believed, the individual psyche can become stagnant, or even neurotic. If the child is shamed, or worse, punished, for such explorations, there will be a lingering fear or resistance to that part of the body, perhaps even inhibiting sexual pleasure later on.

A client told me how her mother discovered her and little friends "playing doctor" under the bed at that age. The mother was a strict fundamentalist who thought the genitals were dirty and shameful. She started screaming and literally dragged the child across the floor from under the bed. For the little child it was a double-pronged trauma; she was physically bruised from the dragging and terrified of the accusing scream from mother, telling her that she was a bad girl. The client told me this story within the context of confronting her sexual embarrassment in marriage. She confessed that she had never been able to really enjoy sexuality because her child's mind still felt it was dirty.

The second chakra holds the basic energy of all creativity. The early child's urge to explore, feel and taste things can eventually evolve into a fluid creativity that might manifest in any form—music, art, architecture and writing.

Third Chakra Development Begins in the Play Stage

The third chakra is located at the solar plexus, which is the area around the middle of the body, from just below the base of the sternum to just below the navel. Its element is fire. Its development begins between ages eighteen months and four years, but is particularly strong between three and four, when various seeds are planted for important lifetime skills. From this chakra we derive confidence in our physical vitality and personal power. It is an important center of will. As with all the chakras, the third chakra and its characteristics will be important throughout life, but especially in the West where ego and power are so valued.

Erickson called this period the *play stage*. He said the learning was *initiative versus guilt*, wherein a child can learn how to act on his own volition.

The play stage marks a multi-leveled development in motor skills, mental and imaginative faculties, creative exploration and expression. Erikson found that "immense new faculties develop in the child at this time." As a child plays, fools around, explores and tests his own abilities he can build a core sense of competence and creativity that will fuel his power to create or initiate things for the rest of his life. He can connect his efforts with a sense of purpose and eventually learn how to set his own goals toward that purpose.

The beginning sense of self and power during this time will eventually develop into a healthy ego. Early psychologists decided a well-developed ego was critical for adult success, and that concept seems to be born out in ordinary life. However, in most spiritual traditions it is claimed that there must come a phase of spiritual progress where ego has to be surrendered to the Divine, or at least to the greater social good.

I consider the play stage as one of great importance for laying foundations of free expression, spontaneity, strength of will and the first developments of ego. While still in a reasonably free state of "playing around," the child can discover so much about his own innate abilities, likes and dislikes. It is during this time that a child can gain confidence in his own power and will.

When a child has a full period of free exploration and initiation on his own, without excessive supervision, rigid rules or schedule requirements, he will have a firm base for initiating his own life-style and life purpose with confidence. Development during this period lays the foundations for later personal power, self-will and self-esteem.

But if a child is forbidden to experience this natural stage of free play he will become unsure of his own abilities, learn how to hold back and feel guilty about free expression.

Toward the end of this stage, approximated at ages five to seven, a child becomes subject to many more influences than the original family: school, community and even the world, through mass media. His field of interaction must expand to include much more information and many more relationships. It is a time that challenges his physical strength, sensory awareness and self-confidence.

Adult Developments of the Third Chakra

An adult with a well-developed third chakra has a strong, *healthy* ego. He has a sense of personal power, and can compete aggressively to preserve that power. In martial arts the "lower *dan tein*," synonymous with the third chakra, is understood as the storehouse of energetic personal power. The martial artist carefully cultivates that power in order to perform remarkable physical feats.

A person with a well-developed third chakra can work toward achieving mastery in his profession. He can set goals and use attention, focus and intention to reach them. Goals achieved invite the setting of bigger goals. Achievements pile up toward great achievement, which can bring the temptation for great ego, and then for great power.

However, great personal power, fueled by ego, is fraught with pitfalls. The axiom "absolute power corrupts absolutely" can certainly be verified throughout history, right up to the present time. At this level of consciousness it is easy to assume that "the means justifies the end."

Soul Lightening Work with the Third Chakra

In our work we emphasize reclaiming personal power, will and the ability to stand up for oneself. Through acupressure and processing, the solar plexus is released from past traumas and strengthened. Often past disempowerments, particularly from childhood, have to be released and reprogrammed. We do a lot of that work in the Inner Child Healing class. The result shows up in an adult with much greater self-esteem, the foundation of a healthy ego and the ability to assert him- or herself.

Co-Dependence as a Third Chakra Issue

Problems of co-dependence have shown up repeatedly in our work. Co-dependence is the habit of placing a lower priority on one's own needs, while being excessively preoccupied with the needs of others. Co-dependency can occur in any type of relationship, including family, work, friendship, romantic, peer or community relationships. It is often associated with low self-esteem, excessive compliance, weak boundaries, or control patterns.

It turns out that many people can become enmeshed in another's emotions or problems and have a hard time telling the difference between the other's emotions and their own. They can have a weak sense of their own identity, needs and boundaries. Often they never really live their own lives because they spend most of their time "helping" other people with their needs or problems, even to the detriment of their own very basic self-care.

It works this way: A friend, co-worker, parent or any acquaintance presents an urgent need or problem. The co-dependent person stops whatever he's doing and jumps to the rescue of the friend. The co-dependent does this with little or no consideration for how it will impact his own wellbeing. And the pattern repeats endlessly, with the same or many other people, until the co-dependent can be completely exhausted, or self-neglected to the point of depression or illness. The extreme example would be that of a person who doesn't know how to swim, jumping into the water to save someone who's drowning.

Co-dependence is a third-chakra issue because the roots of it are usually found in a child's need for love, approval or acceptance. The child who hasn't had those needs fulfilled early on in his development may learn that serving others can bring temporary recognition and acceptance, even the love he craves. That coping skill can then become a lifelong pattern. We have met many adult professionals who operate as good helpers or assistants, trusted envoys, or devoted servants of a family, corporation, or the military.

Fortunately, this pattern can be transformed through concentrated work in the third chakra, which includes recognition and reprogramming of dysfunctional patterns, combined with self-knowledge, strengthening of boundary-setting, and self-care. Until the co-dependent person develops a sense of himself, of his own needs and value, he may become resentful and angry with the people he has cared for or rescued. We have all known the person who complains that he does everything for other people and never gets anything in return, or that others he has "done so much for" abandon or misuse him.

Co-dependence should be differentiated from the caring gestures of a highly developed heart chakra. As we will see with heart development, the person with an open heart will naturally feel loving kindness toward others and want to help or give to them. However, he knows how to care for himself and he has a well-developed sense of his own needs and worth.

The Power of Base Stability: Money, Sex and Power

From the first three chakras we have the energetic, physical and psychological strength to survive and even thrive in the ordinary world. The abbreviated forms for these strengths in our culture have been given as money, sex, and power.

It can also be said that all the propensities and skills needed for war come from the power of the first three chakras: fear of annihilation and the fight to destroy whatever threatens one's life, or the life of his people (first chakra, flight or fight); the vitality and ingenuity to preserve one's life (second chakra); the belief in the superiority of oneself or one's people over others, and the resolve and power to protect them and their territories (third chakra, ego, competition, nationalism). Society on planet earth in general seems to be arrested at this stage of development, when war and the assertion of power over others is still the predominant means for settling conflicts.

So the first three chakras offer human beings all the strengths and skills for physical survival they will ever need. Even basic relationship and social skills can be developed at this level. Humans can get by reasonably well on earth with the strengths these first three chakras provide. Consciousness beyond the first three chakras may not have developed yet on a mass level, but there is so much more potential for the evolution of human consciousness beyond them.

Chapter 12 addresses that further potential beyond the stages of development represented by these first three chakras. As I indicated in chapter 1, there are strong showings now that many people are working seriously to evolve these higher levels of consciousness, for themselves as well as for the planet.

12:
EXPANDING CONSCIOUSNESS THROUGH WHOLE BEING DEVELOPMENT

Spiritual development is an innate evolutionary capacity of all human beings. It is a movement toward wholeness, the discovery of one's true potential. And it is as common and as natural as birth, physical growth, and death—an integral part of our existence.

~Christina and Stanislav Grof, M.D.

In this chapter we will explore the evolution of psychophysical and spiritual consciousness, through development, especially as it is reflected through the chakra system. I will continue to contrast the eastern perspective of chakra development with Erickson's understanding of psychosocial stages and show, where possible, how these systems correlate. I will also address fulfillment of human needs and moral principles as important parts of whole and mature human development.

After we have achieved base stabilization within the first three chakras, we are strong enough to rise into the growth treasures of the heart chakra and the chakras above it. Our orientation to life, including our relationships with other people and the world around us, begins to make a radical shift. Now as we grow beyond the co-coon of conditioning, additional developments become more possible and promising, such as our capacity to give and receive love, express ourselves in more truthful and creative ways, see with more depth and start to develop spiritually.

In the higher chakras we move ever closer to an awareness of life as one infinitely interconnected, alive and evolving fabric. We begin to individuate, according to our innate abilities, but we also begin to understand how we are connected to all people. We can begin to experience ourselves in a new light as members of the family of humankind.

The Fourth, or Heart, Chakra

The fourth, or heart chakra, is located in the chest, in the area of the physical heart. The heart's psychological development begins between the ages of five and twelve, although of course it can continue through a lifetime, perhaps more than any other chakra. Heart consciousness can open and grow through many phases as awareness of its unique ways of knowing and loving progresses.

The heart's most predominant trait is love. As I indicated in chapter 8, the heart offers a wide range of intelligence and feeling. It is understood in Eastern psychology as the place where spirit and matter come into balance, as well as where masculine and feminine qualities gain their own individual balance, regardless of gender. It is also believed that the heart can connect directly to the Divine, or to transpersonal levels.

The heart energy provides a bridge between our lower instincts for basic physical survival and the promise of more advanced human consciousness, which can evolve beyond attachments to ego and power. At the heart, love becomes the foundation for those more refined and mature characteristics that are possible for human consciousness, the qualities and capacities associated with the upper chakras. However, unlike the almost automatic strengths given by the first three chakras, upper chakra development is not assured with physical growth, or simply as the years pass. It has to be cultivated.

Heart chakra consciousness potentials are enormous, beginning with simple affection or feelings of tenderness for another being. Heart awareness can go through many phases, from childhood to death, as the heart opens progressively through life experience, deepening understanding, true reciprocal relationships, spiritual practice, and eventual merging with Divine love.

Progressions of Heart Opening and Love

As heart development progresses throughout life, from school age through old age, the capacity to give and receive love evolves. An adolescent can have the experience of falling in love. This is the experience of romantic love, which can go through many progressions as an individual grows and develops. The heart may open for a brief time; a person experiences the ecstasy, excitement and supreme happiness of being deeply involved with the heart of another. When heart energy is fused with another person's heart and second chakra energy, sexual excitement is ignited.[23] In any case, that first blossom of a heart opening in love can be the beginning of much grander flowerings to come. For example, in tantric yoga, a long practice of physical and spiritual methods can ultimately bring about a fusion of sexual and heart energy that leads to union with the Divine.

---

23 In a recent book, *The Honeymoon Effect: The Science of Creating Heaven on Earth*, Bruce Lipton, researcher of cell biology and neuroscience, explained how to keep that ecstatic state alive for a lifetime.

The first romantic experience can affect a person deeply, sometimes for a lifetime. For example, if a person is especially disappointed or hurt by that experience he may deliberately close his heart, in an effort to protect himself from being hurt again. But a closed heart can block or interfere with full human evolution, because so much of human life involves relationships. It will always be worth the work to open one's heart again after great loss or disappointment in love.

Sometime in early adulthood self-love becomes possible, but it is not inevitable. Self-love, a progression in the young child's self-interest, is one of the most valuable and necessary abilities for personal evolution. It is not to be confused with personal ego, which may be focused on achieving personal power, more a third chakra characteristic. What was narcissistic self-involvement for the adolescent can develop into a true respect and caring for one's own wellbeing, and that of others.

In her book, *The Heart of Healing,*[24] Regina Rosenthal, an experienced physical therapist and Process Acupressure therapist, gives many useful means for developing wholistic self-love and self-care. She explained how she had to learn self-love and self-care for herself after over-giving for many years as a physical therapist. She offers information about how to pick up the signs of over-giving. Then she outlines how to bring awareness back to the authentic self, and how to care for that self, with helpful meditations, journal exercises, and physical and touching exercises.

It is important to understand how self-love is a foundation skill for the ability to fully love and care for another. There's often a quantum leap in our evolvement of love when we are able to truly value, support and delight in the full evolution of another person, such as a partner or a child. A certain amount of age, life experience, personal reflection and individuation must occur before this kind of selfless love is possible.

---

24 Rosenthal, Regina. 2013. *The Heart of Healing: Discovering the Secrets of Self-Care.* Holmdell, New Jersey, Dimensions of Wellness Press.

Soul Lightening Work with the Heart

In Soul Lightening we focus on a person's development of the qualities of life associated with the heart chakra, such as kindness, sensitivity to the hearts of others, and heartfelt giving. We work to
develop the understandings and training for building healthy work
and relationship habits.

Heart awareness and development open up as we use a hands-
on heart acupressure formula. The practitioner touches acupoints
along the energetic pathways of the actual heart, which flow across
the chest, down through the arms and into the hands. Thus the client directly experiences heart energy and associations. Heart acupressure strengthens the physical and emotional heart, and opens
consciousness into a more expansive state.

Acupressure stimulation increases awareness (in both the
physical body and the consciousness) of thoughts, feelings or
memories of past experiences held in the body, some of which
may impede physical and consciousness growth. Since we teach
process skills, explained in chapter 9, from the very beginning of
our training, most students or clients are able to focus their attention on their thoughts or feelings as they arise from the body, and
then stay with them to follow the flow of process. Occasionally
the practitioner can offer questions or suggestions to keep the
process flowing. For example, "What's happening now?" or, "What
are you feeling now?"

In this way, traumas and blocks in the body are released from
childhood, or later, that could impede current adult heart development. We emphasize claiming close contact with heart intelligence
and feeling.

Sometimes we teach a most helpful acupressure *tapping* method to strengthen self-love. This involves tapping along the heart
meridian of either hand while declaring, "I love and accept myself
unconditionally." Scientific studies and much contemporary experience have verified the power of this practice, used in the Tapping
Method or Emotional Freedom Technique (EFT).

The Heart and Spiritual Development

During the heart expansion stage of development, the soul is often more available. For example, some Soul Lightening clients and students discover soul consciousness while working with the heart chakra. Heart intelligence is closer to the essence of a person than the mind. We encourage students to listen for the voice of the heart, or the soul, as the heart opens. And we ask them to test the guidance of that voice in their everyday lives.

As a person evolves through the higher chakras and grows in understanding, a spiritual aspect of the heart can open. A genuine love for many—or all—others, often called *agape,* can become possible. Jesus alluded to this level when he advised, "Love one another as I have loved you." That level of love requires a huge opening of the heart chakra.

The Eastern principle of *ahimsa* (Sanskrit for "do no harm"), an important principle of Buddhism, Hinduism and Jainism, requires heart maturity. Ahimsa means kindness and non-violence *towards all living things, including animals*; it respects living beings as a unity, and believes that all living beings are connected. Mahatma Gandhi strongly practiced this principle. He taught his followers to resist the British military non-violently, as India was struggling for its independence. The practice brought about the end of British colonialism in India. I believe ahimsa is an evolutionary leap in heart consciousness.

The ability to forgive is also an aspect of heart development. A person is able to transcend the wish for revenge (which would be an expression of the first and third chakras, and the Old Testament edict of "an eye for an eye") and extend forgiveness to a former enemy. I have already told of the miraculous power of the simple *Ho'opoonono* statement, "I'm sorry. Please forgive me. I love you. Thank you." It can be said to anyone face-to-face or at a distance, with or without his or her knowledge.

Finally, a spiritual heart attainment occurs when a wide-open heart can love God, the creation, and life itself. A person feels at one with everything—cosmos, nature, other creatures and humans. There is no longer any sense of separation between oneself and All That Is. At this stage a human feels that he is at one with the Tao, or creation. That state can't really be communicated to others with words because it transcends the limits of language. Nevertheless there have been many attempts to describe it and many actual demonstrations of it, so we know it is a possible human development.

Amaji, the Indian female contemporary saint, is a good example of this level of love and total surrender to Divinity (a throat chakra characteristic). She individually hugs one thousand to fifteen hundred individuals per night to deliver Divine Mother love to each. Many of my friends and colleagues have experienced this life infusion from her. Although she is diabetic she persists night after night to deliver love, without a break.

Heart Consciousness and Global Evolution

On the brink of this present time of spiritual awakening it looks like global heart consciousness was arrested at some early stage of development. In his book, *A New Earth: Awakening to Your Life's Purpose*,[25] Eckhart Tolle suggests a way of understanding this: "It is when we are trapped in incessant streams of compulsive thinking that the universe really disintegrates for us, and we lose the ability to sense the interconnectedness of all that exists."

Even though the vast majority of humans will experience some form of love in their lives, we haven't yet been able to organize large social structures with a foundation of love. Most social structures, governments and economies are fueled by energies of the first three chakras, of survivalist instincts and self-interest, and of still struggling with feelings of separation. Success in the world so far is based on these feelings and beliefs associated with the first three

---

25 Tolle, Eckhart. *A New Earth: Awakening to Your Life's Purpose*. New York, Plume, 2006.

chakras. Small utopian groups have tried throughout history to organize around a foundation of love that seeks human harmony, cooperation and peace. Some of these smaller groups endure, but although small, they profoundly influence the evolution of consciousness on our planet.

Fifth Chakra Development

The fifth chakra is located at the throat. Its element is sound and it is associated with a full range of communication, audible or silent. It governs hearing and all forms of attunement with sounds. In yogic philosophy the throat chakra is claimed to be a purifying bottleneck, through which higher consciousness is reached. Remember that the body narrows a lot here at the throat; many energy pathways are compressed in it.

The throat becomes a translator between mind and body; thoughts are differentiated from feelings here. The creative drives first experienced during early childhood and play stages can evolve with the throat and become more advanced levels of creativity. From exploratory and practiced self-expression with this chakra, a creative identity can develop.

The throat chakra imparts the ability to literally "speak one's own truth" and assert that truth in the world. A person's voice often indicates how much throat chakra power a person has *owned*: Is the voice robust and clear, or soft and halting? Can we hear a person's conviction and commitment to his own truth in his voice? Or do we stop listening at some point because we can't sense real vitality there?

The auditory portion of communication—hearing, speaking and singing—becomes more fluent as the energy of the throat develops and strengthens. That ability can progress dramatically as a person learns to debate, write, and deliver oral presentations, or even sing professionally. In most every life there comes a time when claiming one's own voice and telling one's own truth are important.

That stage includes the ability to know what he thinks and say it out loud, to be heard and acknowledged by others.

While growing up, most of us have experienced many barriers to telling our own unique truth. At some point our own experience or inner knowing can run counter to "truths" inherited from our families, learned in school or absorbed from the consensus reality of our culture. Then we must find the voice strength to stand firm and tell our own truth, regardless of what is expressed outside of us. The throat chakra strengthens and matures as one learns to hold firmly to his own experience and inner knowing.

Many writers have told of their struggle to find their own voice, separate from training in writing or modeling other writers. Sometimes it can take several written books before that unique voice is produced.

As we spend more time on the planet we gain skills and experience for increasing energy of the throat chakra. Creativity greatly increases because there are many more expressive abilities to play with. The seeds of creativity that sprouted in the second and third chakras can blossom now in the fifth chakra as a person forms more and more elegant and complex creations. She can more easily take on a professional identity as an artist, a musician or a singer, for example.

Indeed, as we find our own voice and truth, fifth chakra energy becomes healing, regardless of how humble or celebrated that expression may be, from shining shoes to being a world renowned spiritual leader.

In addition, a unique healing ability can sometimes emanate from the throat so that as a person sings, or even speaks, from the opened throat, the vibration of the sound has a healing effect for anyone who hears it. Some music is healing. For example, many people have found listening to the music of Mozart, Bach or Beethoven healing and uplifting. Further, healing sound, through the voice or an instrument, can be focused on particular symptoms or parts of the body to help heal them. Chanting is known to have healing and strengthening effects.

When my daughter Rosalind makes healing sounds with someone who has requested them, that person is deeply soothed, uplifted and sometimes healed. Sometimes even experiences of past lives arise for the person during this sounding. An interesting aspect of Rosalind's ability is that she had to discover and develop it completely on her own, because there was no such training in her Master's Degree in Music. I believe it is a soul talent.

The Fifth Chakra at a Spiritual Level

At a spiritual level, fifth chakra development can open clairaudience, the ability to hear "what makes no sound." For example, one might hear another's thoughts, or a distant cry for help, or even music from heavenly realms. (Beethoven was said to hear such sound.)

It is in the throat that the ability to surrender one's own will to the Divine will happens. A person can sincerely say, and act from, "May Thy will, not mine, be done." This stage of development is eventually required of all true spiritual aspirants. For some it is the greatest struggle of all along the spiritual path because it means putting the ego into its proper function, namely, managing details of earthly life. And when the ego has been carefully cultivated to serve oneself, and even others, it is a huge leap of faith to surrender it. It has often been said that *the ego makes a superb servant but a tyrannical master.* Think of celebrities or famous politicians, social leaders and high achievers. Having worked very hard to achieve their status, and having received much public adulation for it, what a struggle it must be to give all of that attention and importance over to a higher purpose or spiritual law.

Yet some of the finest leaders of our time—the Dalai Lama, Bishop Desmond Tutu, Gandhi, Mandela and Mother Theresa—have evolved to this level in order to surrender to a higher order from where they receive transcendental guidance, and strength, that has a positive, life-affirming impact on large numbers of people. Gandhi said that he took all decisions and actions from God. Amazingly, the strength to carry out very difficult tasks also came from God, not from personal ego or physical strength.

Soul Lightening Work with the Fifth Chakra

Again, we have a specific acupressure formula that focuses on the throat. It stimulates awareness and expression within the throat. We process whatever unfinished business may arise. Often such processing involves bringing emotions up through the throat about something in our lives that has been buried for a long time. When we can fully allow the emotion to come forth, and then give it voice (speak or cry or scream it), the physical and emotional tension releases. There is also almost always a very valuable message embedded within the feeling that we haven't previously been able to know or express as part of us. As children we may have been prevented from expressing some terrifying or infuriating event, such as the frightening experience of a tonsillectomy or other surgery, or experiences of abuse, neglect or wounding. We may have been punished or had love withheld for expressing ourselves or acting out in a certain way, because it would have inconvenienced, embarrassed, exposed, frightened or angered an adult or other person in our lives.

We urge students to tell the truth, to speak up and speak out from that truth, even when it seems a bit edgy. And often when we do exercises such as "chakra tai chi" in the throat, we ask everyone to sing out from her own voice. It's amazing how beautiful and naturally harmonious all those voices are together, as they issue spontaneously from each person's throat.

The Sixth or Brow Chakra

The sixth chakra is located at the brow, on the forehead between the two eyebrows. The element is light, and we can experience how this chakra can shine light on whatever it focuses upon. At this chakra, consciousness can expand and elevate beyond the ordinary.

The sixth chakra is sometimes known as the "third eye," which provides us with the ability to perceive the unity beyond the ordinary duality perceived through our two eyes. When the brow chakra is opened one can see deeply, like a focused laser, into oneself, other people and the patterns of the phenomenal world. Expansive mind qualities of intuition, inspiration, vision, precognition and clairvoyance are associated with the opening of this chakra. True selfless service becomes possible, but is not assured without practice and awareness.

The sixth chakra doesn't automatically develop beyond what we know now as ordinary seeing and brain ability, such as thinking, calculating, planning, reasoning and "figuring things out." Although brow potentials can take a person beyond ordinary thinking and brain power, they are still little known, and rarely encouraged, in the West. We have few authentic models for true clairvoyance. Nicola Tesla was known for his ability to see into machinery, and to visualize how to construct an entire mechanism before it was ever built.

It is also possible to project light from the brow chakra, much like a focused laser, to someone or something. In this way it is possible to send a higher vibration of light into something that has become dark, as in the case of depression, hopelessness, pain, and so forth.

Unfortunately, advanced abilities of the sixth chakra are sometimes pursued and used to serve ego and power. For example, it is possible for a person to use such abilities for power over others—the false guru phenomenon. I first became interested in extrasensory perception when my good college friend, a brilliant woman, told me the story of her "capture" by such a guru. When she attended a metaphysical lecture the guru speaking said there was someone in the audience whom he was destined to teach. Then he pointed her out although she was seated in obscurity, far from the podium.

Their interaction resulted in her leaving her husband to follow this man as his student. She said she learned about paranormal events and some metaphysics from him. But she became very frightened when she realized that he was not only reading her mind, but sending directions to it. She left him straight away. Someone who would use his abilities in that way would have little heart and poor moral sense. Several years later my friend's supposed guru was murdered by disgruntled husbands.

Instead of pure intuition or telepathy, the false guru offers his own projections, fantasies or personal desires as "true vision" or spiritual awareness in a way that might seem to be more than it is. In effect, such a guru uses another person's desire for greater spiritual awareness to manipulate them into serving the guru's will. Think of the extreme case of Jim Jones, who in 1978 took his nine hundred followers to the South American jungle where they established a spiritual community. However, that ended with the tragic mass suicide of nearly the whole community, persuaded to do so by Jones' promise of salvation and enlightenment. Thus, it is very important to pursue sixth chakra evolution carefully, always watching for the possible interference of personal ego and the wish for power.

I am a strong advocate of sixth chakra clairvoyance, and encourage its development in our students because I believe we need this advanced sight to help us see through our enormous global problems to their solutions. Some Soul Lightening students experience clairvoyance as they open this chakra. And some have located their own soul here. The key, of course, is to use that ability under soul guidance, to truly serve others.

Soul Lightening Work with the Sixth Chakra

We use an acupressure formula focused on the brow for this chakra. While applying it hands-on we encourage students to lift their awareness into the brow and explore the images or intuitions they may find there. A number of times people have rediscovered childhood visions or psychic perceptions about other people that were rejected by adults at the time. We encourage these childhood abilities to open up and reveal their true purpose, because the child is not motivated by ego and power. When validated and encouraged by a Soul Lightening practitioner, a person can realize that some of their early visions came directly from the soul; they were prescient and very valuable to the present adult because they can give destiny guidance, similar to the childhood dream. Cassie White, an English Soul Lightening practitioner, reclaimed her childhood paranormal abilities. She said, "The Process Acupressure skills I have been blessed to learn have allowed me to embrace my sensitivity, and my gifts, the skills I already had, and to polish them."

As a child, my process partner, Laura, was often visited by angels or dead people who weren't seen by others. For a long time she had to hide that brow information away, for fear of derision. Now, however, as her higher consciousness advances she has claimed her brow abilities for the valuable information they give. Her visions help her own development and that of others.

The Seventh Chakra

The seventh chakra, or crown, is located at the top of the head, where the *sagittal* sutures come together. The crown connects us with Source, the great unifying order behind creation. Traditionally the element associated with the crown is higher thought, or the ability to access consciousness beyond ordinary thinking. Often pictured as a "thousand-petaled lotus," this symbolism indicates opening to the unlimited information, or infinite intelligence, of the Universal Field. The crown usually opens through adult spiritual practice, although it can burst open as a result of high energy infusion, such as an initiation.

Cosmic consciousness,[26] a state that transcends ordinary reality, can become available. This is the consciousness accessed by prophets, poets, sages and many near-death survivors who received Divine guidance from transcendental realms. Think of Gandhi, Einstein, Nicola Tesla, Martin Luther King and Eben Alexander in contemporary history. Many mystics and philosophers have claimed that infinite intelligence is available to those who seek it.

In our time, it is becoming more common for people to search for higher states of consciousness. Inspiration from higher sources is recognized and welcomed. True connection with the crown enables a person to receive transcendental messages and inspiration. Many connect with transcendental guides or spiritual teachers to help them.

At its best, "channeling" comes from a pure crown level, beyond ego or personal psychology. Marcus T. Anthony, a futurist, coach and writer, claims that he gets most of his life and professional guidance from this level. His book *Discover Your Soul Template*[27] offers a number of valuable tools for attuning to that level.

At this level of consciousness a person is aware of the connectedness of all life and the union of all souls. He realizes that he and all others are sparks of the Divine. A person can begin to feel and identify with the great wave of the creative flow of life, or the Tao.

Soul Lightening Work with the Crown

Since we contact all the chakras in every Soul Lightening session, students or clients are well aware of evolving crown effects in their body and mind. They most commonly contact soul consciousness

---

26 Bucke, Richard Maurice. 2011. *Cosmic Consciousness: A Study in the Evolution of the Human Mind.* Guildford, U.K., White Crow Productions, Ltd. (First published 1901).

27 Marcus T. Anthony, Ph.D. 2012. *Discover Your Soul Template: 14 Steps for Awakening Integrated Intelligence.* Rochester, Vermont, Inner Traditions.

in the crown. As I've noted, we usually ask a client if any soul messages are available at the end of a session.

At the beginning of each class we do Chakra Tai Chi, which ends at the crown. This encourages each person to check in with crown consciousness every day, and progressively builds a familiarity with it.

We work intensely with the crown, through a special acupressure formula for it. When we are working with the chakras in the Anza-Borrego desert where I live, we first open the crown with the acupressure formula and then ask students to walk out into the desert for a day-long or half-day vision quest, during which they focus on receiving transcendental guidance. Similar to the American Indian vision quests, these treks yield remarkable inspiration about oneself, the world and the cosmos. And often they affirm personal destiny.

For example, during one vision quest we asked to receive guidance about how to go forward with Soul Lightening. Following is part of that guidance which we received:

> Reach high and wide into heaven to connect with LIGHT and all your personal higher guides, in order to receive the grace and gifts that are waiting for you. Each of you is an ever-lightening soul on the ground. Together you are a LIGHTHOUSE in the world. Even though money is seen as the bottom line in this culture at this time, in the new world the top line will be strong LIGHT. Your principal focus should be on that top light now. Lots of heaven help is streaming in now to help us co-create the new world. Keep connecting with it, breathe deeply and expand. Each of you needs to ask at that level for guidance and support about your right work with Soul Lightening. You need to *cultivate* hands-on, close-contact work, through study groups, small classes and community outreach in whatever ways are possible. SEVA and

your other for-all-people classes should be spread out like a ground creeper. Wherever each of you are, ask, "What is needed here? What would be the right offering in this environment?"

Of course, when we receive such guidance we act on it to the extent possible at the time. Without accepting it as pure truth we wait and observe what happens in the world. For example, are we moving toward a new world? It's impossible to verify at present with the facts on the ground. Yet, Eckhart Tolle's *New Earth*, Ken Wilber's recent lectures and those of many other current philosophers tell us that we are surely moving in the direction of world transformation.

Consciousness outside the Brain

Thanks to thousands of recent near-death experiences, reported, catalogued and examined by brain scientists, we know that an amazing expansive consciousness exists outside the brain. In several cases, brain scientists have experienced cosmic consciousness while their brains were technically dead. This information has verified experiences of mystics through the ages who claimed a higher mind.

Stanislav Grof, M.D., who has researched extraordinary states of consciousness for many years, points out in his book *The Holotropic Mind: The Three Levels of Human Consciousness and How They Shape Our Lives*[28] , this "perception of the world becomes dominant and compelling. It completely overrides the everyday illusion of Newtonian reality, where we seem to be 'skin-encapsulated egos' existing in a world of separate beings and objects.... We can

---

28 Grof, Stanislav, M.D. with Hal Zina Bennett. 1992. *The Holotropic Mind: The Three Levels of Human Consciousness and How They Shape Our Lives.* New York, HarperCollins

experience ourselves as the whole biosphere of our planet or the entire material universe."

Spiritual Development in Later Life

Although it does not interest all people, commitment to spiritual development can become very important during late adulthood and old age. Both brow and crown chakras can open further with spiritual evolution at this time, providing us with a perspective of our lives that we have never before experienced, one that brings new levels of joy and insight.

Spiritually inclined people will begin to explore their own God questions, or to explore questions that previously seemed beyond their capacity to feel or experience some connection with. Is there really a God? How am I connected to him or that? Shall I just accept whatever religious dogma I was raised with, or should I explore further? With such exploration the crown will begin to open and expand and directly support the process of spiritual evolution.

It is interesting that in the traditional Indian culture people are freed from the role of "householder" (taking care of family and culture) at age sixty-two. Then one is free to devote themselves full time to spirituality. Some men withdraw at that age to live at an ashram or study with a guru. Aspirations for that part of life are traditionally very different from the West, though this pattern is changing as tens of thousands of people in the West enroll in meditation, yoga and spiritual studies, particularly in their retirement years.

As the East becomes more westernized and the West imports more of the traditions of the East, these traditional patterns are changing; we are seeing more older people in the West dedicating their retirement years to spiritual study and practice.

In many cultures in the East, a person will hope to reach enlightenment, or at least higher consciousness, in the last stage of life. The achievements of wisdom, compassion and kindness are valued far beyond those of third-chakra aspirations, such as money, ego and personal power.

Carolyn Myss, the American psychospiritual teacher who commands large audiences, had an interesting description of this period of life when crown opening could be spiritually important:

> (This is a period) when you reach a point that you have cleared your personal agenda so that you can be trusted spiritually. (You have) clear sight and the ability to heal. The ability to give up a private agenda with power. Then you can receive the power to heal others at a distance. When you have no agenda with power it all comes to you. Truth is no more than a prayer away at all times. You are working for the first time with the technical side of your soul. Prayer is the highest form of accessing high voltage guidance. The moment you utter a prayer it is answered instantly.[29]

Soul Lightening's Direct Work with Chakras

Our aim in Soul Lightening is to clarify and empower all the chakras and stages of development, at a pace dictated by the individual soul. We believe that only the soul can know its own appropriate growth and pace.

Every aspect of whole human development—in body, energy, mind, emotions and soul—is reflected in the chakra system. Thus we work through the tapestry of physical, energetic and psychological factors that contribute to complete human development.

Chakra balancing is built into the Basic Acupressure Protocol of every session. This assures that chakra awareness is constantly cultivated and supported, energetically, physically and in

---

29 Myss, Carolyn. 2006. *Invisible Acts of Power: Channeling Grace in Your Everyday Life.* New York, Atria Books

consciousness. Much like the regular practice of meditation or Tai Chi, consciousness is continually enhanced. At the end of a session we ask the client to bring consciousness through all the chakras, from crown to root. In this way a person can notice the energetic, physical or emotional messages from each. Gradually our students and clients are oriented toward chakra balance within their own bodies, consciously and unconsciously.

As personal growth and transformation progress, we often become aware of areas in our development, and in the development of our chakras, that need further processing or strengthening. We can then pause at those areas and focus more specifically on work we might need to do to in those places. For example, we might work with obstacles, or holes in our development and related beliefs, or perhaps process traumas still held in our consciousness, by strengthening the appropriate chakras in the body. In our advanced classes we work specifically with each chakra, with special chakra acupressure formulas, and with various states of consciousness. Chakra Tai Chi, performed in every class, stimulates the chakras energetically and also awakens chakra consciousness in each one.

At the core of our work is alignment between heaven and earth. Through our acupressure formula that activates energy through the Great Central Channel (which connects all the chakras through the spine, from root to crown), we constantly reinforce each person's direct alignment through the center of their own being. This practice also supports each person's soul and access to Source.

Erik Erickson's Stages of Psychosocial Development

Now we will consider Erik Erikson's *stages of human development*, which for the past several decades have proven invaluable for parents, progressive educators (notably the Montessori schools), as well as psychologists and teachers of personal and spiritual development. As a psychologist and psychoanalyst, Erikson (1902-1994) made a huge contribution to our understanding of the stages involved with developing a healthy ego and being able to enjoy a fulfilling emotional life. I have found that his contribution provides insights and knowledge that can serve us extremely well as guides for self-assessment and even self-parenting. For further awareness, I correlate them here with chakra development, where relevant, so that we can see which physical and spiritual characteristics are needed for each stage.

School Age, 6-12 Years

The stage of development which Erickson called *school age* corresponds with the beginning period of heart development, when relationships become more varied and important. The child encounters interaction with others beyond the home and separate from parents. Most of a child's initiation into the world is through pre-school or elementary school or play groups.

Erickson described the most significant learning, or conflict, of school age as *industry versus inferiority*. By this he meant that healthy development would naturally stimulate motivation to accomplish things, to learn and grow, all of which would result in self-confidence and a growing sense of personal competence. Those skills are encouraged in good elementary schools as well as pre-schools.

However, if for any reason these skills aren't developed, perhaps because of poverty, lack of good schooling, or any other factors, then the child would begin to experience him- or herself as inferior or "less than," compared with his more capable fellows.

During this stage between the relative freedom of early childhood and the hormonal upset of adolescence, we're becoming increasingly aware of the world beyond our individual self and what we need to do to function well within that world. Through our participation in school, community, and even the awareness of the global community that we experience through the mass media, we encounter a greater variety of influences and demands on us that we didn't experience in our original family. We become more aware of our own impact on others and start learning that we can make choices about our own behavior in order to achieve different results. Our field of influence and interactions expand to include more information and many more relationships than we ever would have encountered in the nuclear family alone. This is a time that increases challenges to our physical strength, our sensory awareness and our self-reliance.

Mental and sensory learning increase exponentially as does the child's natural desire to learn. This includes learning how to use her or his own mind to investigate things outside the direction and guidance of parents and other authorities. The child learns how to study and work, and is usually delighted with the task, discovering her own inherent capacities, though not always self-confidence, to reach beyond rote learning that is too often required by most schools. She explores and develops her abilities to think independently. She is able to direct her curiosity and her own powers of concentration. She takes command of her own initiative.

During this stage the child starts to develop a social personality, learning to interact effectively with others and to feel personal satisfaction from these interactions. This period offers experiences of what works and what doesn't work with others. A social self is developing during this time that can form the foundation for later adult social interactions. Very elementary relationship awareness begins in infancy, and progresses to relationship and affection skills between the ages five and twelve. A school age child can learn the ability to accomplish things on his or her own and experience deep pleasure with herself; she is able to experience pleasure in her collaborative experiences rather than simply competing.

The strengths of all three base chakras are needed for growth during school age and the heart begins to open as the child starts to establish and value relationships.

Adolescence

Erickson placed adolescent development between the ages of twelve and eighteen years, the usual high-school period. He named the crisis of growth as *identity vs. role confusion*. Adolescents need to develop a sense of self and personal identity. An identity struggle is complicated by the disruptive physical and emotional stresses of hormone upheaval in the body.

I taught psychology to late adolescents in the 1970s and got to see this crisis played out in Wide Screen Hi-Definition 3-D. I tried to empower students to claim their identities and true talents with some of the best principles and methods of psychology at the time. I watched them flourish in self-confidence and power as they were supported and became aware of their own identities. I watched them experiment with many roles as they tried to find themselves in their right place. I also listened to the huge struggles they went through with parents, friends and authorities. At the same time, I was parenting my own adolescents at home. I came to learn that these beautiful young people had enormous potentials within themselves that were impossible to manifest in adolescent bodies, and that were often discounted by adults. For example, one girl was clearly clairvoyant, but that valuable innate talent, yet untrained, only resulted in confusion and sometimes derision from others. I did my best to encourage and support the students for who they were, which was not always appreciated by school administrators. From that experience, I saw first-hand how many conflicting themes and powerful forces adolescents deal with. I concluded then that adolescence is one of the most exciting, promising and difficult stages of human development. Now, in our time, adolescent growth surges are surely much more complicated and challenging.

There are many roles to play as the adolescent experiments with identity. Over time, personal identity will hopefully evolve into the ability to love oneself fully and wholesomely, remain true to self and learn to be a skillful collaborator, even in the face of objections, conflicts, restrictions and highly complex obstacles.

As an aside, I recently had a conversation with a friend who is acquainted, through his business, with several consultants working with Fortune 100 companies. Under the guise of helping employees develop greater creativity, initiative and collaborative skills, these consultants draw from ancient spiritual teachings. For example, they teach meditation and getting in touch with one's own body feelings. They have adapted forgiveness processes for resolving conflicts between co-workers and within work teams. My friend noted, too, that in defining the abilities these Fortune 100 companies most valued in their employees, they listed the following six attributes: 1) having a solid sense of self; 2) being creative and able to exercise initiative; 3) being skillful collaborators; 4) having excellent communication skills; 5) having an ability to maintain their individuality while collaborating with others; 6) having the ability to solve complex problems and handle complex working relationships, even when it involved people and end-results they might never meet or see firsthand.

My friend also reminded me of Steve Jobs, co-founder with Steve Wozniac of Apple Computers, who is credited with being "the father of the digital revolution." Though one of the most successful entrepreneurs of the century, he was also, to his dying day, a serious practitioner of Zen Buddhism, who went on long meditation retreats at the Tassajara Zen Mountain Center. He once stated that people who didn't share his spiritual and counterculture roots had difficulty with his way of thinking and working.

It's interesting to note that the six expressed attributes valued by corporations, which I listed above, are very consistent with Erikson's developmental psychology. My friend also stated that the consultants he worked with often reported that people in their corporate trainings occasionally had profound spiritual breakthroughs as the result of exercises they had learned. In fact, there were cases where breakthroughs brought employees into conflict with corporate practices they felt they could not support, leading them to lodge significant protests or resign. Perhaps these breakthroughs are baby steps in the evolution of our collective consciousness, often difficult to see because they can so easily be overshadowed by darker aspects of greed that drive big business.

Claiming and honoring one's own voice (fifth chakra), and learning how to speak up for oneself while simultaneously valuing others, are important attributes at this time of our evolution. It is heartening to discover how this aspect is also valued in the six attributes above.

There is usually tremendous interest in sexual relationships during this stage of development. Sexuality erupts in exciting and complicating ways as the heart chakra opens more fully and often stimulates the sexual energies of the second chakra. Heterosexual and homosexual exploration can go on.

You have probably realized that this period calls upon all the first five chakras. In the case of my clairvoyant student the sixth chakra was also trying to develop.

Young Adultood, ages 18-35

Erickson called this stage *young adulthood*. It is one that often coincides with learning a trade, going to college, earning a living and starting a family. Erickson said that during this period a person could develop *intimacy,* or else *experience isolation*. In this beginning stage of adulthood we seek companionship and love, a progression of the heart love that began earlier.

As we begin seeking mutually satisfying relationships, primarily through dating, marriage and friends, we may also start a family. Relationship skills become increasingly important, especially with marital partners and friends. The ability to love and care for others can strengthen. Through mastering the characteristics of this stage we can experience intimacy at a deep level. And there are plenty of opportunities to explore, practice and develop these relationship skills at this period of beginning adult life.

If we don't develop these relationship skills, conflict, frustration, dissatisfaction and alienation develop as a result, and our world begins to shrink. If these patterns continue to build, with no efforts to change them, we may be tempted to develop a defensive attitude of superiority toward others. Then we increasingly experience isolation, distancing ourselves from social interaction and avoiding intimate relationships.

During this period families and society expect a person to be able to care for himself independently. Residing in one's own home and attaining financial independence are all synonymous with adulthood in the United States. Yet in the last decade so many young adults still live with parents, some from lack of employment opportunities, others from continued dependence on parents for adult survival resources. Fourth and fifth chakras are of special value during this time.

Middle Adulthood, ages 35 to 65

Erickson placed middle adulthood between ages thirty-five and sixty-five. He claimed that during this time a person could become *generative*, creative and productive, or devolve into *self-absorption* or *stagnation*. The strengths that could be developed were productivity and caring.

At this period of mid-life, creativity, meaningful work and family are very important. We are now willing to "be in charge." A significant task is to perpetuate culture and transmit its values, through the family. A person works toward establishing a stable environment, not only for one's own family but for the world. Significant relationships are within the workplace, the community and the family. Strength comes through care of others and production of something that contributes to the betterment of society. If we don't attain meaningful productivity during this stage we can become self-absorbed and stagnant, fearing that life is meaningless. Fourth through sixth Chakras can be cultivated here.

Characteristics of Adult Mastery

By the end of young and middle adulthood, adults can be expected to master the following characteristics:

- Self-control - restraint, emotional control.
- Stability - stable personality, strength.
- Independence - ability to self-regulate.
- Seriousness - ability to deal with life in a serious manner.
- Responsibility - accountability, commitment and reliability.
- Method/Tact - ability to think ahead and plan for the future; patience.
- Endurance - ability and willingness to cope with difficulties.
- Experience - breadth of mind; understanding.
- Objectivity - perspective and realism.

Old Age and Maturity, ages 65 to Death

Erickson placed this last stage from age sixty-five to death. He named the developmental outcome of it *integrity vs. despair.* He said that one had the possibility of attaining wisdom during this time. He felt that much of life was preparing for middle adulthood, while the last stage was recovering from it. Perhaps that was because older adults can look back and realize the tremendous energy, effort and endurance the middle years took.

By this time, a person can review life with contentment, feeling fulfilled with a deep sense that his life had meaning, and he made a contribution. Probably such a generative person will be continually learning and growing, right up until death. He can have a feeling of integrity within himself. Strength comes from wisdom that he can have a detached concern for the whole of life, accepting death as its completion. The significant relationships of this period are with the Divine and all of mankind.

Some adults may reach this stage without having reached their goals, dreams or made any significant accomplishments. Then they might despair at their lack of accomplishments and perceived failures, fearing or resisting death as they struggle to find a sense of purpose, wondering, "What was it all worth?" Or, conversely, an older person may stop exploring or questioning anything and simply settle back into rigid dogmatism, assuming that they already have all the answers, and only their views are correct.

In these last stages of life the crown chakra can become an important doorway to higher guidance and wisdom. A crown-connected person knows that the universe has a benevolent order and that he is a valuable part of it.

Fulfillment of Human Needs Dramatically Affects Full Development

Development progresses as a person receives what he truly needs at each stage. As we saw, the infant must receive adequate nourishment, oxygen and shelter or he will die. Later, a school-aged child needs appropriate factual instruction, experience of his abilities and competencies, and mental stimulation for the brain to develop.

Actually, human needs continue, perhaps with diminishing importance, throughout life. When they are satisfactorily met, an individual can flourish to full potential; conversely when they are not met his full development is impeded.

The renowned American psychologist Abraham Maslow studied the full range of human needs throughout life and came up with the most thorough description of them that we have at present. He developed what he called a *hierarchy of needs* chart, which was published in his book *Motivation and Personality.*[30] His hierarchy of needs gives a very important index for evolutionary development, in both individuals and society, because it describes needs for the highest human development, starting with survival and extending to creativity and spiritual development. I correlate it loosely with the chakra development we have been considering in this chapter.

Maslow's hierarchy of needs is presented as a pyramid chart that establishes five levels of development, from meeting sheer survival needs such as food, shelter and sex, all the way up to self-actualization, including creative, moral and spiritual development. Just as we have seen in the developmental stages, needs on the lower levels (survival) must be met, to at least some minimal degree, before one can evolve to higher development. People can get stuck at one or several levels, and some may never reach higher levels because of deprived or highly dysfunctional circumstances in their lives.

The five levels Maslow named are:

Physical or Physiological: This first level of needs includes shelter, oxygen, food, water, rest and elimination, all of which are vital to a person's life and essential to survival. (First chakra)

Security or Safety: This second level involves not only actually being secure and safe, but also having the feeling of safety and security. This level is typically claimed in infancy and early childhood. It helps lay the groundwork for developing other skills and moving up to the next step in the ladder. (First and second chakras)

Social (Love and Belonging): This third level goes beyond simple physical survival. It involves developing friendships and eventually relationships

---

30 Maslow, Abraham. 1954. *Motivation and Personality*, see also *Toward A Psychology of Being*

that are emotionally-based, such as sexual intimacy and a supportive and communicative family. (Second and fourth chakras.)

Esteem: A person develops self-esteem and confidence. According to Maslow, all humans need to receive respect in order to develop self-respect and respect for others. Also, a person needs to engage in life activities that give him a sense of contribution, to the family and society, in order to gain recognition. Second through sixth chakras.

Self-Actualization: The highest level one can reach, according to Maslow, was self-actualization, in which one's fullest potential is realized. This attainment is very similar to Jung's description of individuation and the East Indian description of self-realization. (Fourth through crown chakras).

Maslow described the following qualities found in a self-actualized person:

- An ability to embrace the facts and realities of the world (including themselves) rather than denying or avoiding them
- Spontaneity in their ideas and actions
- Creativity and the ability to find new solutions on one's own
- Having an interest in solving problems, which can become a key focus in their lives
- Feeling close to other people, and generally appreciating life
- Embracing a system of internal morality that is independent of external authority
- Having the discernment ability to view all things in an objective manner, free from prejudices.

(These achievements of self-actualization would require development of chakras four through six, and even the seventh.)

Maslow claimed that most people accomplished the two lower levels in their lifetimes, but many got stalled on upper levels.

I believe Maslow's hierarchy of needs is a useful instrument for assessing not only individual needs, but social and global evolution as well.

Ethical or Moral Development

Human development isn't complete without a code for *right behavior*. Instruction in right from wrong commonly starts with our families as we are growing up. Such codes are emphasized or enhanced at school, in various organizations we might be involved in when we are young, by neighborhood and tribal interactions, and from the more direct spiritual teachings of elders.

All moral systems have evolved naturally from first-chakra needs—that is, we don't want other people doing hurtful things that we wouldn't want done to ourselves —the Golden Rule. And it's essentially the fears and issues of comfort and wellbeing that are involved with the first three chakras that keep us in line, not rules of morality recorded in the bible or in other religious writings.

Moral behavior has been prescribed from spiritual or religious sources all over the world, from early history right up through the present time. Various alterations and idiosyncrasies creep into all of them, but the core directions are consistently the same:

Tell the truth, don't lie
Don't steal
Don't kill

In the West and Middle East, the earliest records of a moral code can be found in religious teachings such as we find in the story of Moses and the Ten Commandments. These commandments are fundamental to Judaism, Islam and Christianity. In addition to including the three laws above, the Ten Commandments include reserving a holy day for worship, worshipping only one God, and prohibiting idolatry, blasphemy, murder, theft, deception, and adultery. The Ten Commandments echo and expand upon the Golden Rule:

- Do unto others as you would have them do unto you,
- Love your neighbor as yourself.
- Turn the other cheek.

In the East, ethical guidelines come from Hinduism, Buddhism and Taoism. Many of them are the same as the Ten Commandments. They also include prohibitions against blasphemy, deception and adultery, with a few embellishments.

In addition, Hindu morality includes instructions for liberation of an individual from the cycles of birth and death (in other words, life on earth) through elimination of all karma, negative or positive, and moral duties for the wellbeing of society in general.

From the East come some interesting moral and ethical teachings based on accepting human conflict as a reality; however these teachings are not governed by rules. Among these are some amazing tracts on how to wage war as long as humanity continues to "require" war.

Buddhist and Taoist ethics are essentially the same, with the addition of refraining from the use of intoxicants.

Many Taoist writings add prohibitions against receiving "unrighteous wealth" and against misrepresenting good and evil, maintaining harmony with ancestors and family and never disregarding kin, supporting people who do good deeds, supporting the unfortunate, and harboring no thought of revenge when harmed. It might be noted that the Taoists also advise against thinking "depraved thoughts." This is the only moral code I've found that directly counsels about regulating thought, although the Buddhists certainly work ceaselessly with the mind.

In all societies there's an expectation that the family, the educational system, society and religion will teach moral conduct as we are growing up. When such indoctrination is not accomplished through those sources, then the state is left to create a system of laws for exacting punishment when the moral and legal codes, as well as the "rights of the state," are violated.

How Right Behavior Correlates with Chakra Evolution

As we travel up the chakra scale we can recognize how the capacity for right behavior is enfolded within it.

- The first three chakras give us an attachment to life, feeling and personal power.
- As we reach heart level, love widens perspective and opens the ability to love the self and others, and to be empathically attuned to them.
- Telling the truth keeps the throat chakra strong and allows creative talents to flourish, whereas lying stunts the development of the throat chakra.
- At the brow we can perceive what is true and real. We learn to differentiate the true and real from illusion or false teachings. We choose to speak truth.
- From the crown we know we are one with the great Order behind creation, which is beyond our own comprehension. We are reverent of life and therefore have no impulse to destroy any of it.
- Ideally a sense of right behavior comes from within oneself. We are prompted by the soul's attunement with Source. Unfortunately, not all humans have retained that connection.

Now that we have looked at the full range of the developmental stages of human life, I want to propose characteristics of a whole and mature human being. I know of course that, in the future, more advanced minds, with greater scientific knowledge and long-lived wisdom, will alter and improve this proposal. Nevertheless, I risk articulating it here:

A Proposed Description of a Whole and Mature Human Being

A whole and mature human would:

- have awareness of, and take responsibility for, his whole self—body, mind, emotions, spirit and action—not only for his basic survival but for his own wellbeing (chakras one through three);
- tell the truth to the best of his ability (chakra five);
- have transformed most, if not all, past traumas, especially those from childhood, and harvested them as teachings on his unique path (chakras one through six);
- have accomplished the eight life tasks of Erickson's stages—trust, autonomy, initiative, industry, identity (or ego), intimacy, generativity (productivity), and integrity—so that the teachings of life have been integrated into identity and actions. (All chakras with the possible exception of crown);
- have a kind and compassionate regard for self and others. (chakra four)
- be able to forgive oneself, as well as others, for past hurts and failures (Chakra four);
- respect the rights and possessions of others, and therefore would not steal (Chakra four);
- have a reverential regard for the cosmos, or the laws behind the universe, as Einstein meant when he said, "Everyone who is seriously involved in the pursuit of science becomes convinced that a spirit is manifest in the laws of the Universe—a spirit vastly superior to that of man, and one in the face of which we, with our modest powers, must feel humble." (Brow and crown chakras);

- not destroy life, except as necessary for nurturing and protecting life. (Chakras three, four, and crown);
- have reverence for all of life and hold the intent, at all times, to protect and honor it (Chakras three and four).

Jurriaan Kamp, the publisher of *The Intelligent Optimist* magazine, reported in a recent article how an Indian master once told him that the greatest journey we can make is the journey within. "That journey," Kamp continued, "begins with feeling, listening, looking and experiencing, and sometimes by taking a moment in our busy lives to experience our connection with creation, to invite the future in, to discover that happiness is more than matter or property, to learn that health is, first and foremost, an individual, inner experience.... Come, let's invest in our dreams of a world renewed, trusting that a new era is now supporting our longing."[31]

It is my hope and my dream that whole-being development, as we've explored in this chapter, can serve us all in that mission, deepening our awareness not only of ourselves but of our relationship to our planet and the universe. Many years ago, the French philosopher Pierre Teilhard de Chardin reminded us that "we are collaborators in the creation of the universe." And he spoke further of our responsibility "to behave as though limits to our ability do not exist."

---

31 Kamp, Jurriaan. "The Revenge of the Spirit," Theoptimist.com, Jan/Feb, 2013.

13:
INNER CHILD HEALING
WORK

*The growing child's mind, including its sense of self,
is plastic; it will tend to take on whatever messages
are given to it by the outside world. It doesn't know
any better.*

~Marcus T. Anthony

The Evolution of Soul Lightening Inner Child Healing

The inner child is that most pure creative source within us, offering an inexhaustible stream of inventiveness. The child arrives in life with the vibration of an immortal soul that has history, but it is still unconditioned in this life. The newborn knows no limitation of imagination, no yes and no of propriety, no too small, too large, too outlandish, too loud, too quiet, too colorful, too unusual, too bad! It is our inner child who cooks up the artist's shapes and colors, the writer's inspirations, the architect's visions, the mother's inventions for her children. The free, magical child carries a clear soul vibration, that knows who she is and why she's here, before conditioning.

I have worked for many years to help clients and students regain their spiritual birthright by freeing their inner child from the limitations placed on it by the conditioning of family, ancestry and culture. Inner child healing is one of the most powerful methods available for bringing about present change. As I contemplate the present world situation I am reminded of the Dalai Lama's words that I quoted at the beginning of this book:

> Although attempting to bring about world peace through the internal transformation of individuals is difficult, it is the only way.

I am convinced now that true transformation, personal and global, starts here, with healing the wounded child within each of us. Further, that work has shown me that it is possible and necessary to heal inner children on a broader scale, beyond personal therapy. In this chapter I describe a method of healing the inner child that has proved successful in private practice and with groups for twenty years.

During the first five years of our lives many directives and patterns are laid into our brains, nervous systems and body tissues. Once set in, these patterns guide or even control our thinking, our emotions and our behaviors for most of our lives unless or until we consciously heal and change them. Freud, and later followers in twentieth century psychoanalysis, taught that we are unconscious victims of the past, particularly of our early childhood experiences, until we are able to access those unconscious memories and change their impact on our present lives.

Early in my private practice I encountered many traumas of my clients' inner children. Those traumas were very real and they created obstacles in the adults' lives. As one student said, "I'm a child walking around in an adult body." In fact, very often the needs and patterns of the person's inner child were running her adult life in ways that were anything but healthy or productive. Sometimes inner child's wounds and needs were so great that the adult found herself juggling persistent demands from the inner child while attempting to fulfill adult responsibilities, which frankly caused a great deal of distress in her life. Typically the adult child felt like a victim of her past.

I have listened to horror stories of childhood neglect, abandonment and outright physical and sexual abuse that adults were still carrying around with them. Whenever a client told me such a story, he or she would feel acknowledged and would receive some comfort just from having another person hear him, as in confession or sharing intimately with a friend.

But it became clear that just verbally telling the childhood story, or dwelling on it unnecessarily, could actually reinforce adult suffering. Telling the story often evokes the same feelings, the same nervous system reactions that the original experience caused. Sometimes we call this re-traumatization. Also, the story seldom gets to the mechanism that caused adult suffering, and it doesn't change the dysfunctional adult behavior.

I studied widely, beyond my Ph.D. in psychology, to learn what other psychologists or teachers know about childhood conditioning. I learned that a great deal was intellectually known about how early conditioning influenced adult behavior. The topic had been analyzed in hundreds of ways. But I found little about how to complete these experiences and actually heal them. I found that the principal method for dealing with that early conditioning was still through mental analysis and the "talking cure," as Freud had originally designed it. But even during the time I was first studying childhood conditioning, it was becoming increasingly clear to me, and many others, that talking about it alone wouldn't bring freedom from its shackles.

Contemporary therapies have demonstrated that changing childhood imprints requires emotional work and often direct body work. Wilhelm Reich's early work on body armor (physical defenses against threats) eventually led to *Bioenergetics*, by Alexander

Lowen, who said, "No words are so clear as the language of body expression," and on to John Pierrakos' *Core Energetics*, and so forth, until today there are many body- and energy-oriented therapies that often address early childhood traumas. Within the last thirty years many body- and energy-oriented methods have evolved that go beyond mental analysis to heal childhood.

No matter what the type of childhood trauma a person might have endured, the negative impact is deep and lasting. I developed whole-being methods with Process Acupressure to uncover trauma, bring it to present consciousness and then correct or reprogram the false or obstructive patterns it embodied. These methods were applied with great success whenever a childhood trauma surfaced naturally within the course of a Process Acupressure session. We are not guided by any particular system or required outcome. As with our usual approach in Process Acupressure we simply healed whatever arose organically from the client's body process. As past traumas were healed a person was freer to express his or her true nature. Adults could be released more into their full potential in the present. In addition, valuable teachings and skills emerged from the traumas that could shed light on soul purpose. Consciousness was liberated and transformed into wisdom, love and soul power. Many of my clients made profound progress toward their authentic selves as they were freed from their inner child's suffering. Through this healing of the inner child, one could become whole.

One of our recipients wrote, "I have healed a very wounded inner child and have found a divine magical child within. I am now allowing a process of integration where I can reclaim valuable aspects of myself that I had denied, and yet let go of those traits and aspects of me that simply hinder my wellbeing and keep me small. I have had fun transforming burdens into gifts."

When I first taught Process Acupressure to therapists in the early 1980s I soon encountered the same kind of childhood traumas I had been dealing with in private practice. It became clear that developmental hurdles from childhood were the greatest obstacle to student learning, and to one's ability to claim his own awareness and power. The need for inner child work screamed out at me in every class.

It wasn't enough to explain to a student that his current problem probably originated in childhood, or to advise him to seek counseling. Such intellectual observations didn't do anything to alleviate the symptoms the childhood traumas caused. Conventional research, as in reading books, listening to childhood development lectures or searching the internet typically did not accomplish healing either.

Certainly there are many good psychotherapists who are doing very helpful work with childhood trauma. For example, a friend told me that he had several therapists over the years who helped him uncover childhood trauma, helped him see how it influenced his present behavior and feelings, and then helped him get unhooked from those traumas so that he could see the world and himself very differently, and without the burdens of the early conditioning. This is not to say that he did this exclusively through talk therapy, since he also worked with practitioners of body and energy systems.

If the person's current condition was disabling enough I sometimes recommended psychotherapy. Yet I was amazed when clients who had already done years of psychotherapy came to me with blatant unhealed childhood wounds. I learned that traumas had been talked about, and analyzed, but not often healed. In fact, I found that repeated verbal explanations and examinations of childhood wounds or problems only gave them more power and reinforcement in the psyche, leaving a "wounding" voice, rather than a "healing" one. Now, after observing these phenomena for more than thirty years, I have a better understanding of the difference between talking about something and healing it.

As I listened to many adult children bemoan their fates because of unfortunate childhoods, it became clear that inner child healing and recovery needed a well thought-out program, focused on healing the whole person, one that would uncover indelible hurts or teachings, reveal the mechanisms of their long-term imprinting and then heal them and thus change their impact on the person so he could fulfill his life in adulthood.

I began to develop a method with the tools I already used in private practice that could be applied in seminar or group trainings. Hands-on acupressure promoted energetic balance, a sense of safety and relaxation. From that state of relaxation the person's unconscious became more accessible. It was easier for a person to allow whatever arose during the normal course of the acupressure session or class practice. Altered states of consciousness, aided by deep states of relaxation, provided the opening and ease for traumas to reveal themselves, and also for reprogramming the mind and nervous system. The effect of this state is similar to hypnotherapy, which is one of the most effective in changing events and behavior. But the altered state of consciousness is brought about here with the ongoing hands-on support of acupressure.

Soul Lightening's present four-day Inner Child Healing class was the result of this study and experience. Over a ten-year period our methods were perfected with private clients and students. In our Inner Child Healing class hundreds of students have learned how to heal childhood experiences or teachings that had obstructed their development. They now have the skills to heal themselves and also help others. And their accumulated experience is why I feel confident in presenting our methods here for your reflection. It's clear that you can't get the same effects from a book that you can from sessions that include actual hands-on acupressure, but you can certainly consider the concepts. Maybe you will even want to try our Inner Child Healing class sometime.

In our class and private practices students and clients were able to move beyond merely retelling their stories of crippling early childhood experiences. Instead of getting caught up in repeating their stories endlessly, they were able to greatly reduce or completely free themselves from the influences of those experiences on their present lives. They learned that when the adult self is liberated from the emotional suffering of the wounded child it can move forward into the present without the burden of a crying inner child. And it was demonstrated time and again in class that any given trauma could be healed and reprogrammed in such a way that the painful experience could actually result in the growth of spiritual strength.

I heard from a number of our Inner Child Healing students that the class had resolved significant problems and that their lives had changed in other ways since the class. Further, they now had the tools to heal their inner children by themselves. One student said,

> I reflected on the work I've done and realized most of it failed for lack of either feeling the pain or more often for not expressing the emotions.... Time after time we brought up what was stored in the body but with no processing.... For me this simply became a form of reenactment and left me worse off than when I started.

Another student, Laurie Cahoon, who is an accomplished acupuncture healer and Process Acupressure teacher, kept careful notes of her inner child healing journey, which she willingly shared for this book. Her account gives a grounded report of our work:

An Inner Child Healing Journey

> Through my work with Process Acupressure—in classes, receiving sessions, working with a mentor and working on myself alone—I have become intimately aware of my wounded inner child. She primarily shows up through my emotions, but she also shows up in relationships and in groups. What I have learned is that whenever I am feeling strong disappointment, self-pity or the combination of confusion and nervousness (disproportionate to the situation

at hand or difficult to resolve), I am alerted to the likelihood that my inner child has been triggered.

I have done lots of healing with my dear inner child around the original emotions and relationship dynamics where she was so wounded in the family of origin. She is my dear friend now and I am committed to loving her, being aware of her, protecting and supporting her with the aware adult and loving parent aspects of myself.

I am aware of four distinct aspects of my inner child:

- There is the hurt, vulnerable, fearful child (deflated).
- The adapted child: Early on, I learned to compensate, adapt to my environment and protect her by being reactive with anger and a sense of bravado (inflated).
- Sometimes she is easy going, happy, spiritually connected and naïve (Pleasurable Self).
- The fourth aspect of my inner child reflects my current relationship with her as a work in progress. It includes awareness of the patterns of the other three aspects.

Today, my inner child/vulnerable self can be triggered and with all the awareness I have, I can connect with her, know what she's feeling and what she needs. I can provide her with the resources of my aware adult and loving parent selves, as well as my soul's perspective on her life journey.

From this place I am in healthy relationship with her, teaching her to self sooth, progress her skills and awareness, remember and use her strengths and be in healthy relationships with others. A dear friend calls this part "Sensitive Strong."

Developing this level of awareness and relationship with my inner child has dramatically improved my life. She is a guiding force for my life and an integral aspect of my whole being.

Laurie learned the skills for inner child healing in our four-day class as a serious student. Then she practiced and developed them with an excellent mentor. By further working on herself alone she kept reinforcing the inner child's talents, strength and lovability. Now she is an empowered woman on all levels. The inner child supports that empowerment

Soul Lightening has many such accounts but I truly appreciate Laurie's generosity in sharing hers. I think it will help you get a true sense of what is required: a willing inner child, a loving and caring aware adult who has patience and interest in helping the inner child become empowered.

This chapter briefly describes the principles and methods we use to accomplish inner child healing in body, mind, emotions and soul. Although a much more detailed description and practice is given in our four-day class, the skills reported here can assist your understanding.

The Methods for Healing

Following are the methods we now use to heal inner children. They can be applied in every instance when you find a current problem that tracks back to the child. Only skill and commitment are required. I'm not talking about the skills of a college degree in psychology or an M.D. in psychiatry, but the skills and basic understandings and methods that you can learn from the concepts of this book.

For healing to be effective and complete, it needs to:

- heal and reprogram the original childhood trauma that triggered the present problem or pattern;
- teach the adult skills that can help him heal and reprogram childhood traumas as they arise in present life;
- in present time, help to sort out and correct the problem that triggered the inner child's pain in the first place;
- last long after therapy is over.

Commit to Your Own Healing, Even If It Is Challenging

Believe it or not, many people feel, deep down, that they don't deserve to heal from suffering. In fact, in some cases suffering serves an important function in their lives. Whether from a feeling of unworthiness, guilt or dysfunctional beliefs, they may think they are saddled with their afflictions for life. Author, psychologist and practitioner Gay Hendricks used to ask clients to examine the "payoff" or "secondary gain" from their symptom or painful memory. For example, some people derive a lot of comforting attention for their symptoms, or their payoffs for their suffering are that it gives them reasons to avoid taking responsibility. Others use their painful childhood experiences as justification for destructive patterns in their lives. One of the most common, of course, is the alcoholic who blames his behavior on his terrible childhood.

Often I find it helpful for a person to reflect about his own situation. I might suggest that he ask himself, "Do I believe I deserve healing now?" If he answers that he doesn't deserve it, I point out that he can commit himself to healing anyway by saying, "I am willing to heal. I am willing to move through edgy and unknown territory in order to heal." This commitment alone will initiate a healing process that will clear up a sense of unworthiness over time. For example, one could say a commitment aloud to himself or to a close friend, such as, "I am now willing to heal the childhood wound that triggers this condition, as easily and smoothly as possible and in the right time."

Create a Safe Space to Be with Your Own Process

At the outset of healing it is essential to assure complete safety for the inner child. Usually children were hurt in an unsafe or hidden-away place, with a person who couldn't be trusted or an environment that was threatening. A safe space includes both the physical and the social environment around the person to be healed. That space can be an actual physical structure, like a meditation or healing room, or it can be a healing sanctuary that you create in your own mind. People often seek out a healer or perhaps a workshop in order to find this safe space. But you can consciously create this safe space in your own mind or by literally establishing a physical space somewhere in your life.

Healing also requires concentrated attention. Distractions in the environment prevent such attention. So consciously and deliberately arrange a time and space where you can do this work without being interrupted, giving yourself everything you need to focus on your own process.

In her book, *Repetition: Past Lives, Life and Rebirth*[32], Doris Eliana Cohen recommends a powerful tool that I find most useful. She teaches her clients to create an imaginary magical healing place in nature that is exactly right for them. Even if you have a fear of being alone, particularly in a remote nature place, because you were abused in such a place, assure your inner child that you have created this safe place to be; you are with her now and will protect her. If you find yourself resisting, that could have been the case. Experiment with creating places of safety, perhaps surrounded by people you know you can trust. Cohen instructs her

---

32 Cohen, Doris Eliana. 2008. *Repetition: Past Lives, Life and Rebirth*. Carlsbad, California., Hay House.

clients to place all the things they would like into that space—the right friends or comforters (like a loving grandmother), spirit guides if they have them, loved animals, vegetation, colors, shapes and especially smells, which get the attention of the emotional brain immediately.

I now recommend this method for individual use anytime painful childhood feelings recur. After you have established this safe space in your life, either in a physical space or one in your mind, you will find that it becomes an inner sanctuary that you can access at any time and in any situation regardless of distractions.

Put everything you need or want into this space. It is a place reserved only for your adult self and your inner child; assure the child that no one can enter it without your invitation and full permission. Your child may come here any time. It will become your sanctuary for healing. Explain to your inner child that this is a place of magic where she can play or do anything she wants. If you relate to angels, guides or spiritual teachers you may wish to ask them to join you here.

Honor yourself enough to provide these conditions for your inner child process. It could be one of the most important projects you will ever undertake. And if, at any time, a particular trauma seems too frightening or overwhelming, by all means seek a counselor or psychologist who can shepherd you through the difficult experience.

Accept from the beginning that effective and complete inner child healing requires working with your whole self—body, mind, emotions and soul. You will be exploring your past with a fine-tooth comb when a present problem or pattern arises. By "fine tooth comb" I mean that you, as adult, will pay attention to all of the child's actual experience in body, emotions, pictures and sounds she was, or is having during a painful episode. You will probably feel the painful feelings, see the images, hear the sounds around the child again. Rather than denying or repressing the experience, claim a whole-being healing that results in completion and healing of the trauma. This experience is a direct replay of the actual happening, NOT a mere retelling of it, which is already once removed from the visceral reality.

Although this replay is usually an edgy, even painful process as you travel through it again, it only goes on for just a few seconds or minutes, until the adult consciousness fully realizes what the child experienced, and at last empathizes with him, or comes to his rescue. Unlike repeated *tellings* of a trauma, there is completion, resolution and an end to the powerful influences that episode once held over you. Full healing can happen within this process. Then, finally, the experience falls into past memory rather than being a hot spot that triggers the same pain again and again. That painful experience of the past no longer dictates your thoughts, feelings, behavior or how you respond to the present. Believe me, I can assure you that the outcome on the other side of this experience is expansive and exhilarating; it bears the fruit of health and freedom.

The Difference between *Re-Experiencing* and *Talking about* a Trauma

Talking about and analyzing a trauma usually just reinforces the pain. I have watched this many times with great frustration. This is called re-traumatization or re-enactment in psychology. Recounting the event in words simply reinforces and amplifies the nervous system's imprint of the original trauma. As Byron Katie says, "As if the past isn't horrible enough we want to resurrect it. We talk about it and talk about it and that's as far as the human race has ever gone."

I learned firsthand from a brilliant client that remembering and describing trauma keeps it in the brain (or "in the head" as body workers say), where it is neurologically reinforced with each telling. Here's how it happened.

The Story of S.

When S. came to see me as a client she had been in psychoanalysis for many years, seeing her analyst several times a week. From this training she was incredibly facile at describing everything about her childhood, her family of origin and its relationship dynamics, complete with the subtlest details. She could bring a laser focus to almost any social situation and analyze everyone's behavior within minutes. Not a phrase of dialogue missed her hearing.

S. came to me because she was quite debilitated with chronic fatigue syndrome. As we began to work, other problems came up. Although she was a good artist she kept putting off painting. She had explored several careers but at the last minute they didn't suit her. She wanted a stable relationship badly but kept getting involved with men who were either unavailable or not truly interested in her. When we started our work she was quite depressed about all these conditions.

In our second session S. went back to an early event in her childhood that, on the surface, didn't seem all that severe to the analytical adult, but to the child's consciousness it was deeply painful. She cried in the session. She re-experienced the child's sense of betrayal. For a short time she was lost in the child's emotion of loss and hopelessness.

I urged S. to rescue the child from that painful scene and take her to a safe place. I told her to hold the child and reassure her that she was safe. Once the child was secure within the field of our support, we could proceed with a full healing of the event. I coached S. to comfort the child, to stroke her head and speak to her in gentle tones.

As the child calmed and accepted attention and love we could help her understand the event from another perspective. S. told her that she had done nothing wrong and there was nothing wrong with her. We finished the healing by reprogramming the event in the child's mind so that she ended up with a truthful, updated and positive understanding of it.

At the end of the session S. was in a state of awe. The healing experience had been profound but she was also stunned by the implications of it in her present life. She looked at me in wonderment. She said, "That was a piece I was never able to get to in analysis. I kept searching and searching for the reason I sabotage myself, but the psychiatrist and I could never find it. Now, in this one session we have just uncovered it. I'm blown away. And now I understand!"

This new understanding went beyond thinking and analysis. It included experience and awareness, in body, emotions and mind. The adult self now knew exactly how it had been for the child. Whole-being awareness had brought about a moment of healing for that child which freed S. from some of the limiting behavior in her present life. That whole-being experience, which included supportive, tender feelings and body safety, now filled out intellectual understanding.

True healing and transformation of a trauma happen when the energetic and emotional charges embedded in the body and nervous system are released and expressed. In our work, energetic and emotional charges are accessed and released through hands-on acupressure during the session. These releases automatically bring about whole-being understanding within the adult mind. Such healing cannot be accomplished through the thinking mind; I have observed this time and again with over-therapized people.

The Stages of Inner Child Healing

In the Inner Child Healing class we guide students through the following major stages of healing. Each one includes many smaller stages of learning. We teach them to do the following:

1) Make contact with your benevolent adult or *good parent* consciousness. Make contact with your inner child. Then clearly note the difference between those two consciousnesses, as Laurie did in her account. NOTE: Most of us can contact a

benevolent adult within us, one who is aware, caring, kind and loving, especially to children. However, if you can't find that part, you will need to develop it to be effective with inner child healing. In our class, of course, we can coach and lead each other to find that part.

2) Establish a relationship between the inner child and a benevolent adult or good parent.

3) Have the benevolent adult adopt the inner child and bring him or her to a safe, protected place

4) Bring the benevolent adult consciousness and the inner child's consciousness of a trauma together to *a healing moment in present time* to repair and reprogram the effects of the trauma.

5) Reconnect with the soul and its spiritual resources.

The Five Stages in Detail

Within these five stages we teach explicit action steps that will take students all the way from the pain and chaos of trauma to the freedom and strength of their authentic selves. This process includes unraveling and expressing a specific hurt, connecting it with present difficulties and finally reprogramming it for a positive outcome.

In the following you will find a more complete explanation of how the five stages work.

Stage 1: Make Contact with the Benevolent Adult

This involves making contact with your benevolent adult or good parent consciousness, clearly noting the difference between the perceptions of that benevolent adult and the perceptions or experiences of an inner child.

In Soul Lightening work we teach students how to differentiate between adult and child perceptions, that is, to clearly note that our inner child's early fears are different from our adult fears in the present. We instruct students to notice when the adult fear is unduly influenced by a persistent fear associated with childhood. This helps the adult recognize when an inner child consciousness is the dominant perspective, as distinct from the adult consciousness. For example, when a friend is twenty minutes for a date we've previously made with them, we might suddenly feel hurt and even frightened out of proportion to present circumstances. We might then look at the possibility that childhood memories of abandonment are being triggered and let go of those fears, instead differentiating these feelings from our adult realization that our friend is chronically late.

Learning to differentiate in this way also reveals to us when our inner child is trying to run adult business. The adult will learn how to become a supporter, advocate and benevolent parent to the distressed child, a crucial skill for inner child healing. The adult learns how to do the rescuing, healing and reprogramming required to free the child. As in the above example of our tardy friend, once you recognized that your feelings in the present were triggering old childhood wounds, you'd be able to soothe those feelings (and your inner child) on your own. Without this ability, you might overreact and attack your friend for being uncaring, thoughtless and unloving.

Stage 2: Establish a Relationship between Benevolent Adult and Inner Child

This first step in establishing a relationship with the inner child can be challenging. For example, when I asked one student to relate to her inner child, she said, "No! I hate her."

This is not an uncommon response. In another case when I asked a man to speak with the child, it was the child who came back to him with, "I don't want to talk with you. I don't trust you." This man had denied and misused his inner child's talents—creativity, sensitivity and feeling. In therapy, he had talked about and made promises to his inner child that he hadn't kept. The child was afraid to trust him, and rightly so.

Many adults have become alienated from their inner children. All kinds of conditions and reasons have caused a wall between them: fear of exposure, or re-contacting the pain; guilt about perceived wrongdoing; feelings of unworthiness; on and on. Also, the inner child might be refusing to respond because she or he had been seriously abused or neglected by an untrustworthy parent in her actual childhood.

So the benevolent adult needs to counter such experiences with a loving, kind and accepting interest in the child. It is very important for the adult to locate the kind, loving part of him- or herself that can accept and care for the vulnerable child.

We encourage adult students to make loving contact with the inner child. We ask them to get to know those long-ago children again by talking with them, telling stories, playing games. I remember one student who reported that as soon as she made contact with her inner child, that child demanded, "I want an ice cream cone!" I was so proud of that adult when she took her inner child to an ice cream parlor right after class.

Gradually a sharing relationship between adult and child can be built through repeated loving attention to the child's feelings and needs. Then hopefully they can find familiarity and trust between them through sharing positive experiences. This process can take one afternoon, several months or even years, but whatever effort it takes is greatly rewarded when adult and inner child come together in a mutually nourishing relationship. A child is not just hurt and vulnerable; she is also a genius creator, spontaneous and lots of fun.

A Real Life Illustration of the Above Two Stages

Derek was an attractive, intelligent, top-level executive who attended a Process Acupressure class because he was depressed. Derek's professional achievements would fill pages but they weren't bringing him the inner satisfaction he craved. Despite great ego and financial success in his field he felt unfulfilled. He said he found no joy or creativity in all that he had achieved and was considering early retirement. He felt empty inside. He said he couldn't find his heart. He was looking for the meaning and enthusiasm in life that had eluded him for a long time. He hoped that the class would reveal a way forward.

In a strong Process Acupressure session within the group, Derek started to cry softly. I asked him what he was feeling.

"Sad," he said, and then added, "but it isn't really me crying; it's my ten-year old inner child who was cruelly teased incessantly by my classmates."

I asked Derek to stay with that sad feeling and find out more about what was happening. He said he knew about this scene; he had visited it before with his therapist and it always made him very sad.

I asked him to speak directly with this sad child whose feelings he was experiencing, and find out exactly how it was for him. He said that he couldn't. He was somehow removed from that child. He had tried before to speak with him, assisted by his therapist, but there was always a distance between them.

I didn't say anything for a while, but simply remained in that quiet space of hurt with Derek, while my hands proceeded with acupressure on his body.

Finally I asked him if he could reach out and take the child's hand. He reached one hand forward and clasped the child's hand. Then he cried more. I asked him if he could hold the child close to his heart. He reached both arms out to bring the child to his heart, and then he started sobbing. He continued to sob for a while as he held the child close to his body.

This went on for a while. At first there was only pain, but gradually Derek's body softened. The crying subsided. He patted his heart gently, to comfort the child's heart.

I asked Derek to tell the child that he was aware of how much that teasing had hurt and that he was sorry, but now he was here and that he would be here for the child from now on.

Derek was quiet for some time as he had an inner dialogue with the child.

Finally he said, "That's the first time I've ever been able to actually acknowledge and accept my inner child. Before I have felt his feelings but I was embarrassed by them. I just wanted them to go away; I wanted to avoid his pain. I never actually realized just how it was for him and how much he needed my understanding and help. It feels so good to finally be able to hold him and comfort him."

After this session Derek was exhilarated about making meaningful contact with his inner child. At last he was drawing close to that child, with compassion and understanding. It turns out he had been working to contact his child in therapy for more than a year. Intellectually he understood that healing his inner child was directly linked to finding the joy, creativity and deeper meaning in life he wanted. But intellectual understanding hadn't resulted in the joy he sought. He had been so closed off emotionally from that child in his long years of pursuing professional achievement that a wall had grown up between his adult consciousness and his child consciousness. He and his therapist both felt that after this breakthrough he would move very fast. He would be able to heal the old hurts from childhood that were blocking his discovery of what was really important in his life.

Stage 3: Have the Benevolent Adult Adopt the Inner Child

After a relationship has been established in our Inner Child Healing class, we ask students to adopt their inner children in the present and bring them to a protected place or home that can be a safe haven for comfort and healing instead of letting them return to the original scene of pain.

We teach students how to become their own inner parents, with appropriate, positive parenting skills. Within the class structure a trusted participant can act out the role of loving, trustworthy parent. But this only works after an actual trust has been established between them.

Ideally every adult should develop an inner mother and father to re-parent and reeducate the inner child. Most of us have fantasies about our ideal parents—how we wished our childhood could have been. Or perhaps there were actual parents we observed during our childhood who seemed to us to be ideal. A person in the workshop might start with those ideals and begin dialoguing with her inner child to find out what the child wants or needs in order to feel supported and loved.

This learning process between adult parent and child will evolve as a person continues to work with and support the child. Sometimes an adult has trouble because he truly doesn't know how to "self-soothe" or provide a safe home. In this case the exercise is of optimum benefit to both his inner child and the adult. As adults, we can literally educate ourselves to be the parents our own inner child needed.

Clients have often said to me that they don't know how to re-parent their inner child. How would they know how to do something they haven't experienced? As one person said, "How should I know how to be a good parent? I only know how to do what my parents did and said." That, of course, is true in a great many cases. As so many parents learn after the birth of their first child, parenting doesn't necessarily come naturally. Often we learn to be good parents through our love for these beings who have come to be in our care. A good part of parenting in the modern world has to be learned, through reading books, observing good parents in action, through guidance from a more experienced family member or even by attending parenting classes. Sometimes negative experiences of childhood have driven dedicated parents to learn how to be good parents to their own children. As one student observed, "The love I felt the first time I saw my newborn son was beyond anything

I'd previously experienced or imagined. I had few if any parenting skills when he was born. I think it was my own delight with his delight, and my pain with his pain, that guided me to claim things I didn't even know I knew."

Eventually the caring, supportive, encouraging and disciplining qualities of a good parent will be carried within each of us. When inner parents are dependable, trustworthy and loving, the inner child will never need to feel deprived of those nurturing qualities again.

This relationship-building stage will go through many phases. Hopefully the inner child will continue to occupy more and more of his true self with the nurturing support of good inner parents. And the parents will continue to mature as they encounter the child's suffering, episode by episode.

We teach various good parenting skills in the Inner Child Healing class. Particularly, we teach good parent messages, to counteract many of the negative ones children received. Some of these follow, adapted from recommendations by Jack Rosenberg, Ph.D.[33] Repeat these, or others you create according to the circumstances, frequently to your child as you are re-parenting.

Good mother messages:
- You are a wanted child. I love you.
- I will take care of you. You can trust me.
- I will do my very best to protect you and keep you safe. I love you for who you are and not what you do.
- You are special to me.
- You don't have to be afraid anymore. Your feelings are important.
- It's good for you to have your needs met and it's good to ask for what you need.
- Sometimes I'll say no, and that's because I love you.

---

33 Rosenberg, Jack Lee, Marjorie L. Rand, and Diane Asay. 1989. *Body, Self and Soul: Sustaining Integration*, Atlanta, Humanics Limited.

- I give you permission to be different from me.
- My love will make you well.
- I see you and I hear you.
- You can trust your inner voice.
- I will be there for you even when you die.

Good father messages:
- I love you.
- Your life is very important.
- I will do my very best to protect you and keep you safe. I will be strong for you.
- I have confidence in you. I'm sure you can do it. I will set limits for you and enforce them.
- If you fall down, I will pick you up.
- You are special to me.
- I am proud of you.

Within the container of a mature and healthy child-adult relationship we have the foundation of safety, trust and communication in which to proceed with the serious tasks of uncovering and healing a discovered trauma.

Stage 4: Contact the Relevant Trauma

Contact the relevant trauma within the inner child's mind so that you can learn exactly how it was for him or her. Bring the trauma to consciousness in the present moment so that it can be re-experienced with the whole being, including body sensations, emotional feelings and thought processes. This re-experiencing is very different from re-telling the event (re-traumatization), as I mentioned earlier. Here the therapist has hands on the body with acupressure as the re-experiencing is happening. Loving touch and energetic rebalancing are providing a comforting, visceral medium that the inner child can feel is safe and healing.

Of course, if and when the field of the trauma is too painful or overwhelming, the therapist or inner parent must be able to rescue the child from that environment and bring him or her to a place of safety. We teach a direct rescuing process in class.

Now it's time to bring the child's consciousness of the trauma and the adult loving consciousness together to seize a healing moment in present time.

In this step we maintain a two-track consciousness, that is, we make a point of simultaneously staying aware of the inner child and the loving benevolent adult. While a therapist, or perhaps a classmate in a seminar, could normally take on the role of the loving adult, once we gain confidence in our ability to use this method, we can do the healing alone.

As loving adults in a healing session, we urge the child to contact, move through, and then report the trauma, step by step, as we hold her in unconditional love, with our hands on the body and love in our hearts.

In this way we come to understand the dynamics of the original trauma. The child gets to re-experience and express the full effects of the trauma while being protected and supported by the benevolent adult. The protection and support allow no room or opportunity for re-traumatization; this also keeps the person's awareness in the present moment, which is the only place where true healing and change can be accomplished.

Now we are ready to repair and reprogram the effects of the trauma. By moving through the trauma with the child, stage by stage, a loving benevolent adult consciousness can recognize the components that need to be reprogrammed and updated. Within the container of a trustworthy adult-child relationship, the adult might begin dialoging with the child. This could involve the mother telling the inner child that she loves her and that she recognizes that she is a strong and beautiful person, able to make her own choices. The now-adult parent might even encourage the child to tell the original parent what she might have said and done to provide the love and support that child needed early in her life. The adult can offer comfort and healing words in the healing moment, such as:

- I love you and I will protect you now.
- It wasn't your fault.
- You are a beautiful and strong person.
- That person who criticizes you has her own problems; they are not your responsibility.

Take as long as needed to reframe or update each original negative experience in the present moment of healing. Continue until the child's consciousness has reached a state of relief, self-affirmation, empowerment and understanding. New statements or conclusions about the experience, gleaned from the adult's or therapist's mature comprehension, will now replace the original understanding and conclusions. Of course, since the therapist has hands on the body all during this experience, he or she can feel softening and relaxation in the body as the inner child lets go into a non-threatening, new understanding of the traumatic episode.

If a trauma has been severe and long lasting, this process may require more than one session. If it does, keep building self-affirmation and power in the child with each session.

These methods have helped clients and students heal their inner children so that they are free from repeated suffering over past traumas. They also refrained from retelling their stories, because they no longer see themselves as victims of them but as triumphant spiritual warriors.

Stage 5: Reconnect with the Soul and Its Spiritual Resources

Some traumas cut so deep that they can actually compromise the very foundation of the personality and obscure a person's soul and spiritual resources. For example, when you ask your adult to rescue the child, or think of another solution, she might say, "This adult doesn't know how; the situation is beyond me. I don't have enough power [wisdom, resources, or other capacities]."

Such an experience can seem beyond our capacity to deal with it, either as victim or therapist. This is a time to call for spiritual help stronger than the adult ego. That help could be your own soul, which has more power and wisdom than the ego. Or it could be higher helpers from the spiritual dimension, such as angels, the Divine Mother, or Jesus. One of the Process Acupressure teachers asks angels to enter the situation to heal and correct what seems beyond the reach of humans. In Alcoholics Anonymous, members call on and gather strength from their Higher Power.

In her book *The Gift of Inner Healing*,[34] Ruth Carter Stapleton, one of the foremost proponents of Christian charismatic healing, described how she prayed for the Divine Mother to come into the scenes of trauma. She found that when the Divine Mother's presence was invoked a spiritual force pervaded the victim and usually all the other people involved. For example, the energy of spiritual healing would light up the entire scene, often with a golden glow. This higher love, healing and guidance would touch each person within the scene. Often the child would run into the Divine Mother's arms, where she could feel completely safe, cradled in that infinite love, protection and comfort of the Divine.

I have called upon Divine intervention many times with clients whose traumas were so grievous that their adult consciousness, and mine, could not find a way out.

For example, a client was reliving an early sexual abuse that involved a relative. Suddenly she was in a black sea of ancestral agony. She reported that generations of sexual abusers were trapped in a hell of suffering and remorse. They were crying out for help. The sight was horrendous and overwhelming to her. (In that moment I was reminded of Dante's *Inferno*.) As she witnessed this scene she

---

34 Stapleton, Ruth Carter. 1977. *The Gift of Inner Healing*. New York, Bantam Books.

started crying, almost hysterically. She said, "Aminah, I have to help them but I don't know how!"

Although I didn't know how to help them either, I knew for certain that she couldn't. She had a close spiritual connection to Jesus. I asked her to call on Him for help.

"Yes!" she cried out in relief. "Jesus is here." Immediately she calmed down. Her sorrow turned into awe as she reported, "Jesus says that he will guide them to the light, that it isn't my job. It was only my job to recognize their suffering and this element in my ancestry."

An experience that could have become debilitating actually turned into a showering of grace.

One of the greatest benefits of inner child healing is that it makes room for the soul to become active in ordinary life. When we pierce through layers of wounding and conditioning, back to the original miracle and grace of our beginning, we find all the wisdom we need to explain our predicaments and rectify them. The soul can tap into an eternal time line and universal laws. It knows truth from falsehood.

Without a foundation in spirit, healing can remain in endless mind loops of re-examination for meaning. But once soul contact is realized, healing moves more swiftly and easily to completion. Beyond healing, liberation into wholeness, freedom of being, and creative growth are then close at hand. Access to soul consciousness makes the difference between a mundane life and one fueled by original insight, creativity and personal joy.

Healing and Harvest: The Gold beneath the Tragedy

As in the previous example, sometimes tragic situations can transform into blessings that bring great realization, strength or purpose. Horrible experiences can call forth amazing inner resources. Suffering can force a person so deep that they push beyond fear, pain and rage to burst into the magnificent spiritual power that they actually have. Biographies of remarkable people are full of examples in which traumas or challenges forced them into inner resources they didn't know they had. You have probably had an experience of finding your deepest power and purpose in moments of severe threat.

For example, the great healer and teacher Jack Schwarz, reported that when he was being tortured by his Nazi captors he suddenly remembered, and prayed, as Jesus did: "Father, forgive them, they know not what they do."

In that moment his whole body was seized by a light and power that frightened his captors so much they backed off. Further, the intense illumination of those few seconds brought with it a healing power that stayed with Schwarz for the rest of his life. He healed many, and taught others, including medical doctors, how to use that power.

I have met similar reversals of bad experiences that turned to strengths. For example, a client uncovered early sexual abuse from several family members. These experiences were of course painful and wrong, but the child learned how to separate her consciousness from the body to escape pain and shame. Then she could travel in consciousness wherever she imagined. In psychological terms this is called "disassociation." At its most severe, this state results in a multiple personality disorder. But my client had learned how to use it for her own purposes. As an adult she taught anatomy students how to use a meditative state to travel to all the organs within their bodies.

Healing and Recovery are Different Phases

Successive healings lead to whole-being recovery. Healing and recovery are often used synonymously but there is a distinct difference. So far in this chapter, I have been addressing healing of an actual event, trauma or insult that requires working specifically with the particular moment in time when it occurred. That particular healing may occur in a moment, or evolve over time. After a complete healing the specific wound should no longer be an active sore in the psyche.

Beyond healing, recovery and liberation into wholeness, freedom of being and creative growth are then close at hand. Recovering from the long-term effects of a particular wound, or a damaged childhood, is a continuing growth process. For example, the alcoholic is not out of the woods when he finally renounces alcohol for good. Similarly, the adult who heals childhood wounds still needs to recover, and replace, his early coping strategies, defenses, false beliefs, missed development and behavior patterns that resulted from the wounds, with more self-affirming and empowering patterns. This process can take a lifetime, but it is an evolving process, not a cyclic one.

I was friends with a wonderful Tai Chi teacher and his wife who deliberately spent part of their time "recovering from childhood." That is, when a childhood hurt arose in the course of their every-day lives, they stopped and attended to it with loving kindness to the inner child. My friends were living their lives in this recovery process. How long would it take them? I wondered then. Now, after working with hundreds of inner children, I know time is not the relevant measurement for recovery, but rather the state of peace, happiness and function that an individual is able to come to.

Making Space for the Soul and Its Purpose

Each time a healing experience is taken to a soul level the spiritual channel is strengthened and more spiritual maturity and power are available. Soul wisdom is so powerful because it is connected to universal laws that are part of the infinite Divine plan.

Soul Guidance from Childhood Dreams—Dark and Light

As I explained in chapter 3 about the soul, important clues to soul destiny can come from a childhood dream. The concept was proposed by Carl Jung and pursued by Arny Mindell who progressed it and found it most illuminating for soul purpose and destiny. The idea is that many children have an indelible early dream that says something about their soul purpose or destiny. It is an insistent dream that is either indelible at the time, or is often repeated.

I first learned of the concept while I was studying Process Work with Arny in Zurich where we were doing intense inner work. There I tested this idea in my own history and discovered very fruitful material. I discovered that I had two childhood dreams, one a nightmare that I dreamed in the night and another light daydream that I often acted out with a little playmate.

A Childhood Nightmare

In chapter 3, I described my childhood nightmare in which my father's decomposing body rose out of his grave and reached out to me for help. I had that nightmare when I was about five years old. It is still as indelible as it was on that morning when I awoke from it. Then it was terrifying. I carried it around in my mind, like a monster in a locked closet, until I finally discovered its meaning. Now that dream is illuminating my soul purpose.

When I was in my fifties, studying in Zurich, and learning about the childhood dream, my own nightmare came to the forefront of my consciousness. With processing and inner work I began to understand the nightmare as a statement of life purpose, namely to recognize and help myself and others to rise out of the grave of unconsciousness, or mass brainwash. Long before I deciphered the dream I had engaged in a long process of education and self-examination to train myself in adulthood for this task.

Now, at the age of seventy-eight, the nightmare is just as intense as it was that morning so many years ago, and I see it as part of a process of awakening. I am now grateful for the whole scene that was once terrifying and horrible.

A Childhood Light Dream

There was also a light daydream during that same period. In the daydream I was wandering around everywhere, over mountains and valleys collecting luminous treasures that I imagined were precious jewels. Actually I collected tiny shards of colored glass that I took great pains to bury away in the ground, promising myself I would come back for them at some much later time. I can still see and feel myself on that sandy desert as I carefully gathered those glass pieces and dug their saving places. Now, at seventy-eight, I'm digging up those treasures of the unconditioned, soul-directed child when I know how to truly value them.

I have tested this childhood dream concept with many clients and students who have often found it a valuable key for discovering their life purpose.

As you evoke the soul and follow its counsel, the soul path becomes clearer. In time one can perceive, and act, from that source of wisdom and power within the Self.

Recovery of the Magical Divine Child

The original, natural child, before all the traumas and dramas of ordinary life covered him over, lived from the soul and in harmony with Source. That child was magical, "enveloped in Divine Grace," as Joseph Chilton Pearce[35] said. Often a healing moment can reopen a doorway into the freedom and wholeness where the natural child lived. The inner child of the adult can still access that soul place.

We have learned in Soul Lightening Acupressure that the wounded inner child can be healed. Inner strength and wisdom can replace tragedies. Each healing process refines consciousness skills so that one is able to complete a healing more easily and quickly. And each healing contributes to whole-being recovery.

---

35 Pearce, Joseph Chilton. 1992. *Magical Child.* Plume (Reissue).

Finally, one of the greatest rewards for all this loving effort with the inner child is the recovery of a full-blown creative self that is free and magical. Once again the natural child's freedom of direct discovery and the joy of originality and inventiveness are available.

So far we have focused on the wounded inner child. Appropriately, the approach was one of love, comfort and reprogramming. But once the inner child is liberated from the main burden of wounding, we can start uncovering, supporting and celebrating the awesome magical child who is still close to the soul.

That original, magical child is often obscured by age five, so we need to delve deeper, beneath the characteristics of the personality to find her. She needs recognition and encouragement for her own true nature, talents and creativity, which may be quite different from the cultural norm.

For example, from my inner magical child, who collected treasures and hid them away, I learned my own natural process of collecting inspiration, ideas or materials and then hiding them away for a while, to incubate, to be harvested later. This process is, of course, counter to the one that I learned in school and that is predominant in our culture, namely: Think it out, make goals, add action steps and then accomplish or achieve it as fast as possible! Now I remember this creative style of my own and use it in creative and daily tasks.

As the inner child is healed, and the magical child is reclaimed, the true nature and potential of the whole self are made accessible. The soul path becomes clearer.

Once freed, the original magical child needs challenges to live *up* to her potential. She may need to learn how to "put away childish things," and most specifically, all the hurts and disappointments. *Now* becomes much more important than the past. Now, instead of blocking growth, powerful challenges can help us pierce through our last defenses, shields and inadequacies, so long harbored, to harvest our own true treasures.

In time we can perceive and act from that source of wisdom and power within the Soul.

14:
ANCESTRAL HEALING AND EMPOWERMENT

*I am convinced that these glimpses into the lives of
our parents, grandparents, and even more distant
relatives, can help us better understand, and often
resolve, conflicts in our present lives.*

~Stanislav Grof, M.D.

Why We Need Ancestral Work

As we transit into a new age, we will need to shed and change patterns of the old world that no longer serve our survival. We live in bodies with ancient imprints imbedded in our physical tissues and DNA. The new science of *epigenetics* scientifically verifies what wise people have sensed for centuries. Ancestral imprints carry centuries of recorded history, including traumas, beliefs, cultures and religions.

Ancestors aren't dead or separate from us. They simply support or resist us from another dimension. Usually they offer love and wait for ours in return. Many of the ancestral imprints we carry in our bodies help us survive on planet earth. Others are holding up our chances of building a sustainable world. Most of them couldn't imagine the global problems we have now.

The accumulation of millions of years of planetary experience contains both life-saving information that helps us navigate our time here, and anti-life imprints that hurt us, individually and collectively. In his book about our ancient ancestors, *The Seven Daughters of Eve*, Brian Sykes says, "Our genes did not just appear when we were born. They have been carried to us by millions of individual lives over thousands of generations."[36]

Conditions or issues travel down through generations to influence us in this present life. When a condition inherited from an ancestor is positive (courage, dedication, talent, persistence, physical strength) it is a blessing or empowerment. But if the condition passed on to us is negative (depression, great fear, criminal behavior, hatred) it can be a very destructive influence. Fortunately, what we know now, through bodywork and neurofeedback, is that even these inherited conditions can be transformed consciously, from destructive influence to strength-giving.

In many indigenous cultures people revere or even worship their ancestors. They reach out to ancestors for blessings, guidance and strength. Ancestor reverence has demonstrated through the centuries how we are affected by those whose genes we inherited.

Many Native Americans cultures, for instance, felt close to ancestors who had gone on to another dimension. They communicated with ancestors regularly, asking for help or offering gratitude. They respected the ancestral burial service and respected their burial places as holy ground. In fact, invading Europeans experienced some of the most dangerous battles from the Indians over their

---

36 Sykes, Brian. 2001. *The Seven Daughters of Eve*, New York, W. W. Norton and Company, Inc.

invasion of holy burial sites. Even today some Native Americans believe their ancestors are dishonored and harmed when modern development disturbs holy burial grounds. Federal laws in the United States now demand that archaeological studies be made of any site where the earth will be disturbed. Fights to preserve ancestral burial grounds have now moved to the courtrooms and even boardrooms.

Our colleague, Debra Kaatz, author of *Chinese Characters of the Soul Lightening Acupressure Points*, has traveled to burial grounds and holy sites around the world, and learned of ancestral connections in several cultures. She wrote of the effects of burial sites:

> Great masters are sometimes buried in special ways so they maintain a direct link with the world when they pass away. In Turkey the great Sufi teachers and sheiks are buried in stone coffins that are placed in tombs near or within mosques. One mosque I visited had a very famous sheik buried. People would ask for help and advice from him. They would sit by his coffin in prayer. He always seemed to give people the help they asked for.

> At Lourdes the mother Mary is asked for healing and it is said she has performed many miracles throughout the centuries. In Russia centuries ago there were people who could communicate with the wisdom of the universe. Just before they died they placed themselves in *dolmens* or stone structures. There they would meditate and dissolve in the wisdom of the universe before they died. After they died a small opening would be made in the tomb and anyone could come and sit quietly in meditation and ask for what they needed. The spirit of the person remained to help people for centuries and centuries.

> In Tibet there are *stupas*, which are buildings where the spirit of great Buddhist teachers are buried.

> They are also filled with sacred texts and images. Often they are on high places so all the prayers can flow all over the world. These are beautiful places of pilgrimage and places where people come for advice and help in their lives. When we enter these spaces our minds become linked to the spacious mind of the great wisdom of the teachers, their teachings and the universe itself.[37]

Just as pilgrims to holy places seek wisdom, direction, healing and strength from those who came before, we also respectfully inquire, process and heal with our ancestors in Soul Lightening ancestral work. We learn how to process ancestral material we find in our own bodies. We contact our ancestors and communicate with them. We heal their broken places as we heal our own.

In this psychologically oriented time most of us have experienced or learned that many of our dysfunctional patterns or attitudes came from childhood. In our Inner Child Healing work we address, heal and update those patterns to serve our present adult needs. But when a pattern doesn't release through inner child work, we need to search deeper, into our very cells and bones. When I was in private practice I sometimes worked with clients whose symptoms or conditions didn't release with childhood healing. Ancestral healing was required to free them.

I learned that ancestral patterns release more readily and completely through direct work in the body where those imprints are stored. Intellectual recognition and emotional resonance are helpful but ancestral patterns are carried in body bones and tissues, sometimes even in the soul. Thus, I believe a whole-being approach is most effective.

For example, a woman who had many severe anxieties, which she had already worked with for years in ordinary psychotherapy, found out that these fears were actually ancestrally based. Her

---

37 Kaatz, Debra. Private paper to Aminah in 2010.

presenting complaint was an ache in her back, particularly around the kidney region. In Chinese medicine the kidneys are said to store ancestral energy. But apart from supporting her back directly in the session, I didn't allow my mind to dwell on that information. Instead, I followed her process.

As we worked with the back, she cried and described the hopelessness and fears she had grown up with and that were forever within her family—persecution of the Jews, fears of being seen, of not having a place to settle, and so forth. Through several sessions we processed her own abused childhood with her neurotic parents, who themselves were holocaust victims. Then we addressed the ancestral material passed down to her (still lodged in her body despite other therapy). We changed her scripts about her heritage, from themes of persecution, exclusion and punishment, to inclusion, protection, strong groundedness and creativity. Her body lightened. Eventually she came to a session in which completely new and current energy was flowing through her body. She said, "When the ancestral fears release there is room in my body for life now, and for creativity that originates within me."

Another similar case was sent to me by Leah Matalon, who is a master of ancestral work, in Soul Lightening as well as constellation work. Her report nicely describes some of the ways we work with ancestors in a session. Here is what she reported:

A Young Woman Reunites with Her Maternal Ancestors

A young woman I'll call Rachel, twenty-two years old, was referred by her therapist. She presented with a complex of symptoms, for which she is being treated: chronic fatigue syndrome, major digestive issues, constipation, interstitial cystitis, hormone imbalances, and hasn't menstruated since two years ago. She felt a lack of energy and feeling in her pelvis, first and second chakras.

Her mother had never spoken about her Jewish heritage, until one day she finally whispered to her daughter, "I'm Jewish." By that time, of course, the daughter already knew.

Rachel told me what she knew of her ancestral history: Her great-grandmother on her mother's side, her grandmother, and two sisters, were in concentration camps in Germany. Rachel's great-grandmother got cancer. Then, through some diplomatic exchange, Rachel's great grandmother, her grandmother, and sisters were released to travel to Switzerland. But as they crossed the border Rachel's great grandmother died. Rachel's grandmother was only twelve years old at this time and her sisters were ten and fourteen years old. They were abandoned by their father who had them sent to the U.S.A. to live with other people. Rachel didn't know any more of the story than that.

Rachel's intention for her session was to clear the negative energy of her Jewish heritage around herself and move forward to healing.

When we started the session Rachel went into a deep altered state of relaxation.

During the session we called for her mother and then her Grandmother. They held each other in reunion. Then we called her great grandmother, who had died on the train crossing the border into Switzerland. We reunited that grandmother with her daughter. Then granddaughter and great granddaughter were reunited. The four connected deeply.

It took Rachel's mother (who had resisted admitting her Jewish heritage) a long time to go to her ancestors and join with them, but finally she did. Then Rachel's mother cried.

The session ended with Rachel acknowledging all of those ancestors and their suffering, and her

connection to them. Rachel had connected with people, both living and dead, and after the session she
felt better. By the end of the Great Central Alignment
and chakra balancing there was energy flowing in
her body from the root to crown.

In a follow-up conversation Rachel said she was
feeling a gradual awakening in the pelvis and wants
to do more work.

In our Ancestral Healing and Empowerment workshop we gain
insights, revelations and visions about ancestors through the body.
And as we make discoveries through the body, we heal not only our
own bodies but, I believe, our ancestors' spirit bodies as well.

Through my spiritual practice I have engaged with my own ancestors for more than forty years. I have felt their influences, both
desirable and not so good. I assumed that my spiritual practice
would eventually free me, and them, from unfinished business, as
my spiritual teacher had promised. But I found that working directly with touch and steady inquiry into the body also resulted in
healing.

Some ancestors have already entered a Divine dimension where
they are much freer, more expanded and blissful than they were on
earth. They bless us from that dimension. For example, my beloved
sister Annie, who died almost forty years ago, visited me once when
I was contemplating ancestors while preparing for an Ancestral
class. She showed me the most wonderful, vast, truly heavenly
dimension where she was operating exactly from her own talent,
which was singing. She had always longed to sing in the Mormon
Tabernacle Choir, which had never been possible in her earth life.
But in heaven she was singing with a choir whose heavenly sound
was truly beyond verbal description. I could hear just enough of it
to feel momentarily transported into her dimension.

Annie's love for me, here on earth and in heaven, was and is so
huge that even my process partner, Laura, has felt it, even though
she never knew Annie. "Your sister Annie loves you so much," Laura

said. "She came to me and asked me to watch out for you." Annie has helped me several times when my spirit faltered. She shows me the love and beauty where she is now. It always lifts my soul.

But some ancestors have not yet been released from the burdens and "sins" of their earth life before. Some of them are still healing or being reeducated. Sometimes they entangle us in their unfinished business as they try to get help from us. Sometimes this is the "ghost" phenomenon, wherein sensitive people become aware of wispy human forms hovering around them.

Many of my own female ancestors were oppressed and disempowered by their second-place station in life. They were angry about it. Sometimes they came to literally mistrust and hate men. Anger, hatred, resentment and lack of forgiveness held them here, close to earth. They were still trapped by the magnetic pull of their mistakes, sins, shortcomings and unfinished business. I have felt their ire often in dealing with men in my own life. But I have experienced, through prayer, attunement and processing with them, that they were trying all the time to make amends for these sins related to us; they needed help and forgiveness from the living. Through my inner work they expanded their consciousness about men. They are learning from my experience with my husband and other "new" men of our age, that there is something extremely valuable about that other sex which they had come to hate. They are changing. They are no longer bitter, resentful and martyred. They see a vast new potential in our lives. We now work as responsible women together. And they are grateful, as I am.

Dr. Kenneth McAll, a psychiatrist in England, has based most of his practice on releasing people from ancestral conditions that impinge on the present life. His profound book, *Healing the Family Tree*,[38] describes many miraculous experiences with people who had serious physical or psychic symptoms that hadn't responded to either medical or psychological help. He first listens to their stories as a psychiatrist. If psychiatric interventions prove fruitless he

---

38 McAll, Kenneth. 2013. *Healing the Family Tree.*, London, Sheldon Press.

asks the client to draw a family tree. Dr. McAll and the client study the family tree together and look for disruptions or tragic events in history, such as miscarriages, murder, disinheritance, a loved one un-mourned, a soldier never returned from a war, a lovers' quarrel that had never mended, whatever the situation may be. Once the obstruction is located he engages a priest to join him and the client to perform a Eucharist ceremony for the ancestor, to release whatever unfinished business is held there. Then both the client and ancestor receive prayers for closure and blessing.

Dr. McAll reported many actual cases of cure from serious physical or mental disturbances.

From here, on earth, we can actually help to redeem our ancestors, and ourselves in the process, because healing and forgiveness travel through all dimensions. Now I have come to honor and thank my ancestors time and again for all they suffered and endured so that I now have life. And I have also become aware of their awe as they observe my colleagues, students and me working with them to heal history. We all realize now that we can gift each other in this way. I believe we are supporting cosmic evolution through ancestral work.

Principles We Use for Ancestral Work

In our Ancestral Healing class we create a loving, learning field that can serve both the ancestors and ourselves to explore, clear, update and reprogram outdated ways. Then we call upon our ancestors to join us in this new time when we are receiving new gifts that weren't even on this planet at the time our ancestors were here.

- When ancestors are respectfully invited, they are available for conversation with us *if* our soul consciousness is open enough to hear, see or feel them, and *if* they have not gone very far into another dimension, away from this earth.
- They can be asked directly for assistance, especially when our requests coincide with some talent or strength they had

in life. For example, I had a great grandfather who was quite psychic. I have occasionally asked him for help to refine my own psychic skill. Ancestors may also have wisdom that we haven't earned yet but sometimes they may gift us with some of that wisdom, if it serves the higher good. They have many gifts and blessings, such as strength, love, special talents and a perspective free from the buffeting of the earthly-life dramas and traumas that surround us. The spiritual ancestors—those devoted to God in their lifetime—also have very strong connections to spiritual dimensions. So, just as we might ask a saint to intercede on our behalf, we may ask a holy ancestor.

- Just as we have unfinished business in our lives, ancestors often have leftover unresolved issues they didn't clear up in life, such as anger, hatred, resentment and lack of forgiveness. These issues hold them here, close to earth. They are still trapped by the magnetic pull of their mistakes, sins and unfinished business. They are trying all the time to make amends for these "sins" related to us, but they need our co-operation. For example, when we are unwilling to forgive an ancestor, he or she cannot be freed to move on. Through love and forgiveness we can actually help to release them, and ourselves in the process.

- Ancestors expand in consciousness and potential every time we forgive, honor and love them.

- Ancestors are engaged, along with us, in the future of this world. "The sins of the fathers are visited upon them," through all these thousands of years. The earth field is crowded with sins from the past. I call it earth trash. My students and I have realized over the years that part of our life work here is to help clean up this trash. And we have also learned that we *can* help clear it by doing our own ancestral work.

Soul Lightening Ancestral Methods

As already explained, we do a large percentage of our work in an altered state, facilitated by the acupressure bodywork. Our clients are familiar with expanding into consciousness that encompasses other places and times. Thus, contacting an ancestor is not such a big reach. It's not unusual for an ancestor to appear during the course of a process that involves them. For example, a client is wrestling with an estranged mother who has died; then, either her mother shows up spontaneously, or the client can ask to speak with the mother.

Each of us has an ancestral field around us that extends beyond our personal aura. The ancestral field is a signature of our heritage. It carries energetic vibrations that resonate with ancestral vibrations far back in time. Ancestors can find us through that resonance.

The following case from a student of Soul Lightening work describes the effect of ancestral work on a severe back problem:

> In 1998, I received a Soul Lightening Acupressure session during which I witnessed a long line of paternal male ancestors plunging a knife right through my heart and on into my back. I took the knife and pulled it out of my back and heart.
>
> That session cleared the pain from my upper back that I'd had for twenty-nine years. I had been in a back brace for a year, received cortisone shots regularly, and was on narcotics for many years, as the pain was intense and would recur often. I could not hold my arms above my head for more than a minute, and at times could not lift more than ten pounds. Even with regular exercise, it would flare up on a regular basis and I would always feel tension in my upper back.

The upper back pain, behind my heart, was gone after that session and has never returned.

Whether we are contacting an ancestor in a Process Acupressure
session or in meditation or prayer, the process is simple and
straightforward. For example, a client might ask, "Mother, would
you be willing to speak with me about our estrangement?" Then
we remain very alert for any signal or response—this might come
in the form of a sound, a feeling, mental imagery, intuition, even
a smell or a taste. Not every ancestor will respond in words. For
example, when I ask my mother something, I can feel her love first,
then her answer comes in a block of sound vibration. Ester Hicks,
who channels Abraham, says she receives information in a similar
way; a huge chunk of information comes to her which she must then
interpret into words.

Debra Kaatz, our colleague in France whose writing I gave at the
beginning of this chapter, has suggested a beautiful way to work
alone in meditation with ancestors. She recommends the following:

> Sit quietly in contemplation. Imagine each ances-
> tor before you, one after the other. Ask them if there is
> anything they regret or that needs healing. Send love
> and light and clear that energy. Then clear any nega-
> tive attachments you have to them, any of your own
> angers, jealousies and negative thoughts. Let these
> go and send love to the person. Then let them go, and
> talk with the next person. You can do this over time.

As I've already noted, we approach ancestors with love, gratitude and forgiveness. Bert Hellinger, originator of constellation
work, has done extensive ancestor work in Europe and the United
States. His work is a very powerful and successful group method, in
which people play the roles of ancestors for a particular person so
that an issue can be processed through. One of our Soul Lightening

faculty members, Leah Matalon, also teaches Hellinger's work and has presented some of it in our Ancestral Healing workshop.

Hellinger claims that the principle *wound*, or *barrier*, to unraveling ancestral tangles is the "break in the chain of love." Although I prefer to call it the "stream of love," Hellinger's claim that there is a break in that continuum is a powerful one, verified in our work. When there is a cessation of love between two people—for example, father-son, husband-wife—it is like a rent in the fabric of their wellbeing that must be addressed if there is to be a healing of that relationship. Similarly, with a break in love between two groups of people, as with the people of Israel and Palestine, Hellinger claims this break must be resolved before peace or even sanity can be restored.

Forgiveness is also required for the completion of any piece of ancestral work; this may come before or after love is restored. Moreover, our attitude of forgiving actually attracts ancestors to us and is likely to facilitate the work we want to do with them.

Communication with ancestors requires complete honesty. However, this communication might first involve accusations and complaints, from one or both sides, before the two are able to come together for mutual forgiveness, and finally to bring healing and closure through love. Neither the ancestor nor the living person can truly move forward until forgiveness is complete. When it is, not only are the principal individuals healed but the world, too, is released from a burden; consciousness and love expand.

Once we are in communication with an ancestor we process, heal and ask forgiveness for whatever issues there may be between us, using our regular process method.

15:
PAST LIFE WORK

The soul is constantly in the process of evolving onward, but that evolution begins from the point where it left off.

~Edgar Cayce

Many years ago, when I was first studying and practicing acupressure, primarily to ease body symptoms, I was working on a friend to relieve her back pain. She had been lying quite peacefully on the table, enjoying the deep relaxation that acupressure brings, when suddenly she went into a very strange episode. She rolled back and forth on the table, had a pained expression on her face, and started speaking "in tongues," in some foreign language that sounded like Japanese. Her movements and crying out terrified me.

I took my hands off her, afraid that I had done something to evoke this painful state. She continued to vocalize in this strange language. When I tried to rouse her she looked up at me with a bewildered expression. Her eyes didn't focus on me and I couldn't tell what she was looking at. I became more alarmed and gently shook her. She continued to look at me as if she didn't know who I was. I called her name again and again and tried to lift her off the table.

Finally I was able to sit her up, look into her eyes and call her name. I asked her to be right there with me in the present. She finally looked at me, still in a daze.

"Helen," I said, "what's happening? Where are you?"

"I...I don't know," she said. "Where am I? Who am I?"

By this time I was truly scared. I brought her a glass of water and continued to urge her back into her everyday identity. She was disoriented and I was frightened. After we finally got her oriented back to this time, in her present identity, we seemed to make an unconscious agreement not to pursue the event—not to question it, investigate it, nor even discuss it. We dropped the subject of her "tuning out," on the spot, and never mentioned it again. I didn't offer to work on her again even though she said she would like to try another time.

As I write this today I feel sad that I didn't have the knowledge or skill I have now to help this friend. I simply went into denial out of sheer ignorance. This event occurred long before I studied Process Work or graduate psychology. If I had known how to follow her process, as I am able to do today, I feel confident that we would have uncovered very valuable growth material for her. As I look back on it I realize that we had probably encountered a past life. It would be many years and many trainings before I began to comprehend this. My only thought at the time was that something had gone wrong with the body session.

Many years passed before I was able to integrate this experience and confidently accept that it had probably been a past-life memory. During those years I continued to study, eventually finishing a Ph.D. in transpersonal psychology. I learned about past lives, read many books about reincarnation, and took a number of courses in past life therapy. But I always retained a certain skeptical reservation about the validity of such experiences.

Then, while traveling in Europe and Egypt I began to experience past lives of my own. I finally accepted that we have lived many times before. I studied and experimented with ways to bring that information safely and usefully into consciousness in this life. Past life experiences began to show up in my work with clients. Fortunately, by then I knew what to do with them. Over the course of at least a decade I evolved the Soul Lightening way of accepting, eliciting and integrating past life experiences for the benefit and growth of the life being lived in present time.

The Background of Past Life Therapy

While past lives have been an accepted part of many spiritual traditions for thousands of years, past life therapy, as such, developed during the late twentieth century when past life memories began to emerge in ordinary therapy sessions. Psychiatrists, psychologists and bodyworkers were shocked and unprepared, just as I was, when clients suddenly started speaking in foreign languages and reporting detailed experiences from ancient times. Such was the case for Dr. Brian Weiss, now one of the most prominent proponents of past life therapy and the author of several valuable books on the subject. At the time of his first encounter with past lives, he was a traditional psychiatrist who described his life as "unidirectional and highly academic." He was chief resident in psychiatry at Yale University School of Medicine and had taught and written widely on scientific studies.

Dr. Weiss' practice in psychiatry was traditional, until one of his patients first led him into territory that was to change his life. He tells the story of his patient, Catherine, in his book, *Many Lives, Many Masters.*[39]

Catherine suffered from "fears, phobias, paralyzing panic attacks, depression and recurrent nightmares. Her symptoms had

---

39 Weiss, Brian. 1988. *Many Lives, Many Masters: The True Story of a Prominent Psychiatrist, His Young Patient, and the Past-Life Therapy That Changed Both Their Lives.* New York, Simon & Schuster Inc.

been lifelong," wrote Dr. Weiss, when she sought therapy with him. But after more than a year of conventional psychotherapy Catherine "remained severely impaired," he reported. He could not use conventional medications, like antidepressants or tranquilizers, which she refused because of a chronic fear of gagging and choking. So Dr. Weiss suggested hypnosis to probe for the roots of her symptoms.

Catherine was a good subject who easily entered into trance and uncovered various traumatic childhood experiences that she had not remembered before. Dr. Weiss reports that he was "certain that now we had the answers. I was equally certain that now she would get better." But her symptoms persisted, to the surprise and consternation of Dr. Weiss. Even so, he continued with hypnosis, and finally asked her to go back to the time when her symptoms arose. He reported what happened then: "I had expected Catherine to return once again to her early childhood. Instead, she flipped back about four thousand years into an ancient near-Eastern lifetime, one in which she had a different face and body, different hair, a different name."

Dr. Weiss recounted how this unforeseen event struck him at the time: "I was shocked and skeptical. I had hypnotized hundreds of patients over the years, but this had never happened before.... I knew she was not psychotic, did not hallucinate, did not have multiple personalities, was not particularly suggestible and did not abuse drugs or alcohol. I concluded that her memories must have consisted of fantasy or dreamlike material."

Nevertheless, Catherine's symptoms began to abate when she discovered the roots of them while probing various past lives under hypnosis. Eventually she was completely free of her lifelong struggle. Toward the end of her therapy she went beyond her own healing to become a "conduit for transcendental knowledge," which became a source of wisdom and strength for Dr. Weiss.

So began Dr. Weiss' new education in the history of the soul, an education that would take him far afield from his academic background, lead him through his own soul searching and would estrange colleagues who were following more conventional paths. That entire journey serves him very well now in his practice, and in his writing and teaching about past life therapy, but it was both an enlightening and arduous journey that required much courage.

Many other therapists were having similar experiences to that of Dr. Weiss. Traditional psychotherapy, since the inception of psychoanalysis, had focused on personality development through personal history, primarily of early childhood, of this life. If the soul aspect of being was acknowledged at all, it was thought of as virtually inaccessible. But now clients like Catherine and many others were bringing forth experiences that seemed to uncover soul histories far beyond their present life experiences, often spanning many centuries, perhaps millennia. Some of that history figured into their present lives, explaining character traits or symptoms that had eluded traditional analysis of the present history.

Fortunately, as these experiences continued to surface in various therapies, some courageous psychologists and hypnotherapists began to take them seriously and to study how to probe them for healing and integration into the subjects' present lives. They came together to study and learn and eventually formed the Past Life Therapy Association which now presents workshops and conferences to investigate and therapeutically address past lives.

I studied with the Association, became a member and studied the field seriously for several years before I felt confident enough to incorporate this realm of investigation into Soul Lightening Acupressure. During that time I also worked through a number of my own past lives, with past life therapists and by myself.

A major breakthrough experience in India with Sai Baba led me to finally adopt a trustworthy base and methodology for past life work. This occurred during the last two days of our stay at Sai Baba's ashram in Puttaparti, India. Knowing it would be our last *darshan* (during which Sai Baba dispenses blessings by walking through the temple) for the trip, I silently asked Sai Baba to look into my eyes. Many have claimed that a look from Sai Baba would cause a profound shift in consciousness. I was hoping for this when Sai Baba walked by me. As I looked at his back I felt disappointed that I had missed this chance.

Then he suddenly turned around again and looked straight at me. His eyes seemed to bore into my head. In that moment I felt electrified, galvanized to the spot where I sat.

About three hours later in our room I became violently ill, with vomiting, diarrhea, severe headache and fever. I fell on the bed and held my head. Fritz and our dear friend Deirdre stayed close by, administering what hands-on methods they could when I wasn't writhing on the bed or running for the toilet. Nothing seemed to ease the symptoms.

I fell into a kind of delirium during which many lives rushed past my inner vision in fast forward. It was impossible to catch hold of any one of them and integrate it into my present life. The sensation was that of an ultra-fast roller-coaster. Occasionally I mumbled various strange words (including "Dakau") which were indecipherable to me or Fritz and Deirdre. At one point I vaguely sensed that I might die there. Upon later reflection it was impossible to tell if this feeling was from the actual physical illness or the recurring experience of death after death. This went on most of the night.

Around daybreak I emerged in my consciousness in a tunnel, with light at the end. As I approached the end of the tunnel Sai Baba's form filled it completely, surrounded by a brilliant halo.

"Now!" he shouted at me. "Remember what you are!"

That was a command that I have been investigating and trying to follow ever since that time. Why had Sai Baba said what you are rather than who you are? I continue to try to contact this in meditation and pay attention in my life. It's an ongoing investigation.

By mid-morning of that day I was completely well in my body and sparkling clear in consciousness, clearer than I had ever been in my life.

Why Investigate And Integrate Past Life Information?

There are two good reasons for investigating past lives.

1) An intractable symptom persists after prolonged conventional therapy has not relieved it. For example, Catherine's story clearly demonstrated that symptoms of the present life could have roots far back in time, long before any traumas of the present life;

2) A person spontaneously has an experience that is entirely foreign to his present life's time and space. This can happen as one travels in a country where they have never before been in this life when suddenly a particular city, building or street seems completely familiar and the person has a full blown experience of another time, experiencing life from within another body, being fully aware of another circumstance in that place. Or a past life can emerge spontaneously in bodywork, as it did in the case of my acupressure client in the anecdote I related at the beginning of this chapter, or in depth psychotherapy, as it does with Dr. Weiss, his clients and students. Finding a way to process these experiences enables a person to integrate them usefully into his present life.

People have asked me, "Why is it useful to investigate and heal past lives? Isn't there enough in this life to take care of? Isn't it a distraction or avoidance to mess around in other times and other themes?"

I would have asked the same questions decades ago and no doubt discounted exploring other lives as superfluous. In fact, when I did study past life therapy in my early career, it was more from curiosity than an expectation of really using it in my practice.

But through the years I have encountered too many symptoms, unconscious patterns and unyielding behavioral cycles that didn't change with depth psychological therapy. For example, sometimes a client and I have done extensive and complete psychotherapy on some very early childhood trauma to relieve a current distress, only to find the troublesome situation recurring.

Sometimes, within the deep consciousness states engendered by acupressure, a scenario spontaneously emerged that came from another time and place. After a number of these I had to start taking them seriously enough to explore further.

After I had learned how to work safely and effectively with the material of past lives, through study with the Past Life Therapy Association, I encountered many such experiences of my own as well as others.

One of the early dramatic cases was with a woman I'll call Tess. She came to me for acupressure to relieve painful knees, a symptom that had only recently emerged. At first I used acupressure to open the meridian energy through the knees. Though she had temporary relief, the pain kept returning.

Finally I asked, "When was the first time you experienced this pain?" Immediately her face contorted in agony and she cried out, "They're crushing my knees!" I asked her where she was. She described a scene in a medieval prison where she was being tortured for information. She reported this scene amid sobs of intense pain and shock. Who would betray her, she wanted to know. How could she save herself?

Then she described her captors coming at her with stone hammers. They struck her knees repeatedly as the bones crushed and blood spurted forth. As she told this horror story she grasped her knees in agony as the pain intensified.

I asked her to move forward in time to the period of her death, to get her out of the intense pain. At that moment I was very grateful for the past life therapy I had studied which gave me the skills to follow a life through to its conclusion.

Tess then described the scene of her death, not long after the torture. She had been broken in other parts of the body and was just barely conscious. She welcomed death but her dying thoughts hovered around who and why she had been betrayed. She felt she had failed somehow.

Here was the key. She had brought feelings of failure and be-trayal from that life into this one. We needed to heal them at the source and release her from their effects.

"Okay, Tess," I said, "I want you to go back to that woman and tell her that she did not fail. You in fact triumphed. You didn't tell the enemy the valuable information they wanted to know, thereby protecting others. You were not unworthy. On the con-trary, you died a victorious if horrible death. And now that life is finished."

Tess was quiet for a while. She stopped crying.

I urged her further. "Now, release that woman from the pain and anguish of her death. Bless her and let her go." I then asked Tess to follow her soul out of the body of that past life and into the light where her spiritual counselors were.

Soon Tess' knee pain had completely disappeared. Within the field of the counselors' love, comfort and counsel, she reviewed the life and saw who had betrayed her. She said, "I see that the way to be completely free of that life is to acknowledge and comfort myself and forgive my betrayers and torturers."

I was amazed at this jump in consciousness. "Can you do that?" I asked.

"Yes, I think I can, within this healing field of spirit."

After some time had passed in the session, I helped Tess return to the present time. Both she and I, in a rational state of ordinary reality, were astounded and somewhat doubtful. We could hardly believe what we had just experienced together, and yet we couldn't deny that experience.

Tess had never even thought about past lives before this. She was a highly educated intellectual who wasn't "given to fairy tales or fantasy," as she said. What had just happened?

The next rational step seemed to be to consciously review our experiences in the following session and then see what happened with Tess's knees, which were now completely pain free. In fact, the pain went away permanently, which further verified her experience. This was empirical evidence I couldn't ignore.

After that I decided to integrate past life therapy into my regular practice whenever something that looked like a past life showed up spontaneously during acupressure. I invented techniques to integrate knowledgeable acupressure with the highest quality regression methods of past life therapy.

While bodywork is a valuable facilitator of past life retrieval, most past life material is stored in the energy field just outside the body, though lingering, unresolved trails of past life experiences can lodge in the energy systems, particularly within the chakras, and even in body tissue. The whole-being experience of the past life is more smoothly integrated and grounded in the present body and life through bodywork.

Retrieving the material from the body makes past life information more substantial and identifiable with the current life than it is when it only comes through the mind. In fact, it is my belief, and that of many meditators, that the ordinary mind is not that trustworthy about the facts of life. We now know the left brain particularly likes to make up its own scenarios, theories and beliefs, whether they coincide with factual events or not.

Over time, it became very clear to me that the soul's present purpose can be either greatly obstructed or enhanced by our past lives. I learned that bringing them to consciousness could clarify many obscure factors of the present life and thereby free and empower it.

Benefits of Past Life Therapy

Catherine's and Tess's experiences exemplify one of the many benefits of past life therapy as well as one of the strongest arguments in favor of knowing how to heal past lives. These women's cases demonstrate the strong healing potential of past life work. Beyond simply uncovering past lives, the roots of present life symptoms found there can be healed and released through knowledgeable past life therapy. I learned this over and over in my own practice. In any case, when a symptom or dysfunction persists, despite all therapeutic efforts, it is a good idea to investigate beyond this present life.

It is common in ordinary psychotherapy to search for causes of illness or dysfunction in early childhood. But when distressing symptoms persist, despite careful childhood investigation, it can be productive to ask about a related past life. Many symptoms and dysfunctions may not change with intellectual insight alone.

In my experience almost any symptom or dysfunction can be healed, at its root, whether it happened in this or other lives, when the healing is experienced within the whole being—body, mind, emotions and soul. When these conditions are met the subject can be permanently free of the symptom, in this life and future lives. The one exception is karma, which I will address later in this chapter.

Past life therapy can offer this level of healing because of its pervasive nature. The subject doesn't simply recall, think and talk about a past life; he or she literally re-lives it, in the body, emotions and soul, just as we do in inner child healing. With that whole-being experience the subject has the opportunity to release the toxic imprint and replace it with loving, spiritual energy.

Purposes for Processing Past Lives With Soul Lightening Acupressure

Through the years we have discovered explicit purposes for processing and healing past lives as follows:

- Heal intractable symptoms—physical, emotional, spiritual—chronic or psychosomatic, that resist other therapies.
- Help reclaim soul energies that have been trapped in the past.
- Reclaim talents and strengths of the past.
- Come closer to soul purpose in this life.

- Clear up the unfinished business of past lives.
- Enlighten, free and empower present relationships that have past-life connections.
- Progress soul evolution.
- Illuminate present soul purpose in relation to collective (world) problems and evolution. That is, a particular theme that is being cleared in world karma. Examples include the suppression of women or empowerment of them, violence or eradication of violence, and territorial possession, etc. Thus you help reduce the burden of world karma.
- Gain freedom from entanglements, wounds, bindings of past lives.
- Help to heal the whole person—body, mind, emotions and soul—by updating even those parts that derive from past lives.
- Put death in perspective and in most cases remove all fear of it since we have all died many times already.
- Open new neural pathways in the brain.

Recurring Themes and Patterns in Past Lives

Over the last twenty years past life therapists have discovered themes that recur life after life in a seemingly endless repetitive pattern, until they are healed or resolved. I have encountered many of these themes and have learned that resolving one of them in this life cancels the need to repeat the same experience.

Past life processing and release have often freed a client permanently from some dysfunctional pattern. I don't agree with authorities or theories that claim we are fixed permanently into certain patterns. Nor do I accept that we are condemned to just manage or live with our symptoms and distresses.

Past Life Chart	
Experience from *Past Life*...	Can Lead in *Present Life* to...
Abandonment	Fear of abandonment now; clinging to or withdrawing from relationships
Abuse: emotional, physical, sexual	Becoming victim or perpetrator of same abuse
Anger used for self-service or control	Use of or fear of anger now
Arrogance	Use of or fear of arrogance now
Betrayal	Fear of betrayal now
Control, oppression, dominance	Becoming victim or perpetrator of same behavior
Loss of loved one(s)	Fear of loss now
Over-caring (co-dependence)	Under-caring (narcissism) or continued pattern of excessive giving, resistance to self-care
Power over or misuse of	Use of, or fear of misuse of power now
Violence	Violence continues or one fears it
Wasted life; didn't use talents	Repetition of pattern; obsessive striving for accomplishment; ambition to make up for former waste
Not belonging	Rebellion; confused about identity; withdrawal from social contact; over
Punishment for speaking out	One is mute or simply always parrots the "party line"

There is one soul factor, however, that can prevent healing or liberation from distressing conditions in the present life: unfinished *karma*. Sometimes unfinished business, or even errors or "sins" (translated as "off the mark") from a past life, are brought over into the present life for completion. A "sin," of the past must be completed, updated or resolved. Usually these issues can't be completed until the person has accepted full responsibility for the original error and rectified it, as well as full responsibility for the self in this life.

In his book *The Tibetan Book of Living and Dying*[40], Sogyal Rinpoche describes the karma of present and past lives from a Buddhist perspective: "The word karma literally means 'action,' and karma is both the power latent within actions and the results our actions bring.... In simple terms, what does karma mean? It means that whatever we do, with our body, speech, or mind, will have a corresponding result. Each action, even the smallest, is pregnant with consequences."

Edgar Cayce, who did thousands of past life readings, said that karma was simply patterns of memory stored in the unconscious, from where it can advise us about current decisions. He also said that karma can be corrected by present will and right behavior, toward soul evolution. Past life therapy helps to reveal these phenomena and makes it more possible to accept "un-healable conditions" in the moment. Or, it can show us how to do the appropriate soul work in this life in order to complete the unfinished business or make amends for past errors, to release ourselves from karma affecting our present or future lives.

In the words of Sogyal Rinpoche, "Karma, then, is not fatalistic or predetermined. Karma means *our* ability to create and to change. It is creative because we can determine how and why we act. We *can* change. The future is in our hands, and in the hands of our heart."

It is important to get the learning and updating of old programs into full consciousness, including the analyzing intellect as well as heart love, so that the work can become a permanent benefit in the present life, in future lives and in global evolution. We might say things like, "Let's review what you learned in that life: What themes from it are still working now? Do you see any connections between the timid woman of that life and the scared girl today?"

In our classes we teach an explicit and responsible methodology for processing and healing past lives. Altered states of consciousness are required to access the relevant material of a past life, and

---

40 Sogyal Rinpoche. 1992. *The Tibetan Book of Living and Dying.* New York, HarperCollins.

acupressure is an ideal medium for evoking a safe and balanced altered state. Thus our work is done in combination with appropriate acupressure formulas.

All the relevant players of a life are identified by the person doing the work. When a particular situation, such as betrayal, abandonment or abuse, recurs several times it would be helpful to investigate if a past life, or many, started this theme. And if so, how can the person seek repentance, or forgiveness, to clear the pattern? Problems or traumas that have kept consciousness locked in that life are brought out, worked through and finally resolved. This process might take only one session, but usually several are required. We want to restore the stream of love, and reach forgiveness or a clear understanding of what was not understood at the time.

Integrating Past Lives with the Present

We are careful to integrate the past life work into the present life situations and relationships. During summary and integration at the end of a session, or a series of sessions, the past life information is reviewed in present time, from the present perspective. Or, if the session has been particularly dramatic or traumatic we may postpone integration for a later time, after the client has had time to digest and integrate the material on his or her own. We may also use further methods for digesting and integrating the information, such as dialoguing with persons in that other life, drawing, collaging, journaling or meditating on the themes.

The Soul's Evolutionary Journey

When we consider the soul's long evolutionary journey there is more latitude for detaching from the tight-box perspective of this life's particular history and personality. We can lift our vision from the short-term implications of Mother's neglect or Father's abandonment into a wider perspective of the continuum of soul purpose. We can find greater compassion for self and others.

I've previously mentioned how my father died in a violent, freak accident when I was barely four years old. That part of my own history serves to explain how events such as this impact our lives, not just in the present but also in the ways our lives might unfold in years to come. Father's death was like a cannon shot through my mother's life and livelihood. While I was still a psychology student and client, my therapist, teachers and I concluded that this early loss of my father had left me traumatized and somewhat socially inept in school and society. With that interpretation I often felt abandoned, inferior to my peers who had fathers, and lacking certain father-engendered skills and powers.

Fortunately, later training after psychology school showed me the limitations of our psychological interpretations. I learned acupressure, studied the body and discovered how it carries the records of what actually happened, apart from the mind's interpretations. In my experience, that direct raw data that arrives from the body can be processed through to valid truths.

With these resources as foundation, I deeply investigated the events that actually happened around my father's death from the perspective of my own body perceptions. I ended up with a very different interpretation of those past conditions than the one I had subscribed to throughout psychology training.

Probing true memory with an altered state of consciousness connected to the body, I discovered that I didn't feel traumatized by my father's death at the time. I found that his death did *not* plunge me into grief. I didn't feel abandoned by him (as per the earlier psychological interpretation); rather I had already sensed his receding energy, even before my birth. For example, he almost died in a plane crash on his way to the hospital when I was born. At a soul level he and I both knew, even before my birth, that he wouldn't live long in that body in this life. So at the time of his death, I just flew out after him, to penetrate the veil between this world and the other. In my soul body, I was curious and liberated by the journey, a journey that opened a door in my own consciousness between the worlds. That door to the world of the so-called "dead" has been available to me ever since that time, though it took years for me to become aware of it. I can contact the "dead" quite easily and I find many answers and resolutions from them. This ability has been useful from time to time. For example, if I spontaneously think of Mother, Grandmother or Father I simply ask how they are, what's going on there or for some piece of earth information they might have. I have a strong notion that the door is, or will be, open for many people now.

All spiritual teachings I have studied affirm that life is eternal, whether here in this world or another. We are students of eternity, learning our unique lessons as we go. Sometimes we learn many lessons in one lifetime. In another life we seem to coast along. In some lives we accomplish a great deal in the world. In others we are removed from the world entirely, as are ascetics who live a life of prayer and contemplation.

As souls mature they may choose their preferred lessons before birth. They may also choose friends and family from people they knew before. Some soul families incarnate together life after life, in different relationships. And there are whole soul groups, called soul families by some, that come together life after life for many lifetimes, to accomplish some large world mission. Whatever the assignment, past life work demonstrates that each lesson must finally be completed, in the present or later. And there are seemingly endless ones still to be learned in this world.

16:
WORKING WITHIN
SACRED SPACE

*Keep in mind that all matter is comprised of energy,
or fields of energy: humans, animals, stardust, trees,
chairs...all form is made up of energy at a quantum
level, and this is where the science of our so-called
miracles occurs.*

~Richard Bartlett, D.C., N.D.

Field Awareness

From the beginning, Soul Lightening work was created to align people through the center of their own beings, between heaven and earth, an alignment process that promotes balance of all their chakras as well as giving them greater access to their souls. Through this energetic orientation we combine contemporary academic study with hands-on bodywork to promote individual growth from the inside out. Through stable balance in the body, a person can be grounded on the earth and at the same time receive soul guidance from transcendent sources.

Since we know that the Universal Unified Field encompasses all and everything, we choose to co-create unity and a heightened state of awareness in our classes. Every class is framed in sacred space so that each person is held in unconditional positive regard. We are all harmonized with the environment, including the classroom, the surrounding nature, our own beings and the Field. We have found that this class-contained Field promotes acceptance, harmony and greater personal awareness between all participants. It also encourages personal and group evolution.

Within this setting we can also co-create strategies and interactions within relationships, without conflict or competition, and with much less ego involvement. In fact, when we finish a class everyone feels more acknowledged and inspired than they did at the beginning.

Soul Lightening Methods Strengthen All Seven Chakras

As you know by now, two fundamental concepts are at the core of our methods:

1) We believe every human being contains the wisdom and power within to effectively carry out his or her own life purpose, if adequate resources are available.
2) We believe complete human development is partly a function of the seven central chakras. We use every opportunity to bring more awareness and experience to both of these principles.

Soul Lightening Meditation and Visualization Methods

The Pyramid Meditation was received as an inspiration in 1984. It has been practiced steadily in every class since 1985. The initial inspiration was followed by many clarifications for practical application.

At the beginning of every class, even before personal introductions, the teacher and students visually co-create a pyramid structure in their minds, which we bring around our time and space together. We imagine that the pyramid extends into the ground at its base and reaches up into heaven where its apex is formed. At the apex of the pyramid we ask for unity during our time with each other. We proclaim that the pyramid protects and guides us throughout the class. We ask each person to invite the higher helpers they feel close to, such as spirit guides, patron saints and angels, into the pyramid through its apex, which extends into transcendental realms.

We finish the pyramid visualization by asking students to sweep heavenly energy back down from the apex of the pyramid to its base. As we bring attention back to the ground, we ask students to hold each other in highest personal regard. We know that the protective energy framed by the visualized pyramid creates a container in which we may safely work with each other in respect and clarity. Finally we ask each person to bring heavenly energy down through each of her own seven chakras in the Great Central channel. Then each person is aligned between heaven and earth through the center of her own being.

At the end of each class we release the pyramid energy. One student, Gina Rosenthal, expressed her experience of the pyramid in the following way:

> Our time in the pyramid was filled with awe, joy, laughter, exciting ideas and an incredibly strong sense of community within the pyramid and beyond to our soul and world family.... I saw the top of our pyramid light up and a huge funnel spread out from there. It seemed like a crown chakra opening near the top of the pyramid was sending shooting stars out holographically, farther than I could see with normal vision.

There have been many such reports about the effects of the pyramid, both in class and outside. We have used it at a distance, for healing and support for our community. Eventually the Zero Balancing community also took it up, and it is now used there in most classes. We believe that by creating the pyramid in this way, we are actually radiating balance and sane energy out into the world with this practice.

The Story of the Pyramid

It wasn't until 2012 that a student in a teacher training asked about the origin of the pyramid meditation. That's when I told the following story for the first time.

The pyramid meditation was born in 1984 in Egypt. My process partner, Laura Ramsay, and I went there with Patricia Sun, a California healer and spiritual teacher. We were a group of healers and, indeed, our time together was graced.

We were greeted generously in Egypt and given special privileges, which included an hour to ourselves in the King's Chamber of the Great Pyramid of Giza. I remember climbing up the very narrow and almost dark steps to the top of the pyramid, in single file. When we arrived in the chamber, Patricia had us gather around the sarcophagus of the Pharoah where we proceeded to chant and pray. Imagine the scene: We were dressed in galabeyas, the traditional robes of Egyptians, huddled together, allowing our spirits to ascend within the vibration of the chants. The energy grew more and more intense, and lifted within and around us.

Suddenly I could see and feel a portal open up at the very apex of the pyramid. Light, energy and information from transcendental sources poured down on us through that portal. The feeling was ecstatic. I wanted to retain the information and somehow write it down later because I recognized it as very valuable guidance, even though I knew it was all beyond words. I knew that I would have

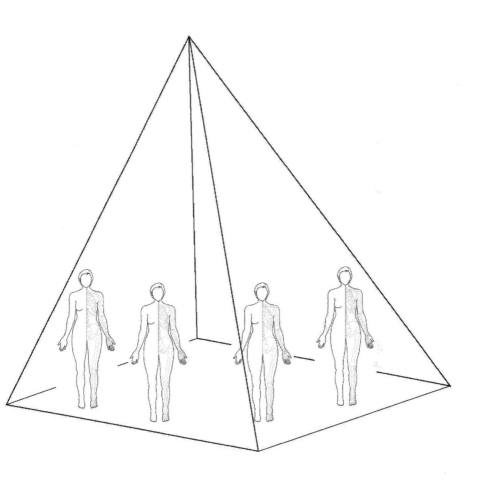

to find a way to translate it.* But once we left the pyramid, all of us in an altered state, we continued with a very intense schedule for days, so I never had an opportunity to write down what had come to me except for the following observation: "There are transcendental sources of information, love and support to you that are available all the time if you will simply open this portal. Everything you need is offered."

Shortly after we got back from Egypt, I was teaching. As I began the morning meditation, in which we always aligned with the Great Central Flow through the spine and chakras, I found myself guiding attention on up from the top of the head to the apex of a pyramid, where there was a portal into higher sources (just as I had experienced in Giza). I remember that at that moment I was *thinking* with my left-brain, "People will think this is weird. Can I get away with it?" But no one raised an objection or questioned the meditation, and the class proceeded as usual. Then, after a while I noticed that there was more harmony, higher consciousness and easier comprehension than usually happened on the first day of a class.

After that class I continued to visually co-create the pyramid with students. The first few times were still edgy for me but I persisted, and there was never any objection. Finally the pyramid meditation became normal and automatic. Later I decided to teach it to our Soul Lightening teachers as a part of our curriculum.

Now the pyramid meditation is known in our entire community, and used in many different contexts, for healing, for strength, for manifestation and for regular guidance. For example, when someone is ill or distressed at any level we visualize a community-wide pyramid over that person. Many people who have been served this way have given the feedback that they felt strengthened and lifted

---

• Some thirty years after that I heard Esther Hicks explain that information was delivered in large chunks to her from Abraham, a collection of beings from "infinite intelligence," and she had to find the words to transcribe the chunks into understandable language for others. That's how it was in the King's Chamber.

up. One member of our community who was undergoing chemo-therapy reported that she felt supported, loved and held in a pro-tected space as we visualized the pyramid over her.

Recently my husband, Fritz Smith, originator of Zero Balancing, and I have started using the pyramid over projects and travels. For example, when we traveled to Esalen Institute, where we were both teaching, we co-created a pyramid over the entire trip before we left home. The trip was complicated, during varying weather, and with many stops, different rooms, beds and commitments. But when we got home we both remarked how smooth the trip had gone. It did feel guided and protected.

In times of widespread disaster, as with recent weather devastation and incredible violence, our community is alerted to join in visualizing a giant pyramid over the entire area, to bring strength and help to the region where the tragedies have occurred.

Soul Lightening and Chakra Tai Chi

Chakra Tai Chi is a whole-body exercise that moves energy through all the energy channels and awakens consciousness to the seven chakras at the same time. It was created to impart a deeper sense of both chakra consciousness and awareness of energy movement for the first Process Acupressure faculty. Chakra Tai Chi is incredibly instructive, and progressive; the longer you practice it, the deeper it goes.

We use the energetic movement of Tai Chi to activate and move each person's energy (chi) through all the chakras. The energetic motion involves a simple movement for each chakra that corre-sponds to the part of the body associated with it. Thus the beginning movements, for the first three chakras, are closer to the ground. The movements for the higher, or last four, chakras—heart, throat, brow and crown—correspond to those parts of the body, traveling from the heart area all the way to the top of the head where the crown chakra swirls.

When a person does all seven movements in sequence she feels stronger, more centered and more aware of her own states of consciousness at the end. And each day that consciousness penetrates deeper. Each class day is usually begun with this practice, so that every person is aligned with her own energy and consciousness before we begin.

Chakra Tai Chi also works well out of the classroom. Some therapists have used it between clients, to clear out the energy and consciousness of one client before engaging with the next. A teacher told me she does Chakra Tai Chi between classes for the same reasons. One woman reported that she did the exercise after a disempowering fight with another person that had upset her greatly. She said that Chakra Tai Chi brought her back to herself and her own values quickly. It also dispelled most of the negative feelings she had toward the other person after the fight.

The Story of Chakra Tai Chi

When I first began teaching Process Acupressure in the late 1980s, I wanted to orient students to the chakras as a template for complete human development. Simultaneously I was studying a simple form of Tai Chi Chuan.

I observed that many students had no familiarity with the chakras, or if they did, it was from a purely intellectual understanding, through books and charts. I wanted them to have the *experience* of chakras in their own bodies and become aware of the states of consciousness associated with each.

It seemed that combining a simple Tai Chi movement method with an awareness of each chakra would accomplish both those aims. As is my style, I first tried this form on myself until I was satisfied that it worked for my purposes. Then I introduced the first faculty members to it and they found the work strengthening and instructive. In fact, many students have by now made it a regular practice in their lives. Now it is used regularly in all classes. It enhances understanding of the energy channels (meridians) as students are studying them intellectually, and it is a constant reminder of the power and placement of the chakras.

Soul Lightening and the Lightening Process Meditation

Another meditative method we use to stimulate and cultivate awareness in the chakras is the Lightening Process Meditation. This process is similar to traditional meditation in that it is done in a sitting position. On the other hand, it differs from ordinary meditation because it elicits the state of consciousness associated with each chakra.

We begin by imagining that we reach up into heaven to receive light from Source. Then we visualize a moving stream of light, pouring down into our bodies. In imagination we let the light build a charge, increasing until it reaches what the soul knows is the right amount. Then we gently imagine nudging the light down into our body. We visualize it forming into a big balloon of light around the top of our body, to encompass the top three chakras: crown, brow and throat. Mentally we hold the light in place there, and trust that it will do its own work. In practice we have found that holding light in a particular place often actuates issues or memories, or brings guidance into consciousness. We simply witness or observe the process, as in traditional meditation, and when ordinary thoughts or feelings intrude, we gently ask them to dissolve into the light. Each part of the process can take between five and twenty minutes. Just as with meditation, we seem to have an inner knowing that tells us when it is finished; there will be no more insights or energy in that place.

Next we imagine the light flowing down into our chest, where it can surround the higher heart and heart chakras. We imagine holding the light steady there to let it work, allowing an influx of love, and dissolving thinking or emotions into it.

When the light feels finished in the chest, we gently visualize it flowing downward to surround the bottom three chakras—third, second and root—and our legs and feet, and then moving into the ground. We imagine the light working there, as we witness its effects for as long as there is insight or energy.

To complete the process we visualize the light expanding out into the surrounding Field, to create a light shield around us. We imagine the light shield forming a space for the soul, to protect and clear our path going forward. We ask for the light to continue blessing and informing us at the right level. To finish the Lightening Process Meditation we thank all the light sources and bring attention fully present in the moment.

For students who are not accustomed to visualizing and imagining in this way, the Lightening Meditation may seem like fantasy at first. Our experience is, however, that as a person keeps doing it, valuable insight, strength and guidance occur. Similar to prayer, it goes deeper with repetition.

Mary Golob, a student from the United States, wrote, "Doing the Lightening Meditation leads me to feeling more grounded, more connected to my soul, more expansive, more conscious of the Divine within me, and more protected from energies that are not for my higher good."

The Story of the Lightening Meditation

As I meditated on the morning of December 31, 2009, light arrived from above my head and descended slowly, sliding down into my body. A cylinder of that energy encompassed my head and hovered there for a time. It felt ecstatic and blissful. After a while the light cylinder slid on down around my chest and remained there, as it had around my head. I felt my heart chakra flare out and at the same time a warm rush of love filled me up.

Then the light cylinder moved down to cover the base of my body and pelvis, the first three chakras, my legs and feet. By this

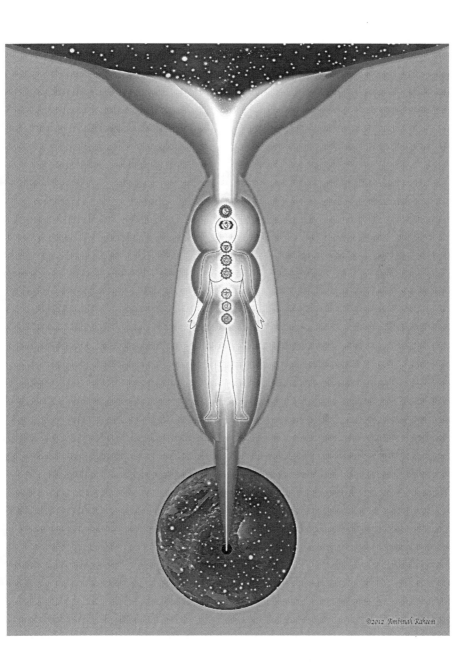

time my whole body was a pulsing, vibrant field. I sat in that light field with a feeling of total ecstasy.

As I repeated this form it became clear that as light hovered around my head it was affecting crown, brow and throat chakras. Then at my chest, it stimulated the heart chakra. Finally at the base of my body it stimulated chakras three, two and one, legs and feet.

At this point I kept saying, "Thank you, thank you, thank you." My soul voice responded with, "You're welcome, but this isn't just for you. Share it with others."

In 2010 I was shown how to work with the descending light more specifically. I learned how to connect with the quantum light field far above my head, how to collect light there so as to coordinate with Cosmic design and evolution, or, in more spiritual terms, Divine Will. The instruction was to place an inquiry or intention at that level and then to let it work for a while, coordinating with Divine Will, before bringing it down into my head, moving on down my body, toward concrete reality on the ground. From this alignment cosmic light can inform my own light and higher chakras about whatever project is being worked on.

The inner soul voice explained, "Working from the light field down will take your mission all the way from heaven, through the earth plane, the-way-it-is-here, and finally to a graceful landing on earth."

As light worked in my head I began having more conscious clarity about the project at hand. Then when I brought the light down into my chest and heart I could feel how light and love informed the project and me. Finally when light landed on earth, I could see how that landing would spawn roots that would foster more growth shoots down into the earth.

I haven't taught this particular work yet, but I can envision that it is a perfect complement to the conscious light work with meridians and organs that we have done for many years in class but which I have not addressed in this book.

It seems to me that this meditation is a template for manifesting anything into the earth plane from a higher level of inspiration, namely heaven or Divine Order. Many inspirations and visions that are received at a crown or brow level never reach earthly manifestation because they don't become activated in the lower chakras. Also, through this trajectory there is much less influence of personal ego. And in a world that is far too dominated by un-clarified egos, this is a good thing.

Since that morning I have taught the original form in a few of my classes. Once a student said, "That transported me to an elevated, wonderful space," and the feedback has always been positive.

I have used the meditation as a standard method for myself ever since it was given to me in 2010. Through it I have had many insights about my own life and projects, in all aspects. I have also received inspirations for teaching and even for this book. For example, only this morning I received, "Make it interesting to read, personal and fresh. Tell stories. It isn't supposed to be another textbook, or how-to book; there are already plenty of those. Only you know the full chronology and story of Soul Lightening."

So, dear reader, for your sake, I am following that counsel.

17:
CONCLUSION

If there's any possibility for enlightenment, it's right now, not at some future time. Now is the time.

~Pema Chodron

Just after the September 11, 2001, bombing of the Twin Towers, the Dalai Lama sent counsel to people all over the world through newspapers and other media. He wrote the following:

> The events of this day cause every thinking person to stop their daily lives, whatever is going on in them, and to ponder deeply the larger questions of life. We search again for not only the meaning of life, but the purpose of our individual and collective experience as we have created it—and we look earnestly for ways in which we might recreate ourselves anew as a human species, so that we will never treat each other this way again.

Combined with the Dalai Lama's words that I quoted at the beginning of this book—"Even though it seems very difficult, world peace can only come about through individual transformation"—these two statements could easily stand as a manifesto for our work in Soul Lightening.

I have described how we work with people in Soul Lightening to facilitate individual transformation, which is our primary purpose. Through transformed individuals we hope to contribute to world transformation, our mission being "to cultivate soul actualization and purpose in the world, to further human evolution, health and awakening, for the preservation of the family and the global community." It is our hope that Soul Lightening can act as a lightning rod from Source to earth, with each individual serving as a single lightning bolt, consistent with their own unique nature and purpose.

As we view the immense challenges of our world, and our incalculable powers of destruction, it would seem that our planet must surely be headed toward total annihilation. And yet, many great thinkers steadfastly argue just the opposite. For example, Ken Wilber, the author of *A Brief History of Everything*, and a prominent contemporary philosopher, believes that the rise of higher consciousness is presently greater than it has ever been in history. Other sociologists, scientists and educators are researching and writing optimistic books about the future, claiming that we will not only overcome but transcend our present state. Only recently Christiane Northrup, eminent physician and champion of women wrote:

> This summer I feel as though I am dying to my old life—and so many aspects of it. All births are always accompanied by deaths. When you give birth to a baby, you die to your old carefree self. And a mother is born. But once your children are grown, you have to labor your own soul into a new life. We are deeply into this process on so many levels now. Can you feel it?

> There is a new exciting raw vibrant spiritual-
> ity rising from the roots of planet Earth these days.
> Women all OVER the planet are rising like yeast—and
> truly feeling their oats. Sera Beak, a Harvard trained
> scholar of Comparative Religions is the perfect exam-
> ple of this feisty new energy. We are reclaiming our
> own spiritual authority as never before in recorded
> history. And this reclamation has the power to af-
> fect every cell in our bodies—as well as the kind of
> healthcare that makes sense to us.

In his most recent book, *The Honeymoon Effect*, Bruce Lipton, eminent cell biologist and recognized leader in bridging science and spirit, wrote, "Humanity's options are quite clear: We can continue to do what we're doing and go the way of the dinosaurs, or we can change our way of life.... I believe today's chaos will push us to the next stage of evolution where loving, cooperative forces thrive.... I sit here looking at the crises facing humanity and I'm excited be-cause I believe they're a sign that we're on our way to the next level of evolution, a new belief system that will shape a civilization based on harmony and self-empowerment.... Human consciousness is one of the most powerful elements influencing the evolution of this planet."[41]

Many of us hope and believe that beneath the tumultuous waves of destruction another great wave of higher consciousness and spirituality is emerging. The boundless pressure of our possible self-annihilation is igniting a massive call to action for the human species, bringing new resolve to transform our present suffering with sweeping solutions that are barely within our present capaci-ty to even imagine. If the prophets of today are accurate, our threat-ening devastation is actually unveiling the greatest opportunity for positive change in human history. Regardless of the evidence

---

41 Lipton, Bruce. 2013. *The Honeymoon Effect: The Science of Creating Heaven on Earth.* Carlsbad, California, Mountain of Love Productions, by Hay House, 2013.

of horrible things happening in the world today, global spiritual change continues.

Thus it seems very important that those who are following a path of personal and spiritual growth and enlightenment hold to the path and not be seduced by the doomsayers. This book, and our Soul Lightening work over the years, may seem like a small contribution in the face of so much world turmoil. But I believe our work is powerful and important, at the leading edge of global change. We're not a mere voice in the wilderness; each of us is committed to continuing our part in world transformation.

The Promise of Soul-Guided Development

When a whole being—body, mind, emotions and soul—wakes up and comes alive, a rare human shows up, one who is committed to her own continued evolution and that of all human beings. One of our aims in Soul Lightening is to facilitate that state in individuals, and we believe such transformed individuals can become a soul voice for global health.

I hope a time will come when whole human development is guided by the individual soul, in touch with Universal Spirit. That consciousness would claim unity with, and surrender to, the Great Source of order and meaning (or the Tao) that infuses all of Creation. Then one could "flow with the Tao," a state impossible to explain in words, because it is a whole-being state that transcends words. But we have felt it many times.

Since I started this book, many remarkable stories have come to me about how Soul Lightening work has transformed individual lives, with greatly improved physical, mental and spiritual health. For example, here's a recent letter I received from Anna Winzenreid, a Swiss Soul Lightening therapist and teacher:

> For more than twenty years I have been using Soul Lightening Acupressure in my work with single

persons, pairs or groups. I would say the effect has been astonishing as well as touching. It is truly healing in all aspects that cover human beingness.

In my practice the majority of clients are between twenty and thirty-five years old. Most of them arrive in a quite desperate state—they feel betrayed by society (parents, teachers, political leaders, authorities). Often they are full of frustration, mistrust, anger or even depression, where any creativity or liveliness is denied. I often hear the words, "I have not been told the truth about life. I don't fit. I am not able to find my place. I do not belong. No one cares. What can I do here?" Often they have retreated from ordinary life to go into drugs, depression, body pain or they simply remain in opposition to everything.

If such people meet a supporting field that not only allows them but encourages them to be curious, to feel and express their feelings, to see, to speak, to find out, to use all their senses, to believe in what they discover, to change and let go what no longer serves them, to decide what suits them, a field that believes in growth and in unlimited possibilities, a field which isn't scared of diversity, then they start to relax, to wake up, and stand up. An incredible life force starts to show up and take the lead. Within this process they start to connect with their innate wisdom, with that part of the human being that is connected to the bigger picture, to the subconscious, and to the Universe. This is when soul consciousness comes in. It is almost unbelievable what effect this has.

I have seen this so many times and it is an absolutely wonderful part of the work: A huge creativity starts to express itself in all fields. Shy and uncertain people might become leaders because they have something to say now; the once called disinterested start to study and learn things; persons that hardly spoke use their voices—in words or sound. People become poets, painters, musicians, etc. They now accept being part of society and dare to bring in their abilities and share their jewels. They leave the drama of their childhood, the conditioning of their ancestors and celebrate life in their own way.

I have seen such processes take place in only six months' time, but they might also take up to several years.

Soul Lightening's World Work

Our world work spreads out from individual transformation because as individuals evolve they care about and reach out to others; they begin to realize the oneness of all life and want to help preserve it. They naturally want to serve.

Toward these ends we have created and taught SEVA stress release and Acupressure for Anyone classes to hundreds of students in the United States and Europe. Both are instruments of healthy and safe holistic care that can be used on oneself alone or given to others.

The Story of SEVA

Just after September 11, 2001, the Soul Lightening faculty was meeting in Baltimore, Maryland. Leah Matalon, who lives in New York City, was very upset, still shaken from the horrible impact of human suffering, crumbling skyscrapers and toxic smoke resulting from the Twin Towers devastation. We talked of that awful event during most of the first day of our meeting.

That night when I went to bed the voice of Sai Baba came to me: "You have skills. Do something!" The next morning I reported this message to the faculty. They responded immediately with the resolve to create an acupressure formula on the spot that could be delivered to the first responders who were still working at ground zero. Then they spent most of that night creating a profound but simple acupressure formula to relieve stress.

Here is Leah's account of that time:

> On September 11, 2001, the world was stunned by the attack on, and collapse of, the World Trade Center. Three thousand people were killed and America was changed forever.
>
> SEVA stress relief was born from the ashes of that enormous disaster. Soon after the attack a small group of Process Acupressure teachers met in Maryland with Aminah Raheem, at the home of Betsy Baker. I was the only one who lived in NYC and related, as best as I could, what it was like to be there.
>
> Aminah asked in the pyramid meditation for us to create a counterpoint to the horror, something we could give from our work to the world in service.
>
> That evening Betsy Baker, Claire Franck, Angelique Priscilla and I put together a protocol that we called Shock/Stress Release. We presented it to Aminah as a gift, born from the work she had created.
>
> That protocol has since become SEVA (Sanskrit for selfless service) stress release and it is taught and practiced all over the world, wherever our teachers go, in small communities, in classrooms, in underdeveloped countries, in hospitals, in offices, community centers, to seniors, children, therapists, and healthcare providers.

I know that the day SEVA was created all my work with Soul Lightening came together. We were guided by something higher. It remains a light in the darkness of those events that will continue to burn brightly as a beacon of hope.

Leah and others took SEVA to ground zero. They described working with firemen and police officers, right through their heavy uniforms, around guns and boots. They said those men and women were so grateful for ten or fifteen minutes of hands-on stress relief and they thanked our practitioners profusely. It was at ground zero that we first learned how profoundly relieving that acupressure formula could be.

Later, Soul Lightening teachers taught the formula to people who wanted to relieve the stress of soldiers, dying patients, teachers and even children. Cathy Miller, our brilliant and devoted president, created a program to deliver SEVA to staff people at Walter Reid Military Hospital in Baltimore. Evaluations and Records were kept there that verified how valuable the work was to recipients.

Results were so excellent in these early trials that we decided to offer classes of SEVA in as many places as possible, so that its balancing and soothing effects could be widely spread.

As of this date we have taught over 200 SEVA and Acupressure for Anyone classes throughout the United States and in Switzerland and England. One of our practitioners even taught women fabric workers in India.

A number of our practitioners have demonstrated how doing SEVA on themselves alone can be extremely helpful in times of crisis or high stress, and some even do it regularly on themselves to maintain health.

One of our teachers, Gina Rosenthal, wrote, "I recall blessings received using SEVA with myself during 2008-2010, when challenges made me question why to remain here on Earth. The pain within and outside me was greater than I had ever experienced." Gina retained stability and worked through her challenges.

The Reason for Acupressure for Anyone

Another of our world work projects teaches simple acupressure formulas for many common complaints, such as headache, colds, digestive problems, insomnia, and so forth. This work came about because of our long-standing success with applying acupressure for everyday conditions, without pain or risk. We realized that anyone could learn simple methods, just as I had in the early 1970s that would help immensely with individual or family complaints, without long and costly professional training. We have since taught many classes in this useful household therapeutic method. And beyond symptom relief, we have found that the formulas promote the same energetic balancing, calming and centering effects that we experience in our more advanced classes.

Our work is growing creatively every year, with new courses, new investigations, and services for the human conditions on earth.

Reverend Paul Sibcy has been with our learning and service from the very beginning. I doubt that anyone has served more fully with our work than he. As a minister of a holistic church and health center, he serves many people every week. He is also a Soul Lightening teacher and therapist. He wrote the following:

> Process Acupressure has been a godsend to me ever since I met Aminah Raheem and her work in the mid-1980s. I had been on the search for a truly holistic and integrative work for years, after a spiritual awakening had drawn me to the task of finding healing and wholeness for myself and my clients. When I experienced Aminah's work, I knew it was what I sought.
>
> Although I am one of the founders of a good-sized holistic health center in Palo Alto, California, I have never encountered a method that comes close to what Process Acupressure does—bring awareness and healing to all aspects of our human nature and

bring it under the guidance and support of our soul. It has helped me to integrate and become whole, as it has thousands of others.

As a practitioner and teacher of Process Acupressure, I have been practicing and using Process Acupressure for over twenty-five years. I realize now that Dr. Raheem's work was far ahead of its time. Implementing the energy healing of acupressure with process work allows us to access our deepest wounds as well as our highest potential, and integrate them in service to our soul destiny. It does that for me, and it does that for the many people it has touched.

As this book was going to the publisher, my process partner, Laura Ramsay, asked me to include her statement about Soul Lightening:

> Your work enables one to dive as deeply, to fly as high as one wishes, all of the time being held completely safely and securely in the grounded brilliance of the system. It enables the practitioner as well as the client to untangle knots that heretofore seemed hopelessly engaged.
>
> Dr. Aminah Raheem has the ability to access the wisdom of the Ancients and bring it through in such a way that every single person touched by it can benefit. This is a rare gift, so rare, in fact that I can say quite truthfully that she is, hands down, the single Best teacher I have ever known. Her Work is a great Treasure desperately needed in our time. Soul Lightening is literally capable of lighting our ways Home.

Thank you, dear reader, for staying with Soul Lightening on this journey. May your own soul journey flourish throughout your life.

18:
AFTERTHOUGHTS

The two worlds, the divine and the human...are
actually one. The realm of the gods is a forgotten
dimension of the world we know.

~Joseph Campbell

Considerations toward the End of Life

Toward the end of life, when some or many of our plans and accomplishments have been completed, there may come a fertile opportunity to pause and reflect about what has been finished and what is to come.

As longevity and life expectancy continue to rise, we have greater opportunities for gaining wisdom than did our parents and grandparents in their time. After a long life of rich experience and self-reflection we can perhaps reach a deeper understanding of self, others and life in general. Science has now discovered that contrary to the common expectation of a deteriorating brain/mind, older brains can consolidate information and reach deeper and more expansive understanding and insight than in their younger years. We know now that we can have healthy and active brains, brains that make new connections and synthesize new ways of thinking and being, right up to the last days of our lives. Minds can continue to learn and grow, right up to the moment of death. For example, from the science of neuroplasticity we know that neurogenesis (creating new brain cells and connections) doesn't stop at a certain age. But our brains do tend to lose function in short term memory, such as finding it difficult to remember names or even words. The discovery of the century has been that we can do things in our later years to start creating new connections, new brain cells. We can learn in ways we never have before and integrate the experiences of our lives in exciting new ways. These benefits may not occur easily or naturally, but we now have the knowledge and practices for doing so. We may need to learn how to learn in new ways to get into these deeper spaces of our minds. But we *can*.

In Celebration of Elders

In some cultures, particularly indigenous ones, older people are honored for the wisdom that they have gained through their life experience, and through living thoughtful, "mindful" lives. Imagine the effects those elders could have on culture and history. What would the state of our world be like if there were a large body of elders, like the Grandmothers I wrote about in Chapter 1, from whom we could seek wise guidance and sane management? Imagine the effect those elders could have on the out-of-control adolescence we seem to be living in our world now.

In an introduction to her course on elderhood, Angelus Arrien[42], anthropologist, author and spiritual teacher, wrote:

---

42 Arrien, Angeles. 2007. *The Second Half of Life: Opening the Eight Gates of Wisdom.* Boulder, Colorado, Sounds True, Inc.

These extra years, even decades, extend the blessings of life, yet in many ways we are not prepared to
live them fully. Unfortunately, a dominant cultural
perspective is that latter life offers only decline, disease, despair, and death. Elders are not valued the
way they are in traditional cultures around the world.
Instead, they are marginalized or rendered invisible,
their wisdom lost to future generations. Neglected,
too, are the rites of passage that help us transition
into being wise elders, living deep and fulfilling lives.

Arrien has become a wise elder herself, even after growing up
in our culture, which doesn't teach about, nor typically honor, our
elders. I hope she continues to teach what she has learned about the
evolution of wisdom and service.

For a number of years Arny and Amy Mindell have been teaching people the skills of true elderhood every summer on the Oregon
coast.

In my own life I have been blessed with many beloved elders.
Some of the most beloved teachers I have known in my life are, or
were, elders. From an early age I was drawn to "old people," who
had a long experience of life, whose hearts were open and loving
and who were patient enough to teach and guide me. My grandmother saved me in childhood. A longtime friend of our family, Bill
Reynolds, was an older rich prospector who had taken on the sur-
rogate role of father to my mother, and who served the esteemed
role of grandfather to me. I learned so much from him before I ever
went to school. He always treated me as an equal and talked to me
as an adult, an approach that later helped defuse negative programming from school on the playground.

Later, all through midlife, I was blessed to have a metaphysical teacher and counselor, Evelyn Sullivan, whose influence I
have written about in my book *Soul Lightning*. I was in graduate
school, in my fifties, when I studied with distinguished psychology
teachers. Nevertheless, when it came right down to wise counsel,

empowering tools and love, I found these in Evelyn. Already in her eighties and not in the best of physical health at the time, she stood out for me as the strongest and most wise life counselor I knew. I miss her still.

And now here in the desert I treasure my friend Barbara Matson, who is understanding, accepting and wise for everyone she knows. She grew past judgment of others decades ago. She believes that everyone is doing their very best, and that whatever they face in life is right for them. She exudes love and promise of the best. In her presence you feel valued, loved and inspired.

Think about elder wisdom in your own life. How do you know when a person is wise? And think of the true elders in this culture at present: former President Jimmy Carter, Nelson Mandela, Mother Teresa, and Maya Angelou. I wish we could call on more of them when many of our present government leaders often seem to be acting from the first three chakras.

Death and Dying

We all must face the inevitable ending of life in our own idiosyncratic ways. Yet, even as the fact of dying looms before us, most of us have only limited preparation for it. Perhaps we could fruitfully pause in our later years to contemplate how we want to take this last journey.

Elisabeth Kübler-Ross was a medical doctor, known best for her depth studies of the dying process. She summarized her findings in the book *On Death and Dying*.[43] She defined what she called the five stages of the dying process, which have helped many healthcare workers, psychiatrists and psychologists assist their patients. Dr. Kübler-Ross had observed that most of us experience at least two of the following stages associated with dying:

---

43 Kübler-Ross, Elizabeth. 1997. *On Death and Dying: What The Dying Have To Teach Doctors, Nurses, Clergy, And Their Own Families.* New York, Scribner.

Denial: "This isn't happening; there must be some mistake."

Anger: "Why me? It's not fair. How could you do this to me?! How could you let this happen to me?" This might include blaming others, like the doctor or medical system, or the polluters of the environment, or even Mom and Dad.

Bargaining: "Just give me two more years...let me live to see_____."

Depression: Extreme sadness, despair, lack of motivation or lack of desire to fight anymore.

Acceptance: "I'm okay with this."

Buddhists and many seekers of higher consciousness claim that one can remain conscious right up to the moment when the soul leaves the body. For this reason they often refuse strong pain medication or other treatment so as to remain as conscious and free of distractions as is possible throughout.

Buddhists have an elaborate spiritual ritual for accompanying a person in death. It begins in the final days or hours before death and continues long after death. The ritual not only comforts the dying but also allows relatives to experience a suitable goodbye.

What Near-Death Experiencers Have Taught Us

Those who have had near-death experiences have brought back much useful information about leaving the physical body and about the soul body ascending into a vast light realm. All of the accounts I've read tell of being welcomed, either by loving dead relatives or by an angelic being of light who guides them on their journeys into the afterlife. Near-death experiencers report an overwhelming love that fills them so completely that there is no grief, sorrow, shame or regret left over.

My incomparable editor, Hal Zina Bennett, described being with his mother in her very conscious dying. He sat by her bed, holding her hand and having an amazing exchange with her, right up through the last few seconds when her spirit left her body. Her last words to him were, "The Quiet," as she described what she was experiencing. And then, as her physical body became still, the room filled with a wonderful energy. One word came to his mind at that moment: "Dispersion—a dispersion of all form and energy and yet something more." Instantly, he was taken back to his own, prolonged near death experience many years before; he had felt guided, certain of the perfection of our lives and of our deaths.

Neurosurgeon Eben Alexander described his "consciousness" while his brain was completely dead:

> While beyond my body, I received knowledge about the nature and structure of the universe that was vastly beyond my comprehension. But I received it anyhow, in large part because, with my worldly preoccupations out of the way, I had room to do so.... It will take me years to understand, using my mortal, material brain, what I understood so instantly and easily in the brain-free realms of the world beyond.... Up there, a question would arise in my mind, and the answer would arise at the same time. [44]

I have read many such reports of near death experiences. Not a single one of them describes the terrifying visions of hell warned of by many religious organizations. Rather, there is always an atmosphere of complete acceptance and love. Alexander's angel-like guide told him:

> You are loved and cherished.
> You have nothing to fear.
> There is nothing you can do wrong.

---

44 Alexander, Eben. 2013. *Proof of Heaven: A Neurosurgeon's Journey into the Afterlife.* New York, Simon & Schuster Paperbacks.

I have read that dying takes energy, or that it is a struggle to exit the body. But when the crown chakra is open, release from the body is said to be easier. In Soul Lightening we understand that usually the soul ascends from the crown chakra during death. Therefore we cultivate the crown energy and its connection with the central channel that runs through the entire spine. Each Soul Lightening session opens that central channel that links all the chakras with the crown at the top of the head. Over time that energetic channel is clarified and strengthened, as consciousness is oriented toward all the chakras. We expect the dying process to be served by this energetic clarification because the soul can ascend more easily from the crown chakra.

Acupressure Helped Her Let Go of the Body

I had a cancer client once who came to a session, with her husband along to support her. He was very eager to help her in any way he could, so I offered to teach him the Basic Acupressure Protocol so that he could provide it to her any time she needed it. He was happy to learn it. I saw them both several times past this initial meeting.

Many months later, following her death, the husband came to my office simply to thank me for teaching him the Protocol. He said, "I've come to thank you so much and tell you that those were some of the most intimate and loving moments of our lives, when I was giving her the Acupressure. We drew closer and closer as she approached death. And I think acupressure helped her let go of the body."

The Life Review

Many near-death experiencers report that they had a life review during their out-of-body journey. They report that they raced through their entire life in minute detail. They re-experienced not only their own feelings and perceptions of events, but also had to feel the reactions of others toward them. That is, if they had said something particularly unkind to another person they felt that person's pain, plus their own shame or regret about the act. In other words, this life review presented a way for the person to spiritually evaluate the effects of the life just past, not to judge but evaluate, in order to sum up the destiny of that life.

Life review seems like a valuable method for getting straight with yourself. So I propose that we not wait until death to do this exercise, but do it in the present as an integral part of our preparation for our last days. Consequently, in one of our advanced classes we meditatively travel through a simulated death and past life review. Students have recovered a number of valuable life teachings from these journeys. For example, Anne House, who is also a hospice worker in the United States, reported the following:

> I became a minister to work with the terminally ill through a hospice. At the same time I was working on Process Acupressure certification and found the work to be immensely helpful with those who were dying and those who were experiencing grief after death, including staff at the hospice, family and friends of the terminally ill. I have an end-of-life protocol that I have used with the terminally ill to ease their transition. I do feel that my ability to work with the terminally ill has greatly been enhanced by the addition of Process Acupressure to my *toolbox*.

I believe our Soul Lightening practices will serve old age well, promoting eldership and helping to make the journey into death an adventure.

BIBLIOGRAPHY

Alexander, Eban., M.D., *Proof of Heaven: A Neurosurgeon's Journey into the Afterlife*. New York, Simon & Schuster Paperbacks, 2012.

Becker, Robert O., M.D., Gary Selden. *The Body Electric*. New York, William Morrow & Company, 1985.

Bradshaw, John. *Homecoming: Reclaiming and Championing your Inner Child*. New York, Bantam, 1990.

Capacchione, Lucia. *Recovery of Your Inner Child: The Highly Acclaimed Method for Liberating Your Inner Self*. New York, Simon & Schuster, 1991.

Cayce, Edgar. *My Life as a Seer: The Lost Memories*. New York, St. Martin's Press, 1997.

Childre, Doc and Howard Martin. *The HeartMath Solution*. San Francisco, Harper, 1999.

Cohen, Doris Eliana, Ph.D. *Repetition: Past Lives, Life and Rebirth*. Carlsbad, California Hay House, Inc., 2008.

Devi, Gayatri, M.D. *A Calm Brain: Unlocking Your Natural Relaxation System*. New York, Dutton, 2012.

Farber, Seth, *The Spiritual Gift of Madness. The Failure of Modern Psychiatry.* Rochester, Vermont, Inner Traditions, 2012.

Goodchild, Veronica, Ph.D. *Songlines of the Soul: Pathways to a New Vision for a New Century.* Lake Worth, Florida, Nicolas-Hays, Inc., 2012.

Grof, Stanislav, M.D. with Hal Zina Bennett. *The Holotropic Mind: The Three Levels of Human Consciousness and How They Shape Our Lives.* New York, Harper Collins, 1992.

Harman, Willis, Ph.D. and Howard Rheingold. *Higher Creativity: Liberating the Unconscious for Breakthrough Insights.* Los Angeles, Jeremy P. Tarcher, Inc., 1999.

Hawkes, Joyce Whiteley, Ph.D. *Cell-Level Healing: The Bridge from Soul to Cell.* New York Atria Books, 2006.

Hawkins, David, M.D. *Power Versus Force.* Carlsbad, California, Hay House, 2002.

Jasson, Jeffrey Moussaieff, *Against Therapy.* New York, Common Courage Press, 1999.

Johnson, Lynn. *The Adventure: A Memoir in Spirituality and Schizophrenia.* Bloomington, Ind., AuthorHouse, 2006.

Judith, Anodea and Lion Goodman. *Creating on Purpose: The Spiritual Technology of Manifesting Through the Chakras.* Boulder, Colorado, Sounds True, 2012.

Jung, C.G. *Memories, Dreams and Reflections.* New York, Random House, Inc., 1961.

Hay, Louise L. *You Can Heal Your Life.* Carlsbad, California, Hay House, 1984.

Hellinger, Bert. *Love's Hidden Symmetry: What Makes Love Work in Relationships.* Phoenix, Arizona, Zeig, Tucker & Co., 1998.

Hoffman, Bob. *No One is to Blame: Getting a Loving Divorce from Mom & Dad.* Palo Alto, California, Science and Behavior Books, Inc., 1979.

Kubler-Ross, Elisabeth. *On Death and Dying.* New York, Touchstone Books, 1997.

Tao Te Ching: A New English Version, translated and with a foreword by Stephen Mitchell. New York, HarperPerennial/ModernClassics, 2000.

Lilly, John C. *Center of the Cyclone*: *The Autobiography of a Journey into Inner Space.* New York, Bantam Books, 1975.

Mate, Gabor, M.D. *When the Body Says No: Exploring the Stress-Disease Connection.* New York, John Wiley & Sons, Inc., 2011.

Martin, Art, D.D., M.A. *Your Body is Talking; Are You Listening?* Penryn, California, Personal Transformation Press, 1997.

McCall, Kenneth. *Healing the Family Tree.* London, Sheldon Press, 1982, 2013.

Maslow, Abraham H. *The Farther Reaches of Human Nature.* New York, Penguin Group, 1971.

McTaggart, Lynn. 2008. *The Field: The Quest for the Secret Force of the Universe.* New York, Harper Collins, 2008.

McWilliams, Peter. *You Can't Afford the Luxury of a Negative Thought.* Santa Monica, California, Prelude Press, 1988, 1995.

Mindell, Amy. *Metaskills: The Spiritual Art of Therapy.* Tempe, Arizona, New Falcon Publications, 1995.

—*Alternative to Therapy: A Creative Lecture Series on Process Work.* Portland, Oregon, Lao Tse Press, 2006.

Mindell, Arnold, Ph.D. *Process Mind: A User's Guide to Connecting with the Mind of God.* Wheaton, Illinois, Quest Books, 2010.

—*Coma: Key to Awakening.* Boston, Mass., Shambhala Publications, 1989.

—*River's Way: The Process Science of the Dreambody.* London, Routledge & Kegan Paul, 1995.

—*Working with the Dreaming Body.* London, Routledge & Kegan Paul, 1985.

—*Working on Yourself Alone: Inner Dreambody Work.* Middlesex, England, Arkana, 1990.

—*Dreambody: The Body's Role in Revealing the Self,* 2nd *Edition.* Portland, Oregon, Leo Tse Press, 1998.

Muller, Wayne. *How Then, Shall We Live? Four Simple Questions That Reveal the Beauty and Meaning of Our Lives.* New York, Simon & Schuster, 1992.

Neal, Mary C. *To Heaven and Back: A Doctor's Extraordinary Account of Her Death, Heaven, Angels, and Life Again.* New York, Crown Publishing Group/Random House, Inc., 2012.

Pearsall, Paul, Ph.D. *The Heart's Code: Tapping the Wisdom and Power of Our Heart Energy.* New York, Broadway Books, 1998.

Pink, Daniel H. *A Whole New Mind.* New York, Riverhead Books, 2005.

Ram Dass, *Still Here.* New York, Riverhead Books, 2000.

Reed, Henry, under Editorship of Charles Thomas Cayce. *Edgar Cayce on Channeling Your Higher Self.* New York, Warner Books, 1989.

Rubin, Lillian. *The Transcendent Child: Tales of Triumph Over the Past.* New York, Basic Books, 1996.

Rusk, Rom, M.D. *Instead of Therapy: Help Yourself Change and Change the Help You're Getting.* Carson, California, Hay House, 1991.

Saputo, Len M.D. and Byron Belitsos. *A Return to Healing: Radical Health Care Reform and the Future of Medicine.* San Rafael, California, Origin Press, 2009.

Szasz, Thomas. *The Myth of Psychotherapy; Mental Healing as Religion, Rhetoric, and Repression.* Syracuse University Press Edition, 1988.

Stepanek, Jeni. *Messenger: The Legacy of Mattie J.T. Stepanek and Heartsongs.* New York, Penguin Books, 2009.

Taylor, Jill Bolte, Ph.D. *My Stroke of Insight: A Brain Scientist's Personal Journey.* New York, Viking, 2006.

Tolle, Eckhart. *A New Earth: Awakening to Your Life's Purpose.* New York, Penguin Books, 2008.

Vitale, Joe, and Ihaleakala Hew Len, Ph.D. *ZeroLimits: the Secret Hawaiian System for Wealth, Health, Peace.* Hoboken, New Jersey, John Wiley & Sons, Inc., 2007.

Weiss, Brian. *Many Lives, Many Masters.* New York, Simon & Schuster Inc., 1988.

Whitfield, Charles, M.D. *Healing the Child Within: Discovery and Recovery for Adult Children of Dysfunctional Families.* Pompano Beach, Florida, Health Communications, Inc. 1987.

Willis, Brad and Bhava Ram. *Warrior Pose: How Yoga (Literally) Saved My Life.* Dallas, Texas, Benbella Books, Inc., 2013.

ABOUT THE AUTHOR

Aminah Raheem, Ph.D. is a transpersonal psychologist, Diplomat of Process Oriented Psychology, a Zero Balancer and Zero Balancing Teacher. As a body/mind/soul therapist, she originated Process and Clinical Acupressure, psycho-spiritual approaches that work through the body's energy systems to assist conscious development and realization of soul purpose.

As the founder and spiritual Director of Soul Lightening International, a non-profit foundation dedicated to soul awakening for the health and wellbeing of individuals and our planet, Dr. Raheem is spreading a vision of harmonic co-existence between humans and nature, and is helping to chart a course for individual and global soul consciousness.

In her long career as a teacher, therapist and author, she has taught thousands in the helping professions to work with a compassionate, client-centered approach to the whole person. She taught at the Institute for Transpersonal Psychology (now Sofia) in Menlo Park, California for ten years where she observed and worked with the process of personal transformation. She teaches body/mind/soul consciousness work internationally, through Soul Lightening International (www.SoulLightening.com) and the International Alliance for Healthcare Educators (see www.iahe.com).

Dr. Raheem's pioneering book, *Soul Return: Integrating Body, Psyche and Spirit*, still stands at the forefront of defining the relationship of body and soul. Network magazine described it: "Aminah Raheem presents a scientific and well-reasoned survey of the role that factors such as love, wisdom, service, and enlightenment play in optimal health."

Aminah lives in Borrego Springs, California with her husband, Frederick Smith, M.D., Originator of Zero Balancing. She has four grown children, seven grandchildren and six great-grandchildren.

ABOUT SOUL LIGHTENING INTERNATIONAL

Soul Lightening International is a 501(c)3, non-profit, public benefit corporation dedicated to world service through the teaching and advancement of Soul Lightening Acupressure, a dynamic and transformative healing modality that integrates ancient teachings with contemporary techniques to promote health and self-responsibility for wellbeing.

Our mission is to cultivate soul actualization and purpose in the world, to further human evolution, health and awakening, for the preservation of the family and the global community. We aim to achieve our mission through the following ways:

- Training workshops designed for people of all ages and professions;
- Professional certification programs and continuing education opportunities for health care practitioners;
- Educational products and support services for practitioners and clients;
- World outreach in the spirit of compassionate service (SEVA) by putting the extraordinary healing gifts of acupressure into the hands of ordinary people;
- Partnership with larger organizations for training, clinical services, and research.

The Principles of Our Work

1. Energy flow in the body promotes wellness and opens new awareness;
2. Touch and the flow of love from the heart are healing and strengthening;
3. Every person carries their own healing wisdom within;
4. The purpose of Soul Lightening Acupressure is to empower that inherent wisdom.

Four Integrated Components of This Program

- *Process Acupressure:* supports health by facilitating consciousness in the body, mind, emotions and spirit;
- *Clinical Acupressure:* addresses common symptoms with specific acupoint combinations;
- *Acupressure for Anyone™:* gives the layperson simple and effective tools to support their own health.
- *SEVA*: this is an easy to apply stress release used in many different situations to bring calm, relaxation, and a sense of self to anyone in distress.

Please contact us for more information, workshop schedules, or for list of practitioners at: www.SoulLightening.com.